# DR. JOHN HARVEY KELLOGG

## AND THE
## RELIGION OF BIOLOGIC LIVING

# DR. JOHN HARVEY KELLOGG

## AND THE
## RELIGION OF BIOLOGIC LIVING

## BRIAN C. WILSON

INDIANA UNIVERSITY PRESS

*Bloomington & Indianapolis*

This book is a publication of

Indiana University Press
Office of Scholarly Publishing
Herman B Wells Library 350
1320 East 10th Street
Bloomington, Indiana 47405 USA

iupress.indiana.edu

*Telephone*  800-842-6796
*Fax*  812-855-7931

∞The paper used in this publication meets the
minimum requirements of the American
National Standard for Information Sciences—
Permanence of Paper for Printed Library
Materials, ANSI Z39.48–1992.

*Manufactured in the*
*United States of America*

*Library of Congress*
*Cataloging-in-Publication Data*

Wilson, Brian C.
  Dr. John Harvey Kellogg and the religion of
biologic living / Brian C. Wilson.
    pages cm
  Includes bibliographical references and
index.
    ISBN 978-0-253-01447-4 (hardback) —
ISBN 978-0-253-01455-9 (ebook) 1. Kellogg,
John Harvey, 1852–1943. 2. Physicians—
United States—Biography. 3. Hygienists—
United States—Biography. 4. Battle Creek
Sanitarium (Battle Creek, Mich.)—History.
I. Title.
  R154.K265W55 2014
  610.92—dc23
  [B]

                                    2014008170

1 2 3 4 5 19 18 17 16 15 14

*For my father, Charles E. Wilson*

Battle Creek philosophy inculcates the idea that the laws of Nature are the laws of God, the unchangeable behests of the Master Creative Intelligence of the Universe. To become acquainted with these basic principles of existence and to render and inculcate obedience to them, this is the dominant aim and purpose of the Battle Creek Idea.

—DR. JOHN HARVEY KELLOGG,
*"The Battle Creek Idea: What Is It?," July 2, 1930*

# CONTENTS

# PREFACE

FROM 1876 TO 1943, Dr. John Harvey Kellogg presided over the Battle Creek Sanitarium, an institution that, at its peak, was one of the largest and best-known health and wellness facilities in the United States, a "combination nineteenth-century European health spa and a twentieth-century Mayo Clinic."[1] Founded in 1866 under the auspices of the Seventh-day Adventist Church as the Western Health Reform Institute, the "San," as it came to be called, grew under Dr. Kellogg's charismatic leadership to include a massive health resort accommodating some thirteen hundred guests, a hospital, research facilities, a medical school, a nursing school, several health food companies, and a publishing house dedicated to producing materials on health and wellness. Legions of health seekers, Adventists and non-Adventists, rich and poor alike, made Battle Creek one of the premier wellness destinations in the United States, if not the world, and celebrities of all kinds, from film stars, writers, and artists to industrialists such as Henry Ford and John D. Rockefeller and even Presidents Taft and Harding, made the pilgrimage to Kellogg's "Temple of Health" in search of the "Battle Creek Idea." For more than two generations, Battle Creek was dominated and defined by the San, and the flamboyant personality of Dr. John Harvey Kellogg presided over all. Even after the sanitarium declined precipitously in the 1940s, Kellogg's influence lingered, as the economy of Battle Creek came to be dominated by the expanding breakfast cereal industry, itself a spin-off from the sanitarium and the doctor's fertile imagination.[2]

Battle Creek Sanitarium and Hospital, ca. 1905. *All images from Community Archives, Heritage Battle Creek unless otherwise noted.*

Today, little remains of Dr. Kellogg's Battle Creek health empire beyond a few spectacular buildings sold long ago to the federal government. Most people who know anything about Dr. Kellogg are apt to associate him either with his most famous invention, the cornflake, or with T. C. Boyle's 1993 comic novel, *The Road to Wellville,* in which he was portrayed as a megalo-maniacal quack. One of the goals of this book is to correct this caricature by contextualizing both Dr. Kellogg's early career and the rise of the Battle Creek Sanitarium within the larger story of the Seventh-day Adventists' abiding concern for physical health, which in turn had its roots in the antebel-lum movement for health reform, particularly that of the so-called Christian physiologists. Seen in this light, Kellogg emerges as less a quack and more an extraordinarily energetic innovator and activist, albeit one constrained by the cultural and scientific horizons of the period just after the Civil War. The Battle Creek Sanitarium should thus be seen as perhaps the grandest institutional expression of a concern for holistic health that ran deep in the American public in the late nineteenth and early twentieth centuries and Kellogg as one of the precursors of today's "health gurus" such as Deepak Chopra and Andrew Weil.

Admittedly, the history of the Battle Creek Sanitarium has been told else-where by both denominational and secular historians, and Dr. Kellogg has been well served by Richard W. Schwarz's 1970 biography, *John Harvey Kellogg, MD*.[3] However, my concerns in this book ultimately focus on an aspect of Dr. Kellogg's career that has not been fully explored in earlier works: his theological development. Inspired by Mary Farrell Bednarowski's *New Religions and the Theological Imagination in America,* a work that takes seriously the intellectual products of those outside the theological mainstream, I see Kellogg as an important example of an overlooked category of theological discourse: the doctor as theologian.[4] Dr. Kellogg's long professional life was balanced on the cusp of massive changes in science and medicine. Over the course of the nineteenth century, the natural sciences came to be dominated by revolutionary naturalistic theories of evolution in biology, geology, and cosmology. These theories presented trenchant challenges to long-held beliefs about the divine origins of human beings, the earth, and the universe itself. Concomitant with the secularization of natural science, medicine also grew increasingly naturalistic in approach, such that the idea of medicine as a religious calling, which was simply assumed in the nineteenth century, was all but lost by the first decades of the twentieth.[5] Indeed, by the time Kellogg died in 1943, American science and medicine had been largely secularized, and the newly dominant paradigm of scientific naturalism not only ignored religious meanings but actively suppressed them. Despite this, Kellogg remained resolutely a man of the nineteenth century, and while the doctor was ever mindful of trends in science and medicine, he nevertheless resisted secularism's totalizing demands to the end of his life. Undoubtedly, Kellogg was not the only physician who faced the challenges of reconciling science with religion during this period, but in many ways his situation was unique.

Kellogg's refusal to give in to the secularizing currents of his day had a lot to do with the fact that he was born and raised in the environment of Yankee sectarianism, specifically that of Seventh-day Adventism, in the small Michigan town of Battle Creek. Kellogg was the son of one of the earliest Adventist families in Battle Creek, which was already noted for its sectarian diversity even before the Adventists arrived. By the time he was an adolescent, his energy and intelligence had brought him to the attention of James and Ellen G. White, whose protégé he became. Steeped in the Adventist subculture from an early age, Kellogg acquired the deep-seated defensiveness characteristic of sectarians, a defensiveness that would allow him to resist the pressures of secular science and medicine later. He also acquired the Seventh-day Adventist propensity for the kind of amateur theologizing that was so prevalent during the early days of the denomination.[6] Without a single authority to enforce theological uniformity, a wide range of theological speculation was commonplace in the pages of Seventh-day Adventist newspapers, journals, and books, and from an early age John Harvey Kellogg felt that he, too, could contribute to this aspect of his tradition. Indeed, Kellogg's training as a physician led him to assume that his pronouncements should carry special weight.

This is not to say that Kellogg remained completely true to the Adventist beliefs of his childhood—far from it. Once exposed to the erosive logic of the natural sciences during his medical training, Kellogg's restless mind would not allow him simply to accept the dogmas of Seventh-day Adventism without synthesizing them with his new scientific and medical knowledge. The eventual result, Kellogg's theology of "biologic living," which "biologized" sin and sacralized wellness, can be seen as an attempt at a via media between the Adventism of his youth and the secular science of modern medicine, a kind of Adventist modernism that replaced a literal biblicism with a nonanthropomorphic theology of divine immanence. As such, Kellogg's biologic living, especially as it was expressed in his major work, *The Living Temple* (1903), represents one of the more interesting products of the Yankee theological imagination to come out of the Midwest. Moreover, Kellogg's attempt to sell *The Living Temple* to the Adventist rank and file culminated in what is known in Adventist scholarship as the "Pantheism Crisis" of 1903.[7] This event is still viewed by the denomination as a pivotal moment in its history. Kellogg's unwillingness to moderate his theological views and bring them more in line with developing Adventist orthodoxy, combined with power politics within the denomination, ultimately led to his disfellowshipping in 1907 and the loss of the Battle Creek Sanitarium to the church. It also accelerated the Seventh-day Adventists' abandonment of Battle Creek as their national headquarters and contributed to their move toward a greater emphasis on doctrinal orthodoxy.[8] At the time of the Pantheism Crisis, Ellen White viewed Kellogg's theological deviations as simply the latest symptom of the doctor's growing independence from, if not contempt for, Adventist control, and in part they probably were. However, the new theology behind biologic living was first and foremost an expression of Kellogg's very real and very personal struggle to reconcile religion with science and medicine. The intellectual life of John Harvey Kellogg illustrates in many ways the spiritual crises of the Gilded Age identified by Paul Carter: the gnawing doubt engendered by the rise of science and Darwinism, the decline in the belief in original sin and the immortality of the soul, the problematic idea of religious progress, the impact of commercialism on religious values, modernism versus fundamentalism, and ecumenism versus sectarianism.[9] Whatever there was of opportunism in Kellogg's "heterodoxy," there was at least as much sincerity. Telling is the fact that once Kellogg had broken with the church and was free to believe anything he liked, the doctor never ceased to be a religious person with roots in American sectarianism, and as he acquired new scientific interests in the second half of his life, specifically eugenics, Kellogg was careful to fit them into his evolving religious worldview.

Kellogg's promotion of eugenics, to which he devoted the last three decades of his life after his expulsion from the church, illustrates clearly how the twin forces of sectarian religion and science continued to mold his theology well into the twentieth century. The result is both fascinating and unsettling. Born into a millennialist sect that, despite the progressive attenuation of its message through institutionalization, nevertheless always taught the imminent end of the world, Dr. Kellogg could never shake the idea that the world was indeed headed for catastrophe, even after he had abandoned a literal belief in the apocalypse by the 1920s. Just as he had increasingly biologized sin under the pressure of scientific medicine, so Kellogg biologized the apocalypse into the concept of "race degeneracy" that foretold a day when the human race would become extinct due to unbiologic living. As in the literal apocalypse, Kellogg believed that a remnant would be saved, though not through any kind of doctrinal orthodoxy, but rather through that quintessential Progressive Era crusade, eugenics.[10] Kellogg's Race Betterment Foundation, founded in 1914, became the primary agency by which Kellogg's eugenic ideas were spread. How Kellogg came to see God operating through eugenics forms the capstone of his theological journey, a journey that took him an intellectual world away from the sectarian environment into which he was born on the nineteenth-century Michigan frontier.

# ACKNOWLEDGMENTS

THIS BOOK HAS BEEN a long time in development. Originally, it began as a religious history of Battle Creek, in which my goal was to determine why, of all places in the Midwest, this small Michigan town became the birthplace of Seventh-day Adventism, today one of the largest of the many new religious movements born in nineteenth-century America. In the course of my research, I could not help but come upon the story of Dr. John Harvey Kellogg and the Battle Creek Sanitarium, although at the time his was to be just one part of the story I was telling. In 2007, however, a diagnosis of leukemia sent me on a two-year run through the cancer mill. The fact that so many of my doctors were openly skeptical about what I did for a living, while at the same time wishing to engage me in theological debate, turned my thoughts increasingly toward Dr. Kellogg and the intersection of religion and medicine. This redirected the focus of my research, the result of which is this book.

I have incurred innumerable debts to people who have helped me along the way. Dr. Kellogg left a voluminous paper trail, and to access it I am indebted to the staffs of the American Philosophical Society Library, Philadelphia; Archives of Michigan, Michigan Library and Historical Center, Lansing; Bentley Historical Library, University of Michigan, Ann Arbor; Center for Adventist Research, Andrews University, Berrien Springs, Michigan; Heritage Battle Creek, Battle Creek, Michigan; Edward G. Minor Library, University of Rochester Medical Center, Rochester, New York; Helen

Warner Branch Local History Department, Willard Library, Battle Creek, Michigan; Resource Sharing Center, Waldo Library, Western Michigan University, Kalamazoo; Special Collections Research Center, Georgetown University Library, Washington, DC; and University Archives and Historical Collections, Michigan State University, East Lansing.

Among those individuals I would like to thank specifically are Professors Amy DeRogatis, David Stowe, and the rest of the Michigan State University Department of Religious Studies American Religions Workshop; Professor Ronald L. Numbers; Professor Mary Lagerwey; Garth "Duff" Stoltz of the Historic Adventist Village, Battle Creek, Michigan; Mary Butler of Heritage Battle Creek, Battle Creek, Michigan; George Livingston, local and family history librarian, Willard Library, Battle Creek, Michigan; Jeffrey Landenberger, public affairs specialist, Hart-Dole-Inouye Federal Building, Battle Creek, Michigan; Richard Merkel; and graduate students Steven Chamberlin, Eric Bowler, Kyle Byron, and Drew Costello. Thanks also to Dee Mortensen, my editor at Indiana University Press, and to her assistant, Sarah Jacobi, for their expert work shepherding this book to press. Finally, I would like to extend my appreciation to my wife, Cybelle Shattuck, for her infinite patience and to Mazel, Beryl, and Thibault for their lack of it.

# ABBREVIATIONS

| | |
|---|---|
| EGWW | Ellen G. White Writings, Ellen G. White Estate (http://www.egwwritings.org) |
| GCA | General Conference of the Seventh-day Adventist Church Archives (http://docs.adventistarchives.org) |
| JHKAM | John Harvey Kellogg Collection, Archives of Michigan, Lansing |
| JHKMSU | John Harvey Kellogg Papers, Michigan State University Archives and Historical Collections, East Lansing |
| JHKUM | John Harvey Kellogg Papers, Bentley Historical Library, University of Michigan, Ann Arbor |

# DR. JOHN HARVEY KELLOGG

## AND THE
## RELIGION OF BIOLOGIC LIVING

# 1

## *Battle Creek Beginnings*

In the summer of 1940 at the age of eighty-eight, Dr. John Harvey Kellogg, seeking to record on paper some of the essential facts of his long life, cast his thoughts back to 1863, a time when Battle Creek, Michigan, was "a very small village of a few hundred inhabitants" and the great Battle Creek Sanitarium was still many years in the future. His mother, Kellogg remembered, had just asked the young boy what he wanted to be when he grew up, to which he had promptly replied, "Anything but a doctor!" Apparently, shortly before his mother's question, John Harvey and some other boys had pressed their faces against a neighbor's window to witness the bloody spectacle of a local sawbones practicing his art on one of their playmates lying on the kitchen table. In the wake of this episode, Kellogg remembered, "I abhorred the medical profession, did not like bad medicine and the bloody surgery." That just a few years later that young boy would find himself a famous doctor—and a surgeon at that—must have given the elderly Kellogg a chuckle, for in addition to his childhood disgust at the sight of blood, he had been at the age of eleven nothing more than an undersize boy working in his father's Battle Creek broom factory, distinguished only by his exceptional manual dexterity sorting broom corn and the fact that his family belonged to a struggling apocalyptic sect.[1]

Significantly, Dr. Kellogg followed this memory with that of another: shortly after his mother had asked him about his future in life, the boy had come upon her praying for his future: "I went in and knelt down beside her and she placed her hand on my head as we knelt there and she dedicated me to the Lord for human service." "From that moment on," the elderly Kellogg said solemnly, "I have never had any desire but to do everything that I could for humanity."[2] As immodest as this sounds to our ears, the statement was typical of Dr. Kellogg's own self-understanding, and its conjunction with the previous memory signals something that Kellogg never doubted: his choice of the medical profession was not a choice at all, but God's choice, and his mission to spread the Battle Creek Idea—"biologic living"—God's will. It was the product of a large ego perhaps, but also the product of the peculiar sectarian "hothouse" environment of Battle Creek's West End, birthplace of the Seventh-day Adventist Church and Kellogg's home from the age of four until the end of his life.

In the middle of the nineteenth century, Battle Creek, from all outward appearances, looked like many another mill town of the Yankee diaspora. Battle Creek, which takes its name from either an epic battle between rival Native American tribes in the distant past or a sordid 1823 skirmish between Indians and American surveyors, lies at the confluence of the Kalamazoo and Battle Creek Rivers in southwestern Michigan. Yankee land lookers arriving at the site as early as 1831 instantly recognized its potential for waterpower and began buying lots. One of the earliest permanent residents, Judge Sands McCamly, built the first millrace in 1834. From then on came the same series of firsts found in many a town chronicle: first log school (1834), first store (1835), first village government (1836), first frame house (1837), with the first newspaper and railroad service both arriving on the scene in 1845. By this time the population stood around a thousand and then quadrupled over the next decade. For all intents and purposes, Battle Creek was in the beginning virtually indistinguishable from any number of comparably sized Yankee settlements in southwestern Michigan at the time.[3]

As part of the Yankee diaspora, Battle Creek's early religious history reflected the patterns of spirituality and church development emanating from the "burned-over" districts of Vermont and upstate New York. Yankees had flooded into the latter areas after the Revolutionary War, making it a "second New England," and then into Michigan, which formed the "third New England," as Yankee Yorkers migrated there in preponderant numbers between 1825 and 1845.[4] Methodists, Baptists, Presbyterians, Congregationalists, and Episcopalians all established churches in Battle Creek in the 1830s and '40s.[5] Because these were precisely the years of religious enthusiasm in upstate

Downtown Battle Creek in 1866.

New York, many of the new settlers brought with them the ethos and concerns of "burned-over district" spirituality. "They came fresh from the New York revivals," wrote one American Home Missionary Society itinerant in Michigan in 1835, "and they still retain much of the spirit."[6]

Nonevangelical groups also made Battle Creek home. Indeed, Battle Creek owes much of the distinctiveness of its subsequent religious history to the leavening presence of Hicksite Quakers, Universalists, and Swedenborgians, who, united by burning interest in social reform, especially abolitionism, banded together in the 1850s to found the Progressionists of Battle Creek, part of the larger Progressive Quaker movement that flourished during this period.[7] Soon, however, the Progressionists caught the Spiritualism bug and converted en masse to this new faith. Now their meetings were just as likely to feature Andrew Jackson Davis, the "Poughkeepsie seer," as abolitionists such as Parker Pillsbury. Pillsbury complained in the pages of William Lloyd

Garrison's *Liberator* that "numerically the Spiritualists [now] predominated" among the Progressionists, ruining the antislavery cause in Michigan by "a morbid, mawkish Spiritualism, that had infested it like potato-rot."[8] His was a minority opinion, however, as the number of Spiritualists in Battle Creek continued to grow. A former Universalist minister, James A. Peebles, was engaged for what the Spiritualists now called the Independent Church of Battle Creek, and he soon turned it into the fastest-growing congregation in town.[9] So attractive did Spiritualism become that several Quaker Spiritualist families founded an intentional community on Battle Creek's outskirts called Harmonia, centered on the Bedford Harmonial Academy. It thrived for a time, attracting such luminaries as Sojourner Truth and former US senator Nathaniel Tallmadge as residents.[10]

Spiritualism, though, was not destined to be the dominant sectarian religion in Battle Creek, although it was probably the tolerance for Spiritualists by the townsfolk that opened the way for the new religious movement that would soon claim that distinction. Sometime in November 1855 a party of travelers alighted on the platform of the Battle Creek train station after a long and jostling trip from Rochester, New York.[11] Although unremarked by the newspapers at the time, the arrival of this weary band signaled a new era in the town's history, for they were led by James and Ellen G. White, the charismatic cofounders of what would soon become the Seventh-day Adventist Church. Today, the church has grown to some seventeen million members worldwide, but in 1855 Seventh-day Adventism was a small, struggling movement defined by what many considered peculiar beliefs about the imminent end of the world and Jesus's Second Coming and a conviction that Saturday, the seventh day of the week, was the true Christian Sabbath. Many Adventists also believed that Ellen White was a prophetess whose visions, known as "testimonies," revealed the will of God. The Whites chose Battle Creek for many reasons, not least of which was that it would serve as a convenient base from which to spread their distinctive ideas to the Midwest and beyond. After years of hectic itinerancy, however, they probably little suspected that this small Michigan town would become their permanent home. Yet here they stayed for nearly forty years, making Battle Creek the headquarters for what would become one of the most successful Christian denominations ever to originate in the United States and, given its focus on bodily health, one of the most distinctive.

## THE BIRTH OF SEVENTH-DAY ADVENTISM IN BATTLE CREEK

The Adventist movement has its roots in the perennial fascination in the West with millennialism, and, more specifically, with the relationship between the prophetic books of the Old Testament such as Daniel and the prophecies of the end times in the book of Revelation. Most Americans of the antebellum period had accepted the optimistic postmillennial interpretation of the latter book; they followed in the tradition of Jonathan Edwards that Jesus's Second Coming would occur after peace and prosperity had been achieved on earth through the agency of human beings. With the success of the Revolutionary War and the establishment of the American Republic, such postmillennial optimism seemed justified. However, beginning in the late eighteenth century in England, premillennial interpretations returned to popularity among certain strata of society, especially after the horrors of the French Revolution, and it was inevitable that such ideas would migrate across the Atlantic. In the United States the combination of the religious excitement generated by the Second Great Awakening with the social dislocations that followed in the wake of the War of 1812 provided fertile ground for the renewed growth of the premillennial ideas that form the basis of Adventism.[12]

The father of the Adventist movement in America was William Miller, a Vermont farmer whose conversion from deism and skepticism to the Baptist faith in 1816 led him to apply the principles of Enlightenment rationalism to prove the reasonableness of the Bible. In so doing, Miller inevitably became interested in apocalyptic prophecy, and after two years of study he became convinced that by employing the numerical clues found in the prophetic books he could predict the year of Jesus's Second Coming: 1843. Miller, however, was initially reluctant to preach his findings, but as the fateful year approached he convinced himself that God wanted him to warn an unwary world. Miller taught that those who were not saved with the coming of Christ would be incinerated in a conflagration that would destroy the earth, a terrifying prospect for believers. In August 1831 Miller went public with his prophetic calculations to a Baptist congregation in Dresden, New York. This led to invitations to preach in other churches, initiating small-scale revivals in many congregations, which in turn led to more preaching engagements for Miller in New York, New England, and Canada.[13]

By the 1840s Miller had gained an energetic publicist, Joshua V. Himes, who opened the way for Miller's preaching in the larger cities of the Eastern Seaboard. This garnered him more followers, including some influential members of the clergy. Himes, meanwhile, was busy creating other avenues by which the Adventist message could be propagated, including a newspaper, the *Signs of the Times* (the first of many such Adventist newspapers). The General Conference was also created, designed to bring together Adventists from around the Northeast to discuss Miller's ideas and coordinate further proselytizing efforts. One of the most important decisions of the General Conference was the promotion of local interdenominational Second Advent associations throughout the region, and although this was not the original intention, many of these associations evolved in time into independent congregations.[14]

Although the number of confirmed "Millerites" during this period probably numbered anywhere from fifteen thousand to perhaps twice that number, interest among the general public remained high and articles on "Millerism" were featured frequently in the secular press. As 1843 approached, Miller was pressured to be more precise about the date. He did so reluctantly by stating that the Second Coming would occur during the Jewish year 1843, which fell between March 21, 1843, and March 21, 1844. Needless to say, the arrival of March 21 was the beginning of a period of tremendous expectation among the faithful and even greater evangelical efforts by Miller and his associates, who expanded their mission to the Midwest.[15]

The failure of Jesus to return to earth on March 21, 1844, was disappointing for the Millerites, but despite this Miller, while freely admitting that his calculations were in error, nevertheless remained firm in his belief in the imminent end of the world. He continued preaching the Second Advent message in upstate New York, Ohio, and Ontario. It was left to another Adventist, Samuel S. Snow, to suggest another date, October 22, 1844, the Jewish Day of Atonement. This caught on quickly among Adventist circles, leading again to another round of tense expectation and, with the passing of that day, a deep sense of despair and exhaustion among the Millerites. Not least among these was William Miller himself, who retreated into abashed retirement, lasting until his death in 1849. Known ever after as "the Great Disappointment," the date marked the watershed event in Adventist history, leading, albeit improbably, to the rise of a vibrant new denomination: Seventh-day Adventism.[16]

Seventh-day Adventism grew from one of the many groups that emerged from the wreckage of the Great Disappointment. All of these groups retained the belief in the imminent Second Coming of Jesus, but they diverged sharply on how they reinterpreted Miller's prophecies and on certain secondary beliefs and practices. One of the most important figures in this process of sectarian formation was a young Methodist Millerite from Portland, Maine, Ellen G. Harmon. In 1844 Harmon experienced a powerful heavenly vision that legitimated the correctness of Adventism, a vision that some accepted as an example of the kinds of "spiritual gifts" to be expected in the end times. Two years later Harmon came into the orbit of the Sabbatarian Adventists, who had adopted from the Sabbatarian Baptists the distinctive belief that the Old Testament observance of a Saturday Sabbath was still necessary for salvation. That same year she met and married a committed Sabbatarian Adventist minister, James White, and together they preached the Second Advent throughout New England and upstate New York.[17]

In 1848 the Whites attended a conference of Adventists in Volney, New York, where, among other issues, there was much discussion over the question of the validity of Miller's prophecies. Some argued that Miller was correct and that Christ did come to earth on October 22, only in spiritual form. Against this "spiritualizing" approach, others such as visionary Hiram Edson taught that the date signified a heavenly, not terrestrial, event, namely, Christ's destruction of sin through the cleansing of the Heavenly Sanctuary, as described in Daniel and Revelation. This, it was argued, was a necessary step in preparation for his return to earth and the reason for Christ's delay. The Sanctuary Doctrine, as it came to be known, continued to be controversial, but a further heavenly vision by Ellen White ratified it as literally correct. For those who believed that White did indeed enjoy spiritual gifts, the issue was settled.[18]

For some time after the 1848 conference, the Whites continued to set new dates for the Second Coming, but in 1850 Ellen White strongly discouraged further date setting by Sabbatarian Adventists. It was enough to know that Jesus's prophecy of the millennial generation ("This generation shall not pass, till all these things be fulfilled" [Matt. 24:34]) applied to them without worrying about the exact date when the prophecy would be fulfilled.[19] Thus began a process by which the apocalyptic fervor of the earlier Millerite movement was attenuated, allowing for the beginnings of institutionaliza-

James and Ellen G. White.

tion of what was now called the "third angel's message" (after the third angel of the book of Revelation, who announced that people should come out
of Babylon, that is, the corrupt churches). By this time James White had become involved in editing a series of newspapers, the most important of which
was the *Second Advent Review and Sabbath Herald,* in Rochester, New York.
Here the growing White family settled in 1852. Millerism had long been a
movement notable for its newspapers and other printed materials, and this
tradition of proselytization would to a great degree come to characterize
Sabbatarian Adventism as well.[20]

  Michigan had not been wholly untouched by the Millerite excitement,
and after the Great Disappointment a few Michiganders retained their con-

fidence in Miller's prophecies. Missionaries representing the various varieties of postdisappointment Adventism were soon active among these believers, with Sabbatarian Adventist Joseph Bates converting a small Millerite group in Jackson, Michigan, led by Merritt E. Cornell. Bates, a former sea captain and something of a visionary himself, subsequently dreamed that he was on a ship bound for some place called Battle Creek. Taking this as a divine prompt, Bates hurried there and soon converted a Presbyterian, David Hewitt, and his wife, Olive, to the new faith, making them the nucleus of the Sabbatarian Adventist movement in the town. By 1853 there was a regular meeting of Sabbath keepers, enough to support a resident minister, Joseph Frisbie, and even attracting a visit from James and Ellen White themselves. Battle Creek now became the center for Adventist evangelization of Michigan and the place selected for the first large-scale tent meetings attempted by the Sabbatarian Adventists.[21]

Meanwhile, one of the first people converted by Jackson's Merritt E. Cornell was John Preston Kellogg, father of John Harvey. John Preston and his first wife, Mary Ann, had migrated to Michigan in 1834 from their home in Hadley, Massachusetts, drawn, like so many Yankees before him, by glowing tales of Michigan's fertility and boundless opportunities. At first the family settled on a farm north of Flint, but financial reverses, including unwise investment in a wildcat bank, forced several moves, first to a smaller neighboring farm, where Mary Kellogg died of consumption, and then, after John Preston's marriage to Ann Janette Stanley in 1842, to a farm in Tyrone Township. Typical of Michigan's Yankees, John Preston Kellogg was something of a religious seeker. After a revival meeting in Flint, John Preston became a professing Baptist following full immersion in the Flint River, and then, after moving to Tyrone Township, he led a Methodist class meeting. Eventually, the restless John Preston left the Methodists to join the Congregationalist Church in nearby Heartland Center in 1843, in which church he was soon ordained a deacon. In the end, however, after the chance meeting with Merritt E. Cornell in 1852, John Preston converted once again, this time to Sabbatarian Adventism. Eventually wishing to live among more of his new coreligionists, he relocated his family to Battle Creek in 1856. Here he opened a small broom factory.[22]

In light of Battle Creek's growing importance to the Sabbatarian Adventist movement, a meeting was held on September 23, 1855, during which

Daniel Palmer, Cyrenius Smith, Henry Lyon, and John Preston Kellogg each agreed to pledge three hundred dollars in order to attract James White's printing operation to the town. The Whites, who had been favorably impressed by Battle Creek on their visit two years before, considered this a literal Godsend and readily accepted. Not only would the move help put the production of Adventist newspaper, tracts, and books on a sounder financial footing, but it would also facilitate Adventist evangelization of the great American West, which the Whites now saw as a more fertile mission field than the East.[23] By the time the Whites and their entourage arrived in Battle Creek in 1855, local Adventists had already built a small two-story frame building to house the *Review and Herald* offices on the corner of West Main and Washington Streets. Printing operations were quickly reestablished, and the first Battle Creek edition of the *Review and Herald*, now under the editorship of Uriah Smith, was pulled from the press on December 4. Within a few years the *Review and Herald* printing operation outgrew the tiny West Main facility with its single handpress and was moved down the street in 1861 to an imposing two-story brick building, complete with a modern steam press. Printing output would continue to expand thereafter, with two identical brick buildings added by the end of the decade, the first of many additions to the physical plant over the decades. In the early years the printing operation would represent the heart of Sabbatarian Adventist activity in Battle Creek.[24]

In addition to the original *Review and Herald* office, a small Adventist meetinghouse had also been constructed on Cass Street just before the Whites arrived in 1855. Reflecting the unsettled state of Sabbatarian Adventist organization at that point, none dared called it a church: it was referred to only as the "house of prayer."[25] Indeed, the issue of whether Sabbath-keeping Adventists should try to organize what had up to that point been a loose coalition of individual congregations united by occasional conferences remained controversial. Many believed that given the imminence of the Second Coming, such organization indicated a lack of faith, while others believed that creating another sect would simply fragment God's church yet again. However, legal concerns over the incorporation of the printing operation and title to church properties forced the issue, as did the desire to license clergy and create church schools.

Both James and Ellen White were proponents of a strong organization, and James would exhaust his health tirelessly working for its creation. Beginning in 1855 a series of conferences were held in Battle Creek in order to achieve what James White called "gospel order." For the next eight years Sabbatarian Adventists debated everything from Ellen White's prophetic gifts, financial support for ministers, the propriety of tithing, even an appropriate name, ultimately deciding on "Seventh-day Adventist" at the 1860 conference. Further organizational steps followed quickly: 1862 saw the incorporation of the printing operation as a joint-stock company and the legal formation of the Michigan State Conference of Seventh-day Adventists, thus encouraging the formation of other state conferences. Finally, the following year, all of the existing state conferences (consisting of New York, Ohio, Michigan, Wisconsin, Iowa, and Minnesota) were gathered into a General Conference, the capstone organization of what was now the Seventh-day Adventist Church. Thus, by 1863 the church now had a firm but flexible organizational foundation and was ready for new growth. Organization, however, would have its price. Not only did it necessitate the further muting of a sense of imminence of Christ's return, source of so much early Adventist energy, but it also created a top-down bureaucracy that, as one Adventist historian put it, "was more Episcopal than congregational, one operated largely by ministers rather than by the laity."[26] Both these costs would have long-term consequences for the development of the church and its tenure in Battle Creek.

It was precisely during this period of the initial organization of the Seventh-day Adventist Church that John Harvey Kellogg spent his boyhood in Battle Creek. Born in 1852 when John Preston Kellogg and his second wife, Ann Janette Stanley, were living on the Tyrone Township farm, little "Johnny" Kellogg was brought with the rest of the family to Battle Creek in 1856 to settle in the Adventist West End.[27] With sixteen children in the home, the Kellogg household was a place of exceeding strictness and little material abundance. John Harvey himself remembered it for its "sad and solemn" atmosphere and his father's unrelenting work ethic. John Harvey was a sickly child suffering from rickets, intensely self-conscious of his slight frame and small stature (as an adult Kellogg would stand only five foot four, although the frame would fill out considerably). He would compensate for his physical shortcomings by energy, assertiveness, and a burning ambition to do something with his life, although he knew this would not be easy for a boy on the frontier. According to Kellogg's later recollections, his parents prevented him from learning to read because, given the imminence of the end of the world, acquiring such

The Seventh-day Adventist Tabernacle, completed in 1879,
a central symbol of the church's growth in Battle Creek.

skills would be a waste of time. Finally, when he was twelve, a local pastor, presumably James White, observed that "if the Lord was going to come soon and end the world, he would be more pleased if he found children in school." Kellogg was then allowed to spend an entire winter term at the neighborhood schoolhouse. Happily, John Harvey was a powerful autodidact from an early age, making up for a very spotty formal education with voracious reading, especially in history, science, and languages.[28]

Exuding a confidence that bordered on cockiness, little John Harvey never passed up an opportunity to prove himself and make himself known. A half century later the Spiritualist minister Peebles would still remember meeting "the bright, sturdy, active, wide awake boy" playing in the streets shortly after the Kelloggs' arrival in Battle Creek.[29] By the time he was twelve, the year after his mother had consecrated him for the Lord's service, Kellogg had caught the eye of James White and was invited to apprentice at the Review and Herald Publishing Association. This must have been an exciting place for such a bookish and sheltered boy. Seventh-day Adventists during the time engaged in unceasing theological controversy and debates with their theological opponents, ranging from Methodists to Universalists. An especially tempting target was Battle Creek's resident Spiritualists, whose "harmonial pantheism" came in for harsh criticism on more than one front page of the *Review and Herald*.[30] It was perhaps during this period that John Harvey Kellogg developed his delight in theological speculation, a delight he would retain to the end of his life. In any case, Kellogg thrived in the bustling environment of the printing house and rose from office boy to editor in four years, indicating that he had absorbed the minutiae of theological polemic and apology with which the paper largely dealt. Fatefully, here, too, he was brought into daily contact with Ellen White, with whom he became quite close; at some point James White confided to John Harvey that his wife had seen in a vision that Kellogg was destined to play an important role "in the Lord's work." This must have been heady stuff indeed for the seeming least of John Preston's many children.[31]

Despite his ambition and his talents as an editor, it took some years before Kellogg decided on the definitive direction for his life. Between the ages of seventeen and twenty, he continued to work off and on for the *Review and Herald* and, inspired by reading Transcendentalist Margaret Fuller, began teaching grammar school. He also completed high school and studied for a while at the Michigan State Normal School in Ypsilanti with an eye toward a teaching certificate. All indications were that John Harvey Kellogg was destined to be an educator, a career choice that he claimed had been ratified to him in a waking vision.[32] It would be another vision, however, that of Ellen G. White, that would be the deciding factor, eventually transforming "Johnny" Kellogg, schoolmaster, into Dr. John Harvey Kellogg, health reformer and superintendant of the Battle Creek Sanitarium.

### ANTEBELLUM HEALTH REFORM

Yankees throughout the diaspora were uniquely susceptible to the currents of health reform that swept the United States beginning in the Jacksonian era of the 1830s. This was a period of the exaltation of the "common man" and distrust of elites. Conspicuous among these elites were medical doctors whose primary modes of treatment, despite their pretensions to higher knowledge, consisted largely of bloodletting and the liberal use of purgatives, especially the highly toxic mercury compound calomel. In response to such "heroic medicine," so called because its reigning metaphor was a violent battle against disease, there arose a number of alternative treatments loosely classed together as "sectarian medicine." The key idea that bound together these treatments was their emphasis on the *vis medicatrix naturae,* or healing power of nature. Sectarian physicians often differentiated themselves from "regular" or "orthodox" physicians by claiming that they worked with nature, not against it, and instead of the diseased body as battlefield, they preferred the metaphor of an unbalanced scale or a musical instrument in need of tuning. Sectarian medicine thus tended to put the emphasis on prevention of disease as much as its cure, and its methods were largely based on a close attention to the balancing of the six Galenic "nonnaturals": air, diet, evacuations, sleeping and waking, exercise and rest, and peace of mind.[33] The popularity of sectarian health reform is indicated by the fact that by 1850, medical licensing laws—that "Apocalyptic Beast [of] the Medical Inquisition"—had been repealed in all but two states.[34]

Of the variety of sectarian medical systems that arose during the Jacksonian period, two of the most popular and widely practiced were Grahamism and hydropathy.[35] Sylvester Graham (1794–1851) was a Presbyterian minister from Connecticut who, through his work as a temperance lecturer, was led

Sylvester Graham from
W. P. Garrison, "The Isms
Forty Years Ago," *Harpers
New Monthly Magazine,*
January 1880, 191.

to develop what was perhaps the most comprehensive system of health reform the country had yet seen. For Graham, all disease was caused by over-
stimulation of the nervous system, which, if left unchecked, led to "diseased
irritability, inflammation, painful sensibility, and, finally, disorganization
and death." Graham is best known, of course, for his advocacy of a strict
vegetarian diet based on whole grains, a by-product of which was the cracker
that still bears his name. Graham also banned all grease, salt, condiments and
spices, tea, coffee, tobacco, and alcohol and felt that the only natural drink
for human beings was cold water. Indeed, Graham prescribed what can only
be described as a rigorous ascetic regimen for all areas of life, including sleep
(the harder the bed the better), waking (the more fresh air and exercise the
better), clothing (the looser the better), bathing (the more frequent the better), and sex (the less of it the better). Through books, newspaper articles, and
lectures, Grahamism, as it came to be called, spread throughout the nation in
the 1830s, and enough people adopted some or all of Graham's principles that
Grahamite boardinghouses, hotels, and spas became commonplace in the
Northeast of the time, especially where there were populations of Yankees.[36]

One of the aspects of Grahamism that should be emphasized is one it
shared with the sectarian health reform movement in general: it was a decid-

edly moral, if not downright religious, crusade. Medicine has always been surrounded with a sacred aura, but this was especially true of early nine-teenth-century health reform, which had been sparked in part by the energies spilling out from the period's fervid evangelical pietism and further inspired by the Christian perfectionism of Charles Grandison Finney.[37] One histo-rian has seen sectarian health reform as a kind of "physical Arminianism" that formed a corollary to the liberalization of Calvinist theology during this period, for just as salvation was now open to all, so too "bodily salvation might be open to all who struggled to win it, and . . . disease and early death were not an ineradicable part of the earthly passage." In other words, with some effort, one could achieve "physiological rectitude."[38]

Many people during the time believed that God visited people with disease as punishment for moral sins. Sectarian health reformers, on the other hand, believed that whereas moral sins led to spiritual diseases, it was "physiologi-cal sins" that led to diseases of the body, and just as spiritual disease could be avoided by following the Ten Commandments, so too physiological sins could be avoided by heeding the "laws of life." Moreover, both kinds of sins ultimately had implications for one's personal salvation, for, according to Dr. Larkin B. Coles, "it is as truly a sin against heaven, to violate a law of life, as to break one of the ten commandments."[39] According to James C. Whor-ton, the connection between moral law and natural law came about because of the long-standing assumption that "natural laws, including those of physi-ology, were of divine institution," and, thus, "the books of revelation and of nature, coming from the hand of the same Author, must be mutually rein-forcing, and . . . in particular natural law cannot possibly be immoral."[40] Thus, as Coles advised his readers, "it is as truly a duty to read and be informed on the subject [of health], as it is to study the precepts of the Bible. The study of the Bible first, and the study of the laws of life next," as "natural law is in direct line with the path that leads to heaven."[41] Of course, the fact that the asceticism implied in such contemporary physiological reforms dovetailed with the long tradition of Christian asceticism also made the connection between physical health and spiritual health seem all the more plausible.

Much more than simply personal salvation was at stake in health reform, however. Members of the American Physiological Association (APA), an organization founded in 1837 to promote Grahamism and other aspects of health reform, emphasized "the importance of yielding a strict obedience to the natural laws, as part of the grand system of Jehovah," averring that "the millennium, the near approach of which is by so many confidently predicted, can never reasonably be expected to arrive, until those laws which God has implanted in the *physical* nature of man are, equally with his moral laws, universally known and obeyed."[42] The millennial aspects of sectarian health reform are best seen in the work of the first president of the APA, William A. Alcott. Alcott, whose brother was the more famous Bronson Alcott, was in his day one of the most prolific of health reformers, producing more than a hundred books and journals on the subject. He was widely considered Sylvester Graham's chief rival. Alcott, who styled himself a "medical missionary" and a long-suffering medical prophet, saw it as his duty to educate the public about the laws of hygiene as "a means of lifting us toward the Eden whence we came." By adhering to the physiological laws, every human being could experience the fruits of God's original design for human beings: perfect health, the total eradication of disease, and a life span of biblical proportions. What's more, considering that one's state of health was bequeathed to one's offspring, "if the individual, in view of the perpetual renovation of his system, can do so much for its improvement, in his own little life time," "how much can be done in a series of generations for the improvement and elevation of the human race?" Nothing less, it seems, than the millennium predicted by the APA. Whorton has labeled Alcott's millennial brand of health reform "Christian Physiology," an ideology that placed "physiology as the cornerstone of the earthly Kingdom."[43]

A decade after Grahamism became popular, another health reform swept the country: hydropathy. Based on the work of Austrian Vincent Priessnitz, hydropathy sought to cure people through the copious use of fresh water, taken either internally or externally through baths, wet-blanket wraps, or showers. The first hydropathic or "water-cure" facility in the United States opened in New York City under the direction of Joel Shew and Russell Thacher Trall, and by the end of the 1840s some thirty water cures were in operation.[44] Typically, as with Priessnitz's original facility, these establishments were run as spas, where patients were expected to spend several weeks in residence for treatment. Hydropathic colleges soon appeared, too, the earliest being the American Hydropathic Institute, founded in 1851 by the Progressive Quaker Mary Gove Nichols and her husband, Thomas L. Nichols. Along with a rudimentary medical education, the Nichols offered instruction in both hydropathy and Grahamism. This combination would thereafter be found at most water-cure facilities, with hydropathy providing a drugless treatment option if the largely preventative approach of Grahamism failed.[45]

The Nichols soon closed their college to pursue their interest in Spiritualism, but American hydropathic pioneer Russell Thacher Trall followed their lead by opening the Hygeio-Therapeutic College in New York City in 1856. He incorporated it as a medical school a year later. This became one of the largest and most successful of the sectarian medical colleges in the country. It offered courses on anatomy, physiology, and chemistry (although not organic chemistry, as this violated Dr. Trall's vitalist beliefs).[46] The emphasis, however, was on hydropathy and Grahamism, and the curriculum fell clearly within the tradition of Christian physiology. As Trall would write in his *Water-Cure Journal,* "Health reform . . . is the veritable corner stone upon which the Christian, the social, the political, as well as the medical reformer must predicate all rational faith in the millennial state of the human family on this earth."[47] Another noted practitioner of hydropathy, Dr. James C. Jackson, owner of the famous hydropathic resort Our Home on the Hillside, in Dansville, New York, also proclaimed the millennial importance of hydropathy: "The Water-Cure revolution," he wrote, "is a *great* revolution. It touches on more interests than any revolution since the days of Jesus Christ."[48] Although Christian physiology was not the only religious approach to health reform that emerged during the period, it was to be the most visible and popular, especially in the Northeast and throughout the Yankee diaspora.

### HEALTH REFORM IN BATTLE CREEK

Elements of Christian physiology came early to Michigan, brought there by the many Yankees who streamed into the area in the 1840s. Grahamism, for example, became popular in part due to the work of such Grahamite missionaries as John Jay Shipherd. Shipherd, a Congregationalist minister, was one of the founders in 1832 of Oberlin College in Ohio, where he attempted to introduce a vegetarian regime to the dining tables of the school. The Oberlin Grahamite experiment was short lived, but Shipherd's faith in the Grahamite system remained unshaken. In 1843 he came to Michigan to found Olivet College in Eaton County. Here, he introduced it to the new school, but, in the words of John Harvey Kellogg, to the misfortune of Olivet, "an army of belligerent mosquitoes carried off the pious pioneer with his ideals, and so the health feature of the settlement, though well initiated, failed to survive the exigencies of pioneer days."[49] Nevertheless, Grahamism had made an appearance and began to be practiced by individuals if not institutions. Hydropathy, too, came early to Michigan, with Trall's and other health reform journals becoming routinely available in the 1840s. The earliest actual water-cure facility in Michigan appears to have been opened in Grand Rapids in 1849 by a Dr. H. T. Seeley. It lasted at most two years, but other water cures were established in Raisin Center (1851), Milford (1852), Coldwater (1853), and Eaton Rapids (1862).[50]

Some of the earliest advocates of health reforms in Battle Creek were the Battle Creek Progressionists, whose quest for universal reform extended in all directions. In the larger Progressive Friends movement, temperance and antitobacco had been part of their platform since 1853, with physical education added in 1859.[51] The Battle Creek Progressionists followed suit. Congruent with their pledge in their 1858 Declaration of Principles to fight intemperance, they also proclaimed that "the manifestations of life being modified by its surroundings, and the body being the medium for the soul's expression, mental and physical culture are necessary in order that a well developed system may be the properly prepared casket for the jeweled soul."[52] In other words, along with proper education of the mind and soul, the body, too, needed to be properly educated in terms of diet and exercise. An earlier declaration from the Progressionists stated that they welcomed all "who acknowledge[d] the duty of illustrating their faith in God by lives of personal purity and deeds of practical righteousness and beneficence."[53] "Personal purity" was code for abstinence from alcohol and tobacco and, though not explicitly stated, probably Grahamism too.

As the Progressionists of Battle Creek evolved into Spiritualists in the 1850s, their interest in health reform continued. For example, in their advertisements for the Bedford Harmonial Academy in the *Battle Creek Journal*, its owners, the Cornells, emphasized the salubriousness of its location, "free from unhealthful causes and the contaminating influences, by which village schools were surrounded." It was also close to a "lake of pure soft water, affording ample facilities for bathing during the warm season of year." Moreover, according to the testimony of one of the instructors, William B. Stone, not one among the institute's staff "used tobacco or intoxicating liquors."[54]

In Battle Creek proper, the Spiritualist minister Rev. James Peebles was a great proponent of health reform. An early convert to temperance and Grahamism, Peebles said he lived most of his long life largely on a diet of fruit and nuts, eschewing meat, grease, alcohol, tobacco, coffee, and tea with equal vehemence. In later years Peebles would acquire a medical degree from the Philadelphia University of Medicine and Surgery (an eclectic institution) and go on to operate health reform sanitariums in San Antonio and San Diego before returning to Battle Creek in the 1890s.[55] Sojourner Truth, too, despite the fact that she struggled with her addiction to pipe smoking, was something of a Grahamite ever since she met Graham himself while she was living at Northhampton, Massachusetts. Often she would pack Graham crackers in her carpetbag to tide her through the long train rides between speaking engagements.[56]

The Cornells' reference to the "pure soft water" of the lake near Harmonia indicates an early interest among Battle Creek's Spiritualists in hydropathy. Both Truth and Peebles were committed believers in the practical benefits of the water cure. Truth had been a patient at the Northampton Water Cure in 1845, where hydropathic treatments, she said, saved her life.[57] Peebles had been a frequent hydropathy patient as well. During his time in Elmira, New York, ministering to the Universalist congregation there, he reported spending many a pleasant hour at the Gleason Sanitarium on Watercure Hill.[58] Perhaps inspired by Peeble's recollections, one of his Battle Creek congregants, the Quaker-Spiritualist Henry Willis, opened "an extensive water cure establishment" on St. Mary's Lake on the outskirts of town in 1858. Managed by Dr. Hiram A. Peterman, a Universalist graduate of the "Ohio Eclectic Medical College" (perhaps the Eclectic Medical Institute of Cincinnati), the St. Mary's Water Cure had accommodations for seventy-five patients and was surrounded by flower gardens, fruit orchards, and woodlands. The St. Mary's Water Cure was often the scene of the yearly meeting of Progressionists, and the facility remained popular among Battle Creek's Spiritualists until it was destroyed by fire in 1863.[59]

## ADVENTISTS AND ANTEBELLUM HEALTH REFORM

When James and Ellen White relocated to Battle Creek in 1855, they found a population already keenly interested in health reform, which perhaps was one of the attractions of the place. Ever since an accident left her an invalid for much of her childhood, Ellen White had been intensely concerned about her own health, and throughout her early ministry she had been plagued by health problems. Sometimes these were so serious that her friends despaired of her life. On at least one of these occasions, her friends rallied around her to pray for her recovery, which, when it occurred, was interpreted as nothing short of one of the miracles promised for the last days. Accordingly, healing exclusively through prayer and avoiding doctors and medicine came to be seen as an act of faith. In fact, in 1849 Ellen White published a broadside targeted at Adventists entitled "To Those Who Are Receiving the Seal of the Living God." It warned that "if any among us are sick, let us not dishonor God by applying to earthly physicians, but apply to the God of Israel," for "if we follow his directions (James 5:14, 15) the sick will be healed." To do otherwise would be to jeopardize one's millennial status because "the sealing time is very short, and soon will be over." After this faith healing for a time became the norm for Sabbath-keeping Adventists, with resort to doctors or to any kinds of medicine stigmatized as a lack of faith. Even Ellen White herself was now seen to have a special power to heal through her prayer.[60]

Ellen White's negative attitudes toward doctors and medicine moderated significantly when, in the mid-1850s, she was implicated in the death of an Adventist woman in Camden, New York, who succumbed to an acute illness after forgoing medical treatment in favor of prayer. According to White in 1860, "Reports [that were] groundless were circulated . . . that we were the cause of her not having medical aid." She protested that she was nowhere near Camden when the death occurred, and when she did go to Camden shortly after, "I was shown in vision that there had been a lack of judgment in regard to the case of Sr. P. in giving their influence against her obtaining medical aid." Local Adventists "had carried matters to extremes, and that the cause of God was wounded and our faith reproached, on account of such things, which were fanatical in the extreme." In order to lay to rest any accusations that she herself was "fanatical" on the issue of medical treatment, she stated explicitly that although "we believe in the prayer of faith," we also "believe it to be perfectly right to use the remedies God has placed in our reach." Ellen White hoped that from then on, faith healing would be balanced with proper health care. Nevertheless, the idea that one could be cured by faith alone would continue to be a part of the Seventh-day Adventist tradition and would occasionally resurface within the church.[61]

Even during the period when she discouraged doctors and medicine for healing, Ellen White nevertheless vigorously promoted other health reforms. She had at least two visions before arriving in Battle Creek enjoining specific health reforms on Adventists: first, a ban on tobacco, coffee, and tea in 1848 and, paralleling the teachings of Sylvester Graham, an injunction in 1854 against rich and greasy food and an exhortation to pay more attention to personal cleanliness. Moreover, James White, who also grew up a sickly child and had an early interest in health reform, used the pages of the *Review and Herald* to campaign against liquor, tea and coffee, and especially tobacco. Soon, giving up smoking and chewing became a test of fellowship among Seventh-day Adventists, although at this point the other diet reforms advocated by both Ellen and James White proved much harder to enforce.[62]

Although Ellen White's health prophecies may appear to have been directly inspired by her own ill health, they may also be viewed in light of certain aspects of Seventh-day Adventist theology and especially against the backdrop of competing understandings of the Great Disappointment of 1844.[63] Ellen White had accepted the interpretation of Hiram Edson, whose own visionary experience had revealed to him that on the day of the Great Disappointment, which had occurred on the Jewish Day of Atonement, Jesus had entered into the innermost chamber of the heavenly sanctuary, which itself was the celestial antitype of the long-destroyed Jerusalem Temple. Having entered the Holy of Holies, Jesus, acting as the antitypical high priest, would cleanse the heavenly temple by blotting out the sins of the saints and then be wedded to the New Jerusalem, as foretold in the book of Revelation. Later Adventists would understand Jesus as having a third task, the "investigative judgment," a process in which the life of each righteous person would be minutely scrutinized in order to deem him worthy of having his name inscribed in the book of life. Once the lengthy process of the "investigative judgment" was completed, then Jesus would physically return to the earth to inaugurate the millennium.

Hiram Edson's was not the only available explanation for the Great Disappointment, however. Another competing interpretation gained a degree of popularity among early Adventists, that of the so-called spiritualizers. The "spiritualizers" believed that Jesus had indeed returned to earth in 1844, but as an invisible spirit who now dwelled in the soul of each believer. This "spiritual" interpretation of the Great Disappointment was roundly rejected by those in the Edson camp, who claimed that the "spiritualizing" interpretation led to exaggerated claims of sinlessness and antinomian behavior. White's own early visions confirmed Hiram Edson's vision. For her, the heavenly realm was a physical place with a specific location in the cosmos, a place where God the Father and his son, Jesus, material beings both, ruled over a court in heaven. There was nothing "spiritual" or metaphorical about this: the material nature of heaven and its inhabitants were to be taken literally, and Jesus's literal work in the innermost chamber of the heavenly temple would form the basis of what Seventh-day Adventists would later call the sanctuary doctrine of the atonement.[64]

The physicality of White's conception of the heavenly realm would have consequences for the meaning of physicality in this world. In the run-up to the millennium, according to White, "while our great High Priest is making the atonement for us, we should seek to become perfect in Christ."[65] For early Adventists, striving for perfection meant accepting the Saturday Sabbath and improving one's Christian character, in part by means of an ascetic discipline and purification of the body.[66] The Adventists' focus on the body had at least three theological sources. The literal, physical nature of God, Jesus, and heaven, insisted on in part to confute the "spiritualizers," necessarily drew attention to the physical nature of the saints in heaven. Based on Ellen White's visions, it was clear that the saints would not inhabit heaven as discarnate spirits, but as fully flesh-and-blood human beings. Moreover, the earliest Seventh-day Adventists were convinced that they would live to experience the Second Coming and, like Enoch and Elijah, be "translated" alive to heaven. Thus, the purity of one's body became an immediate concern in the first decades after the Great Disappointment.[67]

When in time it became apparent that the Second Coming would be delayed and that most Adventists would have to pass through death, the issue shifted from translation to resurrection. The concern for the purity of one's body still remained, however, for the fact of resurrection again pointed to the continual importance of one's physical body in the afterlife. Arguments were volleyed back and forth about whether one's resurrection body would be the same body reassembled or a new one created fresh,[68] but it was clear to all Seventh-day Adventists that human beings existed as indissoluble units of soul and flesh and that God intended for human beings to care for both as one. Some early Adventists therefore became attracted to health reform by the late 1840s for this reason. For example, Dr. Larkin B. Coles, the author of a classic of Christian physiology, *Philosophy of Health: Natural Principles of Health and Cure* (1848), a book said to have sold thirty-five thousand copies in its first five years, was a Millerite; others, such as Millerite Joshua V. Himes, were enthusiastic patrons of water-cure establishments, with Our Home on the Hillside becoming the favorite health resort of Adventists of all kinds.[69]

Meanwhile, among the earliest Seventh-day Adventists in Michigan, sectarian health reform also had its advocates. Even before migrating to Michigan, Joseph Bates had been a practicing health reformer and ardent vegetarian since 1843; by the time he began his missionary work in Michigan, the importance of health reform had become an integral part of Bates's Adventist preaching.[70] Bates, however, would already find Michigan Yankees heavily invested in health reform. Typical of many frontier homes at the time, John Preston Kellogg's was never free of sickness, and the descriptions of his son Merritt G. Kellogg of the medical treatment at the time are nothing short of harrowing. Stricken with an eye infection in 1838, John Preston was treated by a local doctor with "a fly blister on the neck, making a fearful looking sore," and with calomel, which, "salivating him so badly," left "his tongue . . . so swollen that it protruded from his mouth" for several days. Although John Preston eventually recovered his eyesight, he was, according to his son Merritt, bedeviled by "chronic diarrhea" for the next decade. A year before John Preston's first wife, Mary, "began to cough and spit blood" from tuberculosis for which she was routinely bled, but to no avail. Two years later Mary began to suffer massive hemorrhages on a daily basis. Local doctors could do nothing, and she died a week later. Medical tragedy continued to dog John Preston. In 1847 his infant daughter Emma Francis became violently ill and was diagnosed by a local doctor as suffering from worms, and although John Preston's second wife, Ann, insisted that the child was suffering from a lung infection, the doctor went ahead and treated her with a vermicide anyway. The child soon died. Both parents insisted on being present at the autopsy, which revealed that death was indeed caused by a lung inflammation, not worms.[71]

Disgusted with regular doctors and learning of the "Water Cure System," John Preston subscribed to the *Water-Cure Journal*. From then on hydropathy became the treatment of choice for all ills in the Kellogg household. John Harvey Kellogg vividly recalled the treatment some eighty years later:

> I remember very well how violently I shivered when at the age of 10, I was wrapped in a cold wet sheet pack to "bring out the eruption" in an attack of measles. I shall never forget the crude shower bath with its half-barrel tank arranged over a pan with perforated bottom, through which cold water from a deep well poured in frigid streams on my body until the tank was empty, because the door to the little chamber in which I was confined stuck fast so I could not escape, and no one came to my relief until the tank was empty.

"Hydrotherapy in those days," Kellogg added wryly, "was known as the 'cold water cure.'"[72]

About this time, too, Kellogg's family began practicing Grahamism. Again according to John Harvey, "In the forties Graham came to Michigan and gave lectures in various places, and [m]y uncle became a thorough convert to the Graham health reform movement."[73] The Kelloggs' daily fare had "invariably" consisted of large quantities of pork "fried, baked, or boiled," but the uncle, too, must have made a convert, for John Preston soon adopted a vegetarian diet for the entire family. Soon after, a First Day Adventist minister who traveled fully stocked with bags of Graham flour introduced the Kelloggs to Graham gems, the forerunner of Graham crackers. So important did Grahamite reform become for John Preston Kellogg that he sent his oldest sons to Oberlin College primarily because it was one of the few colleges in the Midwest where Grahamism was practiced at the time.[74] From a very early age, then, John Harvey Kellogg had been exposed to the two most important health reforms of the day: Grahamism and hydropathy. He, too, became a lifelong convert.

### ELLEN G. WHITE'S DEVELOPING HEALTH MESSAGE

In June 1863 James and Ellen White traveled to Otsego, Michigan, a small village to the northwest of Battle Creek, to participate in a local Seventh-day Adventist tent revival. The Whites had hoped to find in the Otsego revival a respite from the exhausting burdens of leading a new church. Both were sick and tired, worn out by the monumental task of coordinating dozens of far-flung Adventist congregations into the General Conference, which had met in Battle Creek for the first time the month before. Although successful in creating the Seventh-day Adventist Church, the work took its toll, and Elder White, it was said, looked especially depleted.[75] Little did the Whites know that their brief escape from the cares of Battle Creek and the burdens of leadership would lead to an event that would soon transform the future direction of the new church.

Ellen G. White had long been recognized in the Adventist movement as a prophetess. From her teenage years, she had been subject to frequent visions through which advice and counsel were communicated to her through an angel from God. It was not wholly unexpected, then, that at a prayer meeting in the home of Aaron Hilliard shortly after the Otsego revival, Ellen White fell into a vision that lasted about forty-five minutes. An eyewitness to the event, Martha Amadon, reported that "a heavenly influence filled the room," during which White "was given instruction on the health question." The first part of her vision, the contents of which she only later revealed publicly, hit very close to home: the Lord told the Whites that they needed to take better care of their health by sharing their responsibilities with others. The second part of the vision was a corollary to the first, but implicated the entire church: all Adventists were enjoined by God to "come out against intemperance of every kind,—intemperance in working, in eating, in drinking, and in drugging," and that they should promote to the world "God's great medicine, water, pure soft water, for diseases, for health, for cleanliness, for luxury"—in other words, hydropathy.[76]

This was not the first time Ellen White had prophesied on aspects of health reform, but the Otsego vision made it clear that health reform should now become an integral part of the church and take its place among the other saving truths of Adventism such as the Saturday Sabbath and the sanctuary doctrine of the atonement. From this point forward, health reform would become an increasingly important part of Seventh-day Adventist identity and, along with the Saturday Sabbath, the most distinctive part of Adventists' public witness.

A year after her Otsego vision, Ellen White committed it to paper. Published under the title of "Health," she included it in her ongoing pamphlet series, *Spiritual Gifts*.[77] In addition to the by now familiar exhortation to personal cleanliness and the concomitant condemnation of alcohol, tobacco, caffeinated drinks, and rich foods, she also promoted a plain vegetarian diet in small portions, clean clothes, well-lit and -ventilated houses, plenty of exercise and rest, and, when disease did strike, a patient recourse to "Nature" and "plain soft water," that is, hydropathy, instead of the "mercury, calomel, and quinine" of ignorant physicians. The reasons given for these prescriptions paralleled closely those of the Christian physiologists, who claimed that rich diets and drug taking led to a harmful overexcitation of the body, which not only destroyed physical health by sapping its "vital forces," but also tended to "benumb the sensibility of the mind" such that it "cannot clearly discern spiritual things." This led mankind to sin and progressive degradation to a state "lower than the beasts." "What will be their waking in the resurrection morning?" White asked rhetorically of degraded humanity, knowing full well the prospect would not be a happy one.[78]

If the prescriptions of Ellen White's 1863 vision offered little new, what is remarkable about "Health" is the way in which it casts the entirety of salvation history in terms of health reform. "Health" begins with White's observation that in the beginning, "Adam and Eve in Eden were noble in stature, and perfect in symmetry and beauty. They were sinless, and in perfect health." What a difference now, however: "Beauty is gone. Perfect health is not known. Every where we look we see disease, deformity and imbecility." According to White, when she inquired of her angel why this was so, she was shown a vision of the Garden of Eden where God had given mankind the perfect meatless diet and the ability to eat temperately. But with Eve's sin, she saw, death and intemperance entered the world. Indeed, people then "ate animal food, and gratified their lusts until their cup of iniquity was full," such that God was forced to cleanse "the earth of its moral pollution by a flood." Only after the flood did God give the remnant humanity permission to eat flesh. He did this not only for expedience, all other foods having been destroyed by the waters, but also as a way to continue punishing them by shortening their lives through bad diet. Thus, even after agriculture was reestablished, human beings continued to eat flesh, and White saw that "the race began to rapidly decrease in size, and in length of years." If God's first curse on human beings was the expulsion from the Garden and his second the mark of Cain, God's third great curse on humanity was an appetite for meat.[79] This, after all, was the lesson of the destruction of Sodom and Gomorrah, whose great sexual sinfulness was seen to be due to nothing less than generations of bad diet.

Nevertheless, "Health" was not meant to be a pessimistic document. White also saw that God was not content to abandon human beings to their dietary sins. First, he attempted to cleanse the Israelites of their dietary sinfulness by leading them out of the "fleshpots" of Egypt into the wilderness, where he fed them on "bread from Heaven" and the "purest water out of flinty rock." God also revealed to Moses a set of dietary regulations (the Levitical code) in addition to the Ten Commandments. Still, the Israelites hankered after flesh and impure drink, much to their detriment. Rather than worship God, they made an idol of their appetites.[80] So God next sent Christ to show sinful humanity that, despite centuries of disobedience, they could still resist the physical temptations that pulled them away from God's law. This was the meaning, according to White, of the New Testament story of a hungry Christ being tempted by the Devil, who said, "If thou be the Son of God, command that these stones be made bread," to which Christ answered, "It is written, Man shall not live by bread alone, but by every word that proceedeth out of the mouth of God." Here, White asserted, Jesus referred to the "words of God spoken from Sinai," the Mosaic dietary laws that, if followed, "will give man again free access to the tree of life, that our first parents forfeited all right to by disobedience."[81] And even in these last days, the angel showed White in her vision, this promise still holds. Physical perfection may not be possible in these last days, but after "man has done all in his power to insure health, by denying the appetite and gross passions," he may still "possess a healthy mind, and a sanctified imagination," which he may in safety "render to God" as "an offering in righteousness." Only in this way can one hope to be worthy of translation and escape the apocalyptic wrath to come.[82]

Although Christian physiologists before White had used such biblical tropes, "Health" is remarkable as a sustained application of what we might call the "health hermeneutic." As such, it still remains an influential statement of Ellen White's moral vision for health within the church today. Soon, White expanded on aspects of her health vision by writing a series of pamphlets entitled "Health: or, How to Live."[83] Here, she gave practical illustrations of a vegetarian diet and the use of hydropathy and graphic accounts of the physiological damage done through the use of such things as alcohol, tobacco, and drugs. Many who read White's revelations on health reform remarked on how closely they paralleled the prescriptions of the Christian physiologists. She was even asked if perhaps she had received the health teachings not from God, but from "Drs. Trall, Jackson, and others." White responded that she had not read about any of the health reforms until she had written her own, "lest it be said that I had received my light upon the subject of health from physicians, and not from the Lord." But "after I had written my six articles for How to Live, I then searched the various works on Hygiene and was surprised to find them so nearly in harmony with what the Lord revealed to me."[84] In light of this, Ellen White said, she and her husband decided to republish her pamphlets in book form alongside excerpts from such writers as Jackson, Coles, Trall, Dio Lewis, and Horace Mann. Also called *Health: or, How to Live,* this thin volume came off the *Review and Herald*'s steam press in 1865 complete with a preface by James White defending the originality of Ellen White's health visions.[85]

Even after the Otsego vision and the publication of "Health" and *Health: or, How to Live,* Ellen White still found that the vast majority of rank-and-file Seventh-day Adventists were slow to embrace health reform in its entirety.[86] A few, such as J. H. Waggoner, accepted its divine importance early on. He wrote:

> As mere physiological and hygienic truths, they might be studied by some at their leisure, and by others laid aside as of little consequence; but when placed on a level with the great truths of the third angel's message by the sanction and authority of God's Spirit, and so declared to be the means whereby a weak people may be made strong to overcome, and our diseased bodies cleansed and fitted for translation, then it comes to us as an essential part of *present truth,* to be received with the blessing of God, or rejected at our peril.[87]

For others, apparently, this importance was still hard to accept, because to them the "present truth" consisted exclusively in the imminent end of the world and the necessity of preaching this message throughout the globe. The urgency of this latter task made it hard to expend much energy on such an earthly concern as bodily health. Yet, as Ellen White's vision attested, it was God's will. What was needed, she felt, was greater education in the heavenly meaning and down-to-earth practice of health reform, and for this, again despite the shortness of time, another Seventh-day Adventist institution was required.

# 2

~

## The Rise of the Temple of Health

I n 1865 Ellen White had another important health vision. In this case, God commanded her to create a hydropathic facility in Battle Creek. Although Battle Creek boasted a water-cure establishment at nearby St. Mary's Lake as early as 1858, White said that she first learned about the water cure in 1863 in a newspaper article detailing Dr. Jackson's hydropathic treatment of diphtheria. When her own children were stricken with the dread disease, White used hydropathy to treat them.[1] Inspired by their recovery, the White family made an extended visit to Dr. Jackson's Our Home on the Hillside in upstate New York the following year.[2]

So impressed were the Whites with Dr. Jackson's methods that when James White suffered a stroke in Battle Creek in the summer of 1865, Ellen White rushed him there for treatment. However, this visit would not be so successful. Not only did James not respond to Dr. Jackson's treatments, but after several weeks in residence at Our Home, Ellen White became increasingly irritated by the doctor's religious views. Not only was Dr. Jackson an ardent postmillennialist, but, even more problematically, he believed that when it came to saving souls, health reform should take precedence over preaching.[3] As he put it, "The proper obedience of the laws of nature would so far affect the conditions of human creatures" that "regeneration, or what is called a 'change of heart,' would be so silently accomplished, the transformation being made in so unobservable a way, that the recipients would seldom know the dividing line in their lives." In other words, health reform would replace revivals for the conversion of souls, for according to Dr. Jackson, all the "Christian force as is habitually made from pulpits and platforms, from prayer circles and missionary rooms," is utterly ineffective "until Christians shall intelligently perceive and conscientiously comprehend how important purity of body is to purity of soul."[4] As important as health reform was to Ellen White, it would always be an adjunct to the preaching of the Word, not a necessary preparation for it. Prioritizing health reform as Dr. Jackson did must have struck her as not a little blasphemous. What's more, Dr. Jackson discouraged Bible reading and preaching at his institution in favor of what Ellen White termed "worldly amusements," such as singing, dancing, and card playing.[5]

After a hasty departure and while en route back to Battle Creek, White experienced a vision in which she was told by the Lord that Seventh-day Adventists needed their own health reform institution so that they would not have to resort "to popular water cure institutions for the recovery of health, where there is no sympathy for our faith."[6] Thus was born the idea for the Western Health Reform Institute, which, after approval by the Adventist General Conference in May 1866, became a reality in Battle Creek later that year.[7]

Ellen White had high hopes for the institute, saying that it was "designed of God to be one of the greatest aids in preparing a people to be perfect before God," a place where his physiological laws would be "like a city set on a hill." Unlike other such facilities, the institute's physicians would "be spiritual fathers," always approaching "health reform from a religious standpoint" and, in addition to healing the body, always ready to "point the sin-sick soul to the never-failing remedy, the Saviour who died for them." White stressed that the institute was to be based on "Bible hygiene" and that "the religion of Christ" was "not to be placed in the background, and its holy principles laid down to meet the approval of any class, however popular," for "if the standard of truth and holiness is lowered, then is the design of God not carried out in our Institution." Yet White also intended the institute to be a missionary agency for the Seventh-day Adventist Church, and she was explicit that the institute should be nonsectarian in character, open to all, Adventists or no. The Saturday Sabbath would be observed and prayer meetings available, but no one would be pressured to participate and there were to be no open theological disputes, because "there is an abundance to dwell upon in regard to Bible religion, without objectionable points of difference." White recognized that for some Seventh-day Adventists, such a policy was unwise, but she believed that this was the best way not to frighten non-Adventists away. In any case, the place "to speak of our denominational sentiments" was "the house of God," not the institute. Of course, the institute's staff, especially its doctors, should never lose sight of the fact that it was "established by Seventh-day Adventists," and they should exert a "silent influence" by diligently fulfilling their religious duties.[8]

While the nonsectarian character of the institute bothered some, others caviled at the idea that a church that expected the imminent end of the world should be investing in yet another permanent institution. Such objections, of course, were similar to those that had already been raised over the incorporation of the printing enterprise and the creation of the General Conference. Thus, in the pages of the *Review and Herald*, D. T. Bourdeau assured his brethren that, like those other institutions, the Western Health Reform Institute, too, was a gospel agency and, far from "a denial of our faith in the speedy coming of Christ," "is one of the strongest proofs that the Lord is near. When we see mighty agencies at work to bring about a state of preparation for the coming of Christ, we say the work will go on rapidly, and the Lord will soon come."[9] To that end, in the next issue the editor of the *Review* exhorted his readers to buy stock in the institute, which he assured them would be a safe investment.[10] J. N. Loughborough seconded Bourdeau's view: "Instead of being a denial of our faith to enter zealously in this work, it is to show that our faith is genuine.... This Institution itself, is to me an evidence of the near coming of Christ," because it represents "God's people rallying to get rid of those things that blunt their faculties, that they may be clean vessels, all prepared for translation when the Lord comes." In light of this, he counseled, Sabbath keepers should buy as many shares in the institute as they could.[11]

Despite such protestations, the growing institutionalization of Seventh-day Adventism, with its church structure, publishing house, and now health institute, did represent the attenuation of premillennial urgency so important in the early days of the Adventist movement. This led to the paradoxical situation, in Edwin Gaustad's words, of a denomination "expecting a kingdom of God from heaven," while at the same time "work[ing] diligently for one on earth."[12] In the 1880s and 1890s, there even developed within Seventh-day Adventism the notion that the church should do nothing that

Western Health Reform Institute. *Courtesy of Willard Library Historical Images of Battle Creek Collection.*

might provoke the end prematurely so that more could be converted and saved.[13] Functionally, this was a position that differed little from the optimistic postmillennialism of mainstream American Protestantism, and the church would always have to work hard to differentiate between Seventh-day Adventist institution building and that of the wider world. The subsequent expansion of Adventist health work would continually challenge this distinction, and in time would lead to acute tensions within the denomination.

Several weeks after the General Conference approved the Western Health Reform Institute, the *Review and Herald* reported that its grand opening was set for the following September 5. A detailed prospectus, following the exuberant typographical conventions of the day, promised "a place where disease will be treated on HYGIENIC PRINCIPLES" and "where instruction will be imparted both Theoretically and Practically, to patients and boarders, on the important subject of so caring for both body and mind, as to preserve health." To do so, the institute would be run in accordance with strict health reform principles:

> In the treatment of the sick at this Institution, *no drugs whatever, will be administered,* but only such means employed as NATURE can best use in her recuperative work, such as Water, Air, Light, Heat, Food, Sleep, Rest, Recreation, &c. Our tables will be furnished with a strictly healthful diet, consisting of Vegetables, Grains, and Fruits, which are found in great abundance and variety in this State. And it will be the aim of the Faculty, that all who spend any length of time at this Institute shall go to their homes instructed as to the right mode of living, and the best methods of home treatment.

No less important, according to the prospectus, was the physical site. Six acres located on the outskirts of Battle Creek had been chosen because they were the "highest and driest part of the city, commanding a fine prospect of city and country, within a few minutes' ride of the depot, from which conveyance can be had by omnibus on the arrival of all trains," thus making the facility "easily accessible from all points of the country." The main building, a large two-story Greek Revival farmhouse, was "separated from the street by a spacious and beautiful grove" and its back acreage "diversified with fruit trees, hills, and stream." All was designed for "REST, QUIET, and RETIREMENT," but for those seeking recreation and exercise, "the adjacent rural districts afford abundant opportunities for pleasant walks" and nearby Goguac Lake beckons "with its clear water and shady beach." All in all, "Our Establishment will have plenty of Pure, Soft Water, pure air, good moral influences, and a greater amount of sunshine than any other part of the country can ordinarily boast." Not a little hubristically, the prospectus promised its patients that "WHATEVER MAY BE THE NATURE OF THEIR DISEASE, IF CURABLE, THEY CAN BE CURED HERE."[14]

Concurrent with the announcement of the Western Health Reform Institute, the General Conference also announced plans to produce a monthly journal, the *Health Reformer,* in order "to teach faithfully and energetically those Rules of Health . . . that we may be enabled to heed the apostolic injunction, to glorify God in our *bodies* as well as our spirits." Like the institute, the journal would "not be denominational in its character, but [would] be adapted to the wants of all classes of people everywhere, who are interested in the great question of maintaining health by obedience to Nature's laws." Presumably, the journal would also function as a monthly advertisement for the Western Health Reform Institute and bring it to the notice of a wider clientele.[15]

The opening of the Western Health Reform Institute, which, despite its unfinished state, occurred precisely as projected on September 5, 1866, was reported the following week in the *Review and Herald* under the headline "A Great Fact Accomplished." "In no enterprise ever undertaken," crowed the reporter, "has the hand of the Lord been more evidently manifested than in this thing." Yet, the reporter warned, "we may expect that the enemy will try with all his power to bring reverses, create hindrances, and block the wheels of its onward progress."[16] This prophecy turned out to be true, as the first decade of the Western Health Reform Institute was one of ups and downs. The original facility, despite the advertisements, was far from luxurious and, even with the hasty addition of two new wings, always too small for the demand. Its first superintendent, Dr. Horatio Lay, was a self-taught physician from Allegan with little experience managing such an enterprise, and although the institute did enjoy periods of prosperity and expansion, these were inevitably followed by periods of financial crisis. At times, Ellen White despaired of its ultimate success and was already worrying about the incipient levity and worldliness creeping into its daily life. She had even detected some unbelief among the staff.[17] To make matters worse, the legal incorporation of the institute proved difficult, as Michigan then had no provision for what today would be called a nonprofit. Friends of the Adventists in the state legislature at Lansing managed to tack on an amendment to a law authorizing mining and manufacturing companies, allowing the Western Health Reform Institute to be legally incorporated on April 9, 1867.[18] But such corporate charters were limited to thirty years, a fact that would have significant consequences down the road.

At this early stage, however, the institute's principal problem was that it was woefully understaffed, and those employed, including Dr. Lay, had little or no training. To remedy this problem, James White in 1872 brought in one of John Preston's sons, Merritt G. Kellogg, to help with the work. Merritt was a graduate of Trall's Hygeio-Therapeutic College, which since 1867 had been located in Florence Heights, New Jersey. There, an "MD" could be had within six months.[19] Merritt soon lobbied James White to underwrite the education of more Adventist doctors at Trall's, which, with the approval of Ellen White, he agreed to do. Merritt also insisted that his younger half-brother John

Harvey Kellogg be included in the group sent to Trall's Hygeio-Therapeutic College. To this James White also agreed.[20]

John Harvey Kellogg did not want to go at first. Destined as he thought he was for a career in education (and perhaps because of his continued squeamishness at the sight of blood), it took some persuading by James White for the teenage John Harvey to accept the offer of accompanying the group of Adventist youth to Trall's college. In the end, though, he decided to go. Perhaps Kellogg was attracted by the prospect of learning something of the wider world, but he was also genuinely interested in health reform, both because Grahamism and hydropathy had been practiced in his father's home and because his work at the *Review and Herald* had allowed him to read materials by such Christian physiologists as Sylvester Graham and Larkin Coles.[21] Still, Kellogg did not envision dedicating himself to medicine at this point, expecting to return from Trall's to continue his training to be a teacher.[22]

Bright, ambitious, and not a little censorious, John Harvey Kellogg was not much impressed by the curriculum at the Hygeio-Therapeutic College, which he breezed through with a minimum of effort.[23] Later Kellogg would refer to the diploma he earned at Trall's as "bogus." Dr. Trall, after all, did not even believe in the reality of organic chemistry. Nevertheless, John Harvey's time at the college did whet his appetite for further medical training, this time at "orthodox" medical institutions, an idea he proposed to James White upon his return to Battle Creek. Elder White was reluctant to endorse this project, his attitude being that training at "some doctor-mill" was all an Adventist physician really needed, but Kellogg prevailed, and with White's financial backing, he attended first the College of Medicine and Surgery at the University of Michigan and then Bellevue Hospital in New York City, which at the time was the finest teaching hospital in the United States. Here Kellogg not only learned the latest in regular medicine, including new drug therapies, but under the tutelage of Austin Flint and E. G. Janeway was also introduced to advances in physiotherapy and surgery. Immensely proud of his achievement, Kellogg graduated with a regular MD from Bellevue in 1875.[24] Later, in the 1880s, Kellogg, now completely over his disgust of blood, would take up the practice of surgery in earnest, training first in New York and then in 1883 in Vienna with Adolph Bilroth, whom Kellogg characterized as "the greatest surgeon of the nineteenth century."[25] Over the next three decades, Kellogg would continue to travel to Europe for extended periods to study advances in surgical techniques, and, reflecting his keen interest in the physiology of food and the diseases of digestion, Kellogg became an innovative specialist in gastrointestinal surgery.[26]

### THE EARLY YEARS OF THE BATTLE CREEK SANITARIUM

Shortly after returning to Battle Creek at the end of 1875, Kellogg, now a newly minted regular MD, joined the staff of the Western Health Reform Institute. Much to his surprise, the twenty-six-year-old doctor found himself appointed superintendent of the institute the following year.[27] From the beginning of his tenure as superintendent, Kellogg strove mightily to raise the institute's profile beyond simply that of a sectarian water cure (in later years Kellogg would dismiss the early institute as "an empirical institution, a sort of mixture of water cure, homeopathy, and eclecticism," with "no scientific direction").[28] Despite his small physical size and high, squeaky voice, Kellogg nevertheless exuded a charisma that drew people to him. He also had seemingly inexhaustible energy that allowed him to work eighteen hours a day and to micromanage a dozen different projects at the same time.[29] From the first, the sanitarium was destined for success, if only by the force of John Harvey's will. Very quickly, the doctor became something of a star within the Seventh-day Adventist Church.

From the first, Dr. Kellogg acted with independence. Kellogg's first act as director was summarily to change the institute's name to the Battle Creek Sanitarium, a word of his own coinage. Uriah Smith, editor of the *Review and Herald*, complained that no such word existed in *Webster's* and no one would know what it meant, but Kellogg believed the variant name would better signify "a place where people learn to stay well," instead of "sanatorium," a place were people came only to be cured.[30] Kellogg next began a campaign of extensive advertising of the Battle Creek Sanitarium, placing full-page ads in professional journals, such as on the cover of the American Medical Association's journal, and in popular magazines as well.[31] Along with all the luxuries of a grand hotel, the "San" was touted as offering a carefully monitored vegetarian diet, a variety of physical therapies including "rational" hydropathy, Swedish movements, calisthenics, breathing exercises, and eventually electric, light, and heat therapies. "Rational medicine," an

A young John Harvey
Kellogg, from John Harvey
Kellogg, *Plain Facts for Old
and Young* (Burlington,
IA: I. F. Segner and
Condit, 1881).

idea Kellogg appropriated from Dr. Jacob Bigelow and Dr. Oliver Wendell
Holmes, meant that "disease is not a thing to be antidoted; that it is not be
thrown out of the body by violent means, but that it is a wrong action of the
body, and that it is to be cured by training the patient into a state of health in
a case of chronic disease by helping nature so that the disease may become
acute instead of chronic," and thus cured.[32]

True to the original mission of the institute, Dr. Kellogg was eager to expand the sanitarium's clientele beyond Seventh-day Adventists, and in this
he was extremely successful. Over the next two decades, thousands of Adventists and non-Adventists alike were convinced that a stay at the Battle
Creek Sanitarium was just the cure for their harried lives, especially those
with "chronic nervous disorders, functional disturbances of the stomach,
and other chronic diseases." What's more, those thousands paid hefty fees
for the privilege, typically between ten and twenty dollars a day for room,

board, and two daily treatments (an initial examination and assessment by a physician was included in the price, as were subsequent consultations, but other amenities and services, such as surgery, cost extra). Kellogg realized that a stay at the San was not within the reach of everyone, and therefore offered special rates to "physicians and clergymen and their families, and to worthy objects of charity."[33]

Continuing an emphasis of the Christian physiologists, one of the more unusual features of the sanitarium was Kellogg's insistence that women and men receive identical treatments in terms of diet and exercise. Dr. Kellogg rejected the popular cult of female invalidism of the late nineteenth century and its ideology of the constitutional weakness of women. Whatever physical inferiority was to be found in women in America and Europe was primarily due to improper diet and lack of "regular, systematic, and daily exercise." Indeed, "the physical training of women," Kellogg believed, "should begin in childhood," and a girl's upbringing that ignored such training was nothing short of "criminal." However, "women who have already attained to maturity and find themselves suffering in consequence of inattention to physical culture in their early years may do much by pursuing a course of physical exercise," even if this was done "late in life." Nor should the restricting fashions of the day, which Kellogg abhorred, be an obstacle to exercise; they should simply be abandoned in favor of suitable clothes that allowed "unrestrained action" and freedom of movement.[34] Thus, at the sanitarium women were expected to work out in the gymnasium as well as the men, and if they did not bring with them suitable clothing, such garments could be conveniently secured from the sanitarium's Sewing Department.[35]

Kellogg's vision for the sanitarium proved so successful that the physical plant had to be constantly expanded to accommodate the demand. In 1878 the old farmhouse that had housed the original institute was replaced by a massive 150-foot-long, four-story brick-veneered structure that could house three hundred guests. Dominated by a central mansard-roofed tower that formed the central entryway to the first floor lobby, the new sanitarium boasted a large formal dining room and a "grand parlor," along with doctors' offices, a medical laboratory, and a large gymnasium. Connected outbuildings in the back of the structure housed the hydropathic facilities. In the summertime exercise activities were moved outside to take advantage of the sunshine and fresh air, leading to the eventual development of the grounds for both athletic uses and aesthetic enjoyment.[36] Kellogg was always insistent that beauty be a part of the treatment, and to this end he had constructed an elegant floral conservatory on the second floor of the new San.[37]

The next two decades saw even further expansion and improvement of the sanitarium's facilities, funded primarily by large loans (later in life Kellogg said, perhaps facetiously, that he was advised by "leading brethren" to borrow all he needed, but to make sure the loans did not come due for twelve years, "as before that time the end would come").[38] An addition that almost doubled the size of the building was built on to the south end in 1884, a chapel was added in 1886,[39] a second addition was completed in 1891, and a fifth story was added four years later. Clinical activities were moved in 1888 from the main building to a new five-story two-hundred-bed hospital and surgical ward located across the street, and a nurses' dormitory followed soon after. No aspect of the patients' comfort was neglected. Guest rooms were now supplied with hot and cold running water, and a central heating and ventilation system, partly of Kellogg's own design, filled the rooms with the fresh air the doctor considered so important for health. The main building was also thoroughly electrified. Day care for guests' children was instituted in 1886, the landscaping of the grounds grew more elaborate, and, continuing a tradition that began with the original institute, cottages and a boardinghouse were constructed at nearby Goguac Lake for those desiring a break from city life in Battle Creek. Moreover, given the emphasis on diet, fresh food was a must, so the sanitarium acquired some four hundred acres for dairy, fruit, and vegetable farms to supply its dining rooms directly. All of this, of course, took an army of staff members to run, most of whom were recruited from the Seventh-day Adventist Church and who, out of devotion to the cause, worked for less than the going rate, thus improving the sanitarium's bottom line. All in all, by the turn of the century, the sanitarium hosted some seven hundred patients attended by a staff of nearly one thousand.[40]

Although Ellen White was always worried about the deterioration of the religious atmosphere of the sanitarium, especially as it expanded and brought in wealthy clientele,[41] Dr. Kellogg strove to create an atmosphere of Christian solemnity. A chaplain was always available, Bibles were found in every room, prayer services and Bible classes were conducted daily for both patients and staff, and worship services were available on Saturday and Sunday in the chapel.[42] A rather cranky correspondent for *Cereal and Feed* complained that

Battle Creek Sanitarium, ca. 1890s.

at the sanitarium, "there is one religious institution that we have too much of, and that is the Sabbath. There are two Sundays here, and between the two, I am afraid we do not keep either one. The Adventists are as rigid in their observance of the Seventh day, as the old Puritans were of Sunday, and we are in a measure forced to observe it. Then, when Sunday comes we feel that we have kept our day of rest, and grow lax."[43] Another guest, Mrs. Marion B. Baxter, an official of the Women's Christian Temperance Union (WCTU) who had been visiting the sanitarium off and on for more than a decade, was more reverential, writing in 1897 that she "was captivated by the missionary spirit pervading this place."[44] Observing the gymnasium exercises, she remarked that here "they teach the value of every bone and nerve and sinew, constantly emphasizing that the body is the temple of God, and that to sin against the body is to sin against him." "Pretty good religion this," she added, and, contra the *Cereal and Feed* correspondent, "the more there is of it the better."[45] Fully aware that this was a Seventh-day Adventist institution, Mrs. Baxter nevertheless detected no tension because of it: "Among the seven hundred helpers who come and go, I have heard no arguments on theological questions. They believe in the Bible, and study it carefully. Nurses and helpers are often seen with the Book of books in their hand; they are deeply in earnest, and practise [sic] and love more than they preach."[46]

For Mrs. Baxter, the entire sanitarium, from its lawns to the dining room, was pervaded by the "shine of the Master's face," although nowhere was this aura more evident to her than in the operating room where Dr. Kellogg ("the look and tone" of whom "stirred my soul to its depths") practiced his surgical magic:

> One day, drawn by very strong ties, I found myself in the gallery of the operating-room of the Hospital, looking down upon a strangely solemn scene. Nurses and physicians, capped, slippered, and gowned all in white, moved softly about the place. Not a spoken word, save that of the surgeon-in-chief. Just for a moment he paused, as if in prayer, before a glass-topped table on which lay a young women in a sleep very much like death; and then, with infinite tenderness, he let fall the shining blade that was to send her back to health again. And still she slept on. In and out among the delicate muscles moved the skilled fingers,—with like manner passed out; and as I looked down on this awesome scene, it did seem to me that God was manifest there in power.[47]

Mrs. White said that Kellogg's skill as a surgeon was due to the fact that angels were present in the operating room, invisibly assisting his work, an assertion with which Kellogg publicly concurred: "I know the Lord helps me in operations," he once said, for "any honest doctor . . . who would look up to the great Father to help him would get help." Kellogg long insisted that he and his surgical team begin with a prayer before every operating session, a ritual that Mrs. Baxter found especially inspiring.[48]

Kellogg, of course, was not alone responsible for the success of the Battle Creek Sanitarium. In addition to his army of staff, the doctor was also aided immeasurably by his wife, Ella Eaton.[49] Eaton first came to Battle Creek in 1876 with her younger sister to visit an aunt who worked at the *Review and Herald*. When Eaton's sister came down with typhoid, a sanitarium doctor was called who prescribed hydropathy. Eaton was skeptical of such treatments, but she faithfully carried them out and her sister recovered. Ella Eaton soon discovered that she had a knack for healing and was quickly enlisted to help out when typhoid became epidemic in the West End. It was through her service as a nurse that she met Dr. Kellogg. Impressed with the young woman's education and skill, Kellogg induced her to enroll in his new School of Hygiene and soon after asked her to share editorial duties on *Good Health* (Kellogg had renamed the *Health Reformer* in 1879). A short time later he pro-

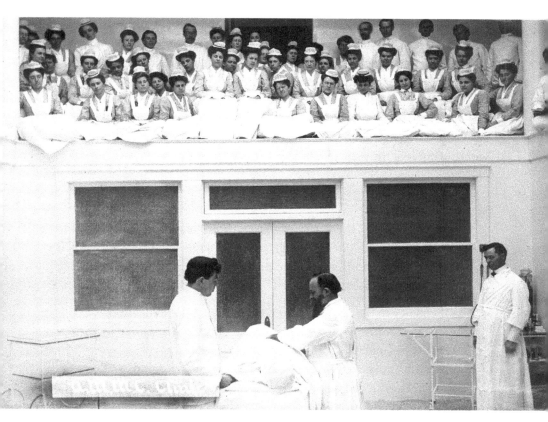

Dr. John Harvey Kellogg in the operating theater, ca. mid-1890s.

posed, and they were married by Lycurgus McCoy, the sanitarium chaplain, on February 22, 1879.

Kellogg's decision to marry Ella Eaton was unexpected and perhaps controversial among the Adventists of the West End.[50] Ella Eaton was not an Adventist, but a member of the Seventh-Day Baptist Church. Such "mixed marriages" were not unknown at the time, but the fact that one of the chief ornaments of Seventh-day Adventism chose to marry outside the faith was an indication of Kellogg's growing independence. However this may have been, Ella Eaton was soon working closely with her husband at the sanitarium, not only in literary work, but also in research into the preparation of vegetarian foods. In this department Ella Kellogg's influence was paramount. She wrote several popular vegetarian cookbooks, started a cooking school that later developed into the Battle Creek Sanitarium School of Home Economics, and devised the menus for the San's dining room. Although theirs was apparently not an outwardly affectionate marriage, Ella Eaton doted on her "nearly perfect husband," whom she routinely referred to in her diary as "Dr. K."[51] Dr. Kellogg, for his part, respected both his wife's fervent Christian piety and her contribution to the sanitarium, toiling as she did "year after year to aid in the working out [of] the principles of 'biologic living.'"[52]

### BIOLOGIC LIVING

According to Kellogg, the single most important key to the success of the Battle Creek Sanitarium was its emphasis on "biologic living," also known as the "Battle Creek Idea." Kellogg articulated the basic rules of biologic living as early as 1875 in an editorial entitled "The Hygienic Platform":

1. Obedience to the laws of life and health is a moral obligation.
2. Mental, moral, and physical health can only be maintained by the observance of mental, moral, and physical laws.
3. A healthy body is essential to perfect soundness of mind.
4. Physical health promotes morality.
5. Morality, likewise, promotes physical health.
6. In the treatment of disease the simplest and safest remedies are the proper curative agents.
7. Nature is the most efficient physician.[53]

Despite his contempt for his education at Trall's and despite his training in regular medicine at Bellevue, Kellogg never lost his respect for medical sectarians such as Sylvester Graham, William A. Alcott, Larkin Coles, Elizabeth Blackwell, and Vincent Priessnitz.[54] He simply believed that their ideas needed to be rationalized and made more scientific. Thus, in terms of practice, Kellogg's biologic living followed closely the old injunctions of the Christian physiologists: sexual restraint; total abstinence from alcohol, tobacco, and caffeine; and a complete commitment to a vegetarian diet. It also consisted of attention to sleep, exercise, fresh air, and proper dress, which, for both men and women, meant clothes that did not in any way constrict the body or prevent the proper functioning of any of its organs. Such a regimen, Kellogg believed, would prevent most diseases, but if disease did strike, drugs and surgery should be avoided as long as possible in favor of less taxing forms of therapy such as hydropathy, radiant heat, or light therapy.[55]

Of all the elements of Kellogg's biologic living, two still seem to evoke the most comment today: his teachings on sex and diet. Kellogg's ideas on sex were largely derived from the Christian physiologists via Ellen White, who had written two pamphlets on sexual temperance based on her visions, *An Appeal to Mothers* (1864) and *A Solemn Appeal Relative to Solitary Vice, and the Abuses and Excesses of the Marriage Relation* (1870).[56] In 1877 Kellogg himself published *Plain Facts about the Sexual Life* (later retitled *Plain Facts for Old and Young*), a volume combining Christian physiological prescriptions with relatively explicit (for the day) discussions of the biology of human reproduction. The goal of *Plain Facts* was to give parents a resource to teach their children "just and religious views of the nature and purpose of the relation which the Creator has established between the two sexes." It would become one of the best-known volumes on sex education in the nineteenth-century United States.[57] Like the Christian physiologists and Ellen White, Kellogg believed that the human body at any one time had a finite supply of vital energy or force and that this force contributed to the state of one's overall health.[58] To waste vital energy through masturbation or excessive sexual activity led to a serious and perhaps permanent decline in one's health.[59] Additionally, Kellogg taught that if couples conceived a child while one or the other was in such a weakened state, this state was heritable and would necessarily impair the constitution of the child. Thus, the doctor warned, having sexual relations in a debilitated state not only harmed the child, but, since heritable, could have a devastating impact on the nation, if not the whole human race. For this reason Kellogg counseled married couples not to have sexual relations above once a month. Both the health of the future child and that of the human race had to take precedence before the satisfaction of mere sexual desire.[60]

Of all the sexual sins, masturbation was the most disturbing for Kellogg, as it was also for many of the Christian physiologists and Ellen White.[61] In children especially, the "solitary vice" could have disastrous consequences for the child's development, up to and including imbecility and sterility. Boys especially, because they were more given to masturbation, were responsible for "undermining the health of the race and sapping the constitutions of our American men."[62] For this reason Kellogg recommended intense parental supervision of children, to the point of denying them privacy. If this did not work, Kellogg was prepared to employ even harsher methods, such as circumcision without anesthetic for boys and the application of carbolic acid on the clitoris for girls.[63]

One of the aspects of *Plain Facts* that troubles today's reader, but would have reassured a Victorian one, was that Kellogg frequently justified his physiological teachings by reference to the Bible, making it clear that human sexuality was a part of God's plan of salvation: "We belong to our Creator, and are accountable to God not only for the manner in which we treat our fellow-men, but for how we treat ourselves, for the manner in which we use the bodies which he has given us." To abuse our bodies in any way was to rebel against God and invite divine retribution. For this reason, Kellogg intoned, "The Bible utters the most solemn warnings against sexual sins." Were not "the inhabitants of Sodom of Gomorrah . . . destroyed by fire and brimstone for such transgressions," and was not King David made to suffer "to the day of his death" because of "a single violation of the seventh commandment"? Of course, the most heinous of all these sins was that of Onan, "who was struck dead in the act of committing" the sin of masturbation.[64] Given Kellogg's firm conviction about the ineluctable connection between proper sexuality, health, and salvation, it is little wonder why sexual asceticism formed a notable part of biologic living. Like every other aspect of biologic living, nothing less was at stake in sex than the fate of one's eternal soul.

Perhaps even more controversial at the time than his views on sex was Dr. Kellogg's uncompromising promotion of vegetarianism. It was obvious to all, Kellogg argued, that animal foods putrefied in the body and deposited poisons, thus unnaturally shortening life.[65] In the wake of the rise of the germ theory of disease, Kellogg taught that this was at least in part because animal foods were always contaminated with harmful bacteria (Kellogg's nauseating descriptions of the unhygienic nature of slaughterhouses predated those of Upton Sinclair's book *The Jungle* [1906] by several years).[66] "Animal foods," it should be noted, included milk, cheese, and eggs, all of which were, according to Kellogg, routinely produced under unsanitary conditions.[67] With progress in sanitary reforms, Kellogg would soften somewhat his strictures against the consumption of milk and eggs, although completely eliminating these animal products from the American diet, as the doctor had done in his own, always remained a goal. On the farm of the future, Kellogg predicted in 1927, nut trees, peanuts, and soybeans would replace cattle and fowl, and the only animals to be found on the farm would be draft horses and perhaps chickens for "decorative purposes."[68] As an additional physiological argument for vegetarianism, Kellogg argued that animals "have adhered far more closely to the divine order established for them than has man" and therefore enjoy a perfection that he no longer does. This was because most animals still eat the vegetarian diet that God prescribed for them in the Garden of Eden, and they, unlike human beings, retained their Edenic purity.[69] Kellogg would later call attention to the great apes, which "have adhered to the old fashioned bill of fare" and "have not degenerated as we have. They have even improved a little."[70]

Kellogg's militant vegetarianism was most prominently and polemically on display in his book *Shall We Slay to Eat?* (1899). As the title suggests, Kellogg added moral arguments to his sanitary and physiological arguments.[71] In earlier works the doctor had taught that the consumption of "animal foods of all kinds, not excepting fish, fowl, oysters, eggs, and milk," had a heating action within the body, which inevitably led to the sin of lustful and intemperate behavior.[72] But in *Shall We Slay to Eat?* Kellogg's moral arguments took a different tack. "The basis for the ethical argument against flesh eating," wrote Kellogg, "is to be found in the fact that lower animals are, in common with man, sentient creatures. We have somehow become accustomed to think of our inferior brethren, the members of the lower orders of the animal kingdom, as things; we treat them as sticks or stones, as trees and other non-sentient things that are not possessed of organs of sense and feeling. We are wrong in this; they are not things, but *beings*." And because animals are sentient beings "into whose nostrils as well as into man's God breathed the breath of life," do they not have "the right to live"? To kill animals for food or any other reason was "simply unprovoked, premeditated, systematic *murder*," "a manifestation of that supreme selfishness that leads man to the egoistic belief that all things were made for own personal pleasure and use." To kill and eat an animal was, therefore, to commit a multitude of sins against God's divine order. At the end of *Shall We Slay to Eat?* an impassioned Kellogg wrote:

It is certainly to be hoped that the time may come when there will be preached, not only in civilized lands, but also in heathen lands, that greater gospel which was sent not to save man out of the world, but to save him from himself in the world, and to save, to rescue, to redeem the world itself,—man, animals, plants, the whole creation,—which, groaning under the burden of sin and strife and carnage and wrong and perversion, awaits the dawning of that new day when Eden shall be restored, and the "golden age" shall have come again, and when man shall love not only his fellow men, but all God's creatures, great and small, in earth, and air, and sea, and when once more there shall arise with each returning dawn one universal hymn of praise, in which all living, sentient things shall join in sweet accord.[73]

Apparently, Kellogg meant this last statement literally. In Adam's time, he believed, all creatures without exception literally sang for joy, and "if universal harmony is once more restored in creation, as I believe there will be, there may yet be beautiful music among all living things,—and there is music in nature, even now."[74]

Enjoining a vegetarian diet on moral and physiological grounds was one thing, but getting people actually to eat it was quite another. Realizing that most vegetarian cooking was unpalatable, Kellogg and his staff, most notably his wife, Ella Eaton, and younger brother Will K., worked long hours experimenting with a variety of new vegetarian food preparations. Their successes included the reputed invention of peanut butter, a grain coffee substitute called Caramel Cereal Coffee, a soy-based meat substitute called Protose, and, of course, ready-to-eat breakfast cereals, most notably Granola and cornflakes. Sold under the Sanitas label by Kellogg's Sanitarium Food Company, Kellogg's vegetarian food products were a modest but consistent moneymaker for the sanitarium during the 1890s.[75] Despite their potential for mass marketing, Kellogg refused to think of his food products as ends in themselves, and quite often when his recipes were pirated, the doctor would celebrate the profitability of his inventions as a victory for biologic living.[76] Kellogg at one point even offered to turn the health food patents over to the denomination, but this offer was refused because it was seen at the time as more of a distraction than an asset.[77] In time, when breakfast cereals became big business, Dr. Kellogg would come to worry that his association with their sale would hurt his professional reputation; it was for this reason that the name Kellogg would not appear on a box of cereal until after the turn of the century, and then it would not be the doctor's, but that of his brother Will K. Kellogg.

As his wariness of commercialism indicates, Dr. Kellogg always remained intensely concerned about his professional reputation among both regular physicians and other health reformers. In 1877, in response to a letter of inquiry from Henry S. Clubb, the Swedenborgian president of the Vegetarian Society in America, Kellogg was at pains to insist on his "regular" bona fides: "Our institution is sometimes incorrectly called a water cure. It is not a water-cure, for we employ all other curative agents as well as water. Our physicians are all graduates of 'regular' schools of the best standing (Bellevue Hospital College of N.Y. and Michigan University). We claim to be entirely regular in our practice, using drugs, when necessary, though we find them necessary very rarely."[78] Beyond simply claiming regular status, Kellogg equipped the sanitarium with laboratories designed to prove scientifically the truth of his physiological theories and the validity of his empirical observations. Despite this, as one of his closest associates observed, Dr. Kellogg was "a born reformer and propagandist rather than a scientist." Another reported that Dr. Kellogg always knew in advance what the results of an experiment should be, and if not satisfied, his response was to "repudiate the entire effort and castigate the laboratory workers for their inefficiency." Moreover, although the doctor's reading in the medical literature was voluminous, he tended to remember (and quote) only those studies that supported biologic living.[79]

This is not to say, however, that Dr. Kellogg was wholly resistant to new scientific ideas: he quickly accepted the germ theory of disease and eventually accepted aspects of evolutionary theory. He was careful, however, never to allow these scientific advances to undermine the core theories behind biologic living, and he worked hard to harmonize new scientific findings with his religious beliefs. For example, Kellogg believed that germs were a special creation in the wake of Adam's fall and that their ability to cause disease was a direct result of human physiological sins.[80] Conversely, the presence of germs was also the reason he continued to believe in the old Millerite prophecy that the world would be consumed by fire after the Second Coming. "The world has to be burned," he said in a lecture to medical students in 1905. "Nothing but fire will ever disinfect the earth. The accumulation of microbes and germs of every description has gone so far that nothing but fire can purify it. . . . There is no way in which disease can be stopped in this world except by a complete renovation, and nothing renovates like fire."[81]

Dr. Kellogg's attitude toward science simply illustrates that biologic living was at bottom a religious and moral system.[82] According to Kellogg, biologic living began with the key insight that motivated Sylvester Graham and other early health reformers such as Larkin Coles, as well as Ellen White herself: "We must recognize as a solemn reality," wrote Kellogg in "The Greater Gospel" (1898), "that religion includes the body, and that the laws which govern the healthful performance of the bodily functions are as much the laws of God as those of the decalogue."[83] Earlier in this article Kellogg made it clear that he meant this literally:

> The gospel of deliverance which Moses taught offered redemption from physical as well as moral degeneracy. In instructing his people in the wilderness, God did not stop at the so-called Decalogue, or moral law, but supplemented it by a code of sanitary regulations which have been the recognized model during all ages since. The sanitary code of Moses included minute instructions about diet, cleanliness, clothing, domestic sanitation, disinfection, and quarantine; and the out-of-door life and constant moving from place to place, the pure diet of manna, and the crystal pure water from the rock afforded the conditions essential for physical regeneration and a return to natural and original simplicity, while the daily instruction in moral principles given by Moses and his associates, was the means of educating a semi-barbarous horde up to the level of a godly people.

Unfortunately, modern man had forgotten not only this greater gospel taught by Moses, but also that of Jesus, whose ministry focused on healing.[84] Thus, "If the church is to rescue the world, it must give the gospel trumpet another and a different tone. It must teach physical righteousness, as well as moral rectitude."[85] Simply put, as Kellogg wrote in 1916, "'Biologic Living' is our 'Supreme obligation,'" for a "man can do credit to his Creator and make the most of himself only in following the natural order of life intended for him."[86] From this premise Dr. Kellogg drew some radical conclusions that sounded much like Dr. Jackson's. For example, God's "wish for the prosperity of the *health* of man is exactly on an equality with His wish for the prosperity of the *soul* of man," Kellogg wrote, quoting 3 John 1:2 as a proof text. When it came to holiness, Kellogg believed, purity of body was equally important for salvation as purity of soul, and, indeed, it would be difficult to heal the soul without first healing the body. It was for this reason, Kellogg asserted, that the Christian doctor was destined for a role in salvation at least as important—if not more so—than that of a minister of the gospel.[87]

## MISSIONARY FOR BIOLOGIC LIVING

For John Harvey Kellogg, the Battle Creek Sanitarium was designed to function as a "gospel agency" to evangelize the world in the principles of "biologic
living."[88] One of the ways the world would be evangelized was through education. From the beginning Kellogg stressed the educational mission of the
sanitarium, referring to it often as a "University of Health." Lectures and
classes for guests in physiology, diet, and cooking formed a regular part of the
daily routine at the San, with Kellogg's own popular lectures and "question
box" sessions in the grand parlor a regular feature in the evenings.[89]

Kellogg also wanted to make the sanitarium the center for the professional
training of those who would become "medical missionaries." In an 1876 testimony Ellen White had pointed out that Jesus used healing in his ministry
because, by looking after people's physical health, "the reception of truth
into their minds was made more likely." Adventists, she believed, should do
likewise and use medicine as part of their ministry to lessen the prejudice
non-Adventists might have against the denomination. Kellogg was enthusiastic about this focus on medical missionaries, and to this end he began
offering Adventists desiring rudimentary medical training a twenty-week
course through the sanitarium's School of Hygiene beginning in 1878. In
time this would develop into the more formal Sanitarium Training School for
Medical Missionaries, and in 1883 the Sanitarium School for Nurses would be
added.[90] Kellogg also felt that more medical missionary doctors with regular
credentials like himself were needed, but it was feared that Adventists who
sought medical training at established medical schools ran the risk of being
corrupted, both in their doctrine (especially concerning the Saturday Sabbath) and in their morals. Moreover, regular medical schools were too heavily dependent on drug therapies and surgery and tended to scoff at biologic
living. An Adventist medical school was obviously needed, and so, as the
educational capstone of the Battle Creek Sanitarium, Kellogg created the
American Medical Missionary College in 1895. A clinical branch was soon
added in Chicago. Tuition was nominal, funded in part by sanitarium profits
and contributions from Adventists, and although the college was open to all
regardless of church affiliation, every student was required to sign a pledge
that he or she would devote his or her career to medical missionary work

and the worldwide promotion of biologic living. The stated purpose of the American Medical Missionary College was to provide "the science and training of the best medical schools guided and permeated by religious sentiment and missionary enthusiasm."[91]

"The opportunity for usefulness for the Christian physician," Kellogg said the year before the opening of the American Medical Missionary College, "is almost infinite in possibilities." For the next fifteen years Kellogg would work hard to make the Battle Creek Sanitarium a recognized center for medical missionary work. Beginning in 1891 Kellogg edited an interdenominational journal called the *Medical Missionary,* and the sanitarium began to host a series of well-attended international medical missionary conferences that ran until the second decade of the twentieth century. Perhaps a measure of the importance of the sanitarium in this regard can be gauged by the fact that in 1907, Dr. Kellogg induced the foremost pioneer of medical missionary work in the United States, Dr. George D. Dowkontt, to retire to Battle Creek to help advise the board of the American Medical Missionary College and to coedit the *Medical Missionary.*[92]

Another way the world would be evangelized as to the truth of biologic living was by domestic missionary outreach to the urban poor in what the doctor called his "Biologic Social Gospel." At a conference at Northwestern University in 1896 where he shared the platform with such social reformers as Jane Addams and C. R. Henderson, Kellogg asserted, "The homeless, destitute man is always a sick man. He is sick morally, mentally, and physically." If one wished to uplift the urban poor, then one must begin by making them physically whole. Kellogg, who had been influenced by a similar urban medical mission opened by Dr. Dowkontt and the evangelist Jerry McCauley in New York City, convinced the General Conference to open a medical mission on Chicago's South Side in 1893. The mission eventually expanded into a network of Adventist medical missions, not only in Chicago but also in several other large American cities and eventually abroad. Each of these medical missions functioned as a kind of "poor man's sanitarium," featuring vegetarian foods, laundry and bath facilities, a clinic for hydropathic and electrical treatments, and nondenominational worship services. Kellogg even created a Chicago settlement house modeled after Hull House, the food needs of which were supplied by a farm south of the city (Jane Addams refused to collaborate with Kellogg on this enterprise because she perceived it as too religious). Such domestic medical missions were meant to complement overseas missions by providing a training ground for future medical missionary doctors and nurses, and they too deserved their own publication. In 1898 Dr. Kellogg launched the publication of the *Life Boat* as both an advertisement and a fund-raising tool for his Chicago missions.[93]

Finally, in addition to his own programs promoting biologic living, Dr. Kellogg was happy to lend his efforts to non-Seventh-day Adventist organizations that pursued the same goals. In the wake of an 1875 vision in which Ellen White was told to reinvigorate the Adventists' concern for temperance, and at the urging of the Battle Creek Reform Club and local representatives of the Women's Christian Temperance Union, Kellogg helped found two organizations, the American Health and Temperance Association (1879) and the Health and Temperance Missionary School (1889), both of which sought to mobilize Seventh-day Adventists in the temperance cause.[94] Kellogg was soon drawn into greater involvement with the WCTU, which he came to call the "noblest of humanitarian organizations."[95] Founded in 1873, the WCTU became, under the leadership of Frances Willard, the nation's most comprehensive and active organization for purity reform.[96] Dr. Kellogg was brought to the notice of the national WCTU by his wife, Ella Eaton, who had long been active in the organization through her contacts in the Seventh-day Baptist Church, long a supporter of the WCTU.[97] Dr. Kellogg was initially invited to address the organization's annual convention in 1882, after which, in the words of Ella Eaton, he became an "honorary member of the WCTU." In 1884 Ella Kellogg helped organize a "Health and Heredity Normal Institute," which brought thirty Michigan delegates of the WCTU to the sanitarium for five days of lectures on a wide variety of purity issues. The institute was a success, and both Dr. and Mrs. Kellogg participated in a similar institute in Washington, DC, later that year. In 1885 Frances Willard invited the Kelloggs to become the national superintendents of the WCTU's new department of social purity, giving Kellogg a national audience to whom he could promote purity through biologic living.[98] For his part, Kellogg devoted pages in *Good Health* to a social purity section edited by Ella Eaton Kellogg, and the doctor also published articles by WCTU officials on issues of purity and heredity.[99]

From the WCTU Kellogg began to participate in the wider national purity movement, which brought together those agitating not only for temperance,

American Medical Missionary College dispensary in Chicago, ca. mid-1890s.

but also for reforms in American sexual behavior. Such reforms included moral and sex education programs, the raising of the age of consent, the abolition of prostitution, and the elimination of venereal disease (euphemistically referred to as "social hygiene"). It also included agitation for pure foods and the prohibition of alcohol and dangerous drugs, all of which, in good Christian physiological fashion, were believed to lead to immoral sexual behavior.[100] In an address entitled "Social Purity" delivered to a large audience at the Battle Creek Sanitarium in 1887, Kellogg decried the "public prejudice and perverted modesty" that prevented reasonable Christian men and women from talking about and confronting the degenerating effects of sexual sins. Such reticence to talk about such matters simply allowed them to fester: "We boast of our Christian civilization. We talk with pride of our foreign missionaries and the conversion of the heathen. We imagine the glorious millennium is just beginning to dawn, while all the time a malignant ulcer is eating at the vitals of our society." This cancer was nothing less than rampant "unchastity," which "is sapping the vital energies, debasing the mental faculties, and blunting the conscience of thousands of youth, who are ignorant of the present and eternal ruin which they invite."[101] Kellogg obviously relished bringing "biologic living" to the national stage in this way and would continue to be a standard-bearer for the national purity movement well into the twentieth century.

## TENSIONS WITH THE ADVENTIST LEADERSHIP

Despite Dr. Kellogg's success, or probably just as likely because of it, not all in the Seventh-day Adventist Church shared his zeal for biologic living. During the 1890s the doctor would often complain to Ellen White that the majority of Adventists, especially the clergy, were not taking the health teachings seriously enough and were actively working to undermine his influence. To make matters worse, at the beginning of that decade the church experienced an upswing in eschatological excitement, which included the return of the kind of faith healing that Ellen White had repudiated decades before. Such Seventh-day Adventist luminaries as A. T. Jones, W. W. Prescott, and J. N. Loughborough began teaching that all that was necessary for health and healing was to be prayed over while maintaining a genuine faith in God's power. The fact that such healings did occur on occasion was again seen to be a powerful sign of the end times. Not only did this undermine biologic living, but Kellogg's anger over such teachings was compounded by the fact that during his extended absence due to illness, faith healing took root in the sanitarium itself, promoted by two helpers, "Drs. Neall and Beilhart." Faced by this epidemic of "fanaticism," Kellogg fired both men upon his return in 1892 and shot off letters to Ellen White begging for her to intervene. White responded by trying to split the difference, writing that "it is not always safe to ask for unconditional healing" in prayer, but that praying for the sick was an important part of the healing process (here she even chided Dr. Kellogg and his physician colleagues at the sanitarium for putting science above God and faith in the promises of the Bible). Although equivocal, White's missive seems to have quelled the episode, and Jones and Prescott backed down from their extreme position on faith healing. They even for a time allied with Kellogg in the promotion of biologic living.[102]

Nevertheless, even with faith healing in check, promoting health reform among the Adventist clergy was still an uphill battle. The fact that Ellen White herself had difficulty maintaining a vegetarian diet was perhaps one of the reasons for the clergy's laxness, although White reiterated in an 1897 testimony, much to Kellogg's delight, that the clergy and laity must take more care in the health reforms. However, laxness continued, a fact that Kellogg witnessed firsthand while lecturing at Adventist camp meetings, where he was furious to find that meat and cheese were openly sold.[103]

The doctor undoubtedly made his own position more difficult by his uncompromising zealousness for biologic living. Kellogg fervently believed that "the Lord intended we [the Seventh-day Adventists] should be medical missionary people" and that the denomination should focus exclusively on being "the medical missionary people of the world."[104] Indeed, at one point Kellogg declared that in these last days, medical missionary work was the heart of "True Christianity" and that "the final test in the judgment" would be whether one had participated in it:

The world is dying, and if ever there was a need of live, earnest, medical missionaries, it is now; if ever there was a time when the truths pertaining to simple wholesome living were essential, it is now; if ever there was a time when the preaching of the whole gospel of salvation for the soul and the body was needed, it is certainly now. If there ever was a time when the medical missionary element of the gospel should appear in its proper place on an equal footing with the preaching of the kingdom as in the commission given by Christ to his disciples, now is the time.[105]

Still, the church never identified itself as wholly with health reform as Dr. Kellogg demanded. As one former General Conference president, G. I. Butler, put it to Kellogg, "It is an excellent thing to heal the sick; encourage the suffering; do good to those who are in great need of help; alleviate pain— that is all good, but my Brother, the salvation of God in his everlasting kingdom, and a preparation for the coming of Christ is more than that."[106]

Ellen White also called for balance. In these, the last days, she said, there is a "tendency to make one line all-absorbing." Dr. Kellogg should understand that "as the right arm is to the body, so is the medical missionary work to the third angel's message, . . . but the right arm is not to become the whole body." In a dig at Kellogg's "Biologic Social Gospel," White cited a concern that too much effort was being expended on the "poorer classes," which, while worthy, were nevertheless limitless, and if they were pursued to the exclusion of other classes in society, the movement to proclaim the third angel's message would decline into "spasmodic and excitable movements," producing "no beneficial results."[107] Kellogg could not have disagreed more, arguing that in these, the last days, Adventists should be like the wise virgins of the Bible, using their fully filled lamps of health reform to light the way for the rest of the suffering world, a cause in which no one should be neglected, especially not the urban poor.[108] Moreover, while both White and Kellogg believed in the imminent end of the world, Kellogg, affected by the attenuation of apocalyptic fervor within the denomination, no longer took literally the prophecy that the world was to end "in this generation." Therefore, unlike White, he apparently no longer felt the absolute urgency in preaching only this message to the world; indeed, like Dr. Jackson, he believed that without proper physiological preparation, however long it may take, such preaching would be useless.[109]

A second way Kellogg managed to alienate the Adventist leadership was his constant assertion that doctors, not clergy, were to be the most respected class of people in Seventh-day Adventism. "Every heathen land," Kellogg wrote in 1894, "is stretching out its hands in pitiful appeal for Christian physicians who, above all other men, are prepared to present the whole Gospel, a symmetrical Gospel, a Gospel capable of saving both soul and body." Thus, "Christian physicians might do more for the moral elevation of man, more for the redemption of the lost ones in the dark places of our great cities than all the priests, preachers, and evangelists of every description combined."[110]

And although "I do not believe that a preacher has any business in a medical institution," wrote Kellogg a decade later, it was different when it came to a doctor preaching: "The doctor should be the best of all preachers. He knows how best to live. . . . So I think the doctor is the natural preacher if coupled with his medical knowledge he has faith."[111] Kellogg had actually refused ordination in 1901, ostensibly because being labeled a minister would have damaged his professional reputation.[112] In the face of such contempt, Ellen White stated categorically that "no enterprise," not even the medical missionary work, "should be so conducted as to cause the ministry of the Word to be looked upon as an inferior matter," and she was deeply concerned that "some have been encouraged to take a course of study in medical lines who ought to be preparing themselves to enter the ministry."[113] Not surprisingly given both Kellogg's and White's pronouncements, tensions between Kellogg and "the preachers" continued unabated.[114]

A final source of tension between Kellogg and the Adventist leadership was the doctor's insistence that the medical missionary work be absolutely nonsectarian in nature. Although the San was founded as a Seventh-day Adventist institution, Dr. Kellogg took advantage of the Battle Creek Sanitarium's 1897 rechartering by the state to create the Michigan Sanitarium and Benevolent Association, which had an expanded number of non-Adventist stockholders and whose articles specifically stated that the sanitarium was an "undenominational [and] unsectarian" institution not to be used "for the purpose of presenting anything that is peculiarly Seventh-day Adventist in doctrine." In terms of his city missions, too, the doctor would also go on to insist that the work be "a Christian and gospel work without any sectarian trammels" and that admission to the American Medical Missionary College be blind to denominational affiliation.[115] Ellen White, of course, had also insisted that the original Western Health Reform Institute be nonsectarian in terms of its clientele, but not that the institution would repudiate its Seventh-day Adventist roots, nor did she see the point of Seventh-day Adventist missions that did not in some way further the third angel's message. White was especially infuriated when she heard after the rechartering that Kellogg refused to share resources with the church's other health institutions.[116] Kellogg said that this was due to the legal conditions of the new charter, but White considered this "a breach of faith" and "not pleasing to God."[117] "Sanitariums," she reminded him, "are to be established for one object,—the advancement of present truth," that is, the Seventh-day Adventist message.[118] "We are not to take pains," she wrote in 1902, "to declare that the Battle Creek Sanitarium is not a Seventh-day Adventist institution, for this it surely is."[119] Moreover, she encouraged medical missionaries to speak freely "upon the points of the present truth, giving the reasons why we are Seventh-day Adventists," and she went on to warn Kellogg that if accepting non-Adventist medical students to the American Medical Missionary College meant that "the peculiar characteristics of our faith [are to be] hidden," then those students should not be admitted.[120]

Throughout the 1890s many in the Adventist leadership came to fear that Dr. Kellogg sought not only to control the denomination's medical missionary work, but to change fundamentally the character of the Seventh-day Adventist denomination.[121] According to Ronald Numbers, Kellogg's presidency of the American Health and Temperance Association in 1899 "symbolized his ascendency to the leadership of the Adventist health-reform movement." From then on the doctor said that he saw himself as "a sort of umpire as to what was true or correct and what was error in matters relating to hygienic reform" within the church, a role he played with gusto.[122] It did not stop there, however. In 1893, at the urging of Dr. Kellogg, the American Health and Temperance Association was folded into the Seventh-day Adventist Medical Missionary and Benevolent Association, which Kellogg then controlled. Not to be confused with the Michigan Sanitarium and Benevolent Association, a separate organization, the Seventh-day Adventist Medical Missionary and Benevolent Association was set up as a department of the General Conference in order to supervise and coordinate all of the denomination's medical missionary work. Here again, Kellogg insisted that the association was "independent of any sectarian or denominational control," and to underscore this point, *Seventh-day Adventist* was dropped in favor of *International* in 1896.[123] Three years later, at a meeting of the association, its nondenominational aspect was reemphasized: its members, according to Kellogg, were "here as Christians, not Seventh-day Adventists," and the organization was "simply the undenominational side of the work which Seventh-day Adventists have to do in the world."[124]

In light of what they saw as Kellogg's systematic denigration of the special mission of Seventh-day Adventism, some in the church's leadership came to view Kellogg's nondenominationalism as a present threat to the very integrity of the denomination.[125] They were perhaps well aware that the debate over whether medical missionary work should be sectarian or not mirrored a similar debate going on within mainstream Protestant Christianity in the United States during the 1890s. Many conservative Protestants still insisted that Christian missions needed to emphasize the doctrinal and historical specificity of Christianity in their efforts to spread the tradition abroad; modernists, on the other hand, wished to minimize the doctrinal differences between Christian sects and to convince non-Christians of Christianity's superiority based on ethics, not doctrine.[126] Kellogg, though never identifying himself as a modernist, nevertheless evidently agreed with this modernist trend, believing that the best way to convert people to his "biologic living" was through a maximum of medicine mixed with a minimum of doctrine.[127] In this he was probably being influenced by his interaction with the missionaries from the many other denominations who attended his medical missionary conferences and who contributed articles to the *Medical Missionary*. It is perhaps for this reason that one Seventh-day Adventist elder characterized the *Medical Missionary* as "the most subtle, deceptive and dangerous publication ever put out by this denomination."[128]

Despite growing opposition, Dr. Kellogg's influence nevertheless continued to grow as the century turned. Addressing the General Conference at the Battle Creek Tabernacle in 1901, Ellen White voiced concerns that because of the proliferation of the institutional structures of the Seventh-day Adventist Church, its work was becoming "confused." She therefore called for a thoroughgoing reorganization of the entire General Conference. The operative goal of this reorganization was to take control of the various departments of the conference from the hands of a few men and to decentralize it into committees with broader membership. This proved difficult when it came to Dr. Kellogg. He now controlled both the Medical Missionary and Benevolent Association and the Michigan Sanitarium and Benevolent Association, and the two together now employed more people than did all the other departments of the General Conference combined and had a larger budget. When the new governing General Conference Committee was formed in 1901, six out of its twenty-five seats were reserved for the Medical Missionary and Benevolent Association, in recognition of Kellogg's clout.[129] Even so, Kellogg asserted that "there is no question that [the Medical Missionary and Benevolent Association] can consider that it needs to refer to the General Conference Committee or the General Conference." This was because, Kellogg affirmed, it "has the power of the entire denomination in it; for it has all the presidents in it, and the whole General Conference in it, and it has something more in it besides."[130] Kellogg even asked the General Conference to grant the association more power, demanding that it be allowed to form the boards of any new branch sanitarium created anywhere in the world, thus ensuring control of these new sanitariums by Dr. Kellogg and his allies. Despite Ellen White's objections—"It is an error to tie up everything possible with the powers at Battle Creek"—the General Conference granted Kellogg's request.[131]

In the face of Kellogg's obvious power grab, White and those many among the Adventist leadership who were not his allies were in a quandary over how best to rein in the doctor. By the turn of the century, John Harvey Kellogg had become the most famous Adventist in America, indeed far better known than Ellen White herself.[132] To alienate him without good reason would be a public relations disaster, and the doctor had threatened to resign on at least one previous occasion when confronted.[133] Yet, given Dr. Kellogg's growing power and independence, his break with the Seventh-day Adventist Church was perhaps inevitable. Significantly, however, what immediately precipitated the break was not the growing tensions over the direction and control of the Seventh-day Adventist medical missionary work, although these issues certainly formed the background. Rather, it was Dr. Kellogg's growing theological deviations that provoked the rupture.

# 3

## The Theology of Biologic Living

Photographs of Dr. John Harvey Kellogg taken during the 1880s and '90s show an avuncular figure with a full beard, still exuding the unbounded confidence of his youth. These were indeed decades of spectacular success for Kellogg, with the Battle Creek Sanitarium growing in popularity and fame, both nationally and internationally. Yet because of his success, Kellogg the physician and Kellogg the Seventh-day Adventist came under increased scrutiny from both the medical profession and the church. Kellogg was sensitive to both, and he apparently felt increasingly pulled in two directions: toward either scientific respectability or religious allegiance.

In 1886, in what was the gravest threat yet to his professional reputation, Kellogg was brought to trial by the Calhoun County Medical Board for, among other things, promoting ideas "unbecoming to a regular physician," that is, biologic living. The trial ended in a hung jury, and the charges were dropped, only to be revived the following year by the Michigan Medical Board, with the charges withdrawn just before trial.[1] After this harrowing experience, Kellogg redoubled his efforts to protect his status within the medical field, and this in part accounts for why he began to insist on the nonsectarian mission of the San. It was perhaps also not coincidental that during this period, Dr. Kellogg began to move decisively away from many of the specific dogmas of Seventh-day Adventism and to equip his biologic living with a more modernist theological rationale. Kellogg was not about to abandon the religion behind biologic living; as the product of the Adventist

Dr. John Harvey Kellogg, Ella Eaton Kellogg, and adopted children, ca. 1890.
*Courtesy of Willard Library Historical Images of Battle Creek Collection.*

subculture, he retained too much of the Yankee sectarian spirit to be bullied out of religious belief, yet the doctor did become increasingly anxious to make his beliefs appear "scientific." It must be said, however, that although Dr. Kellogg's professional problems accelerated this process of theological reformulation in the 1890s, it had already begun in his youth.

### KELLOGG'S EARLY THEOLOGICAL DEVELOPMENT

It is clear from Dr. Kellogg's reminiscences and those of his friends that, despite his Adventist upbringing, he always harbored a streak of skepticism and a tendency to question articles of his faith. Kellogg was fond of telling the story of when he was seven or eight years old and had been sent out of a Sabbath-school class for impertinence: the young John Harvey had dared to ask the teacher why an all-powerful God created the Devil bad instead of good. Upon returning home, Kellogg asked his father the same question but was quickly silenced. "This set me to thinking deeply," wrote Kellogg later, "and I wondered why in the world they didn't tell me" the answer to this and other theological questions.[2] From then on, Kellogg would make up his own mind about theological questions.

Apparently, Kellogg's tendency toward skepticism only deepened with his medical education, and it is clear that his first exposure there to the philosophical materialism of the natural sciences had an immense impact on his approach to religion.[3] According to Merritt G. Kellogg, John Harvey's older half brother, both boys were exposed to "infidelity" at Trall's, including the "infidel doctrines of evolution, Darwinism, etc."[4] Kellogg would get an even bigger dose of materialism when he began his studies at "regular" institutions. In one of his student notebooks dated 1874, for example, Kellogg recorded at length the lecture of a Dr. Palmer, presumably Alonzo Palmer, one of the earliest members of the faculty at the University of Michigan Medical School and an attractive figure due to his advocacy of many natural treatments.[5] Although Dr. Palmer felt that "the office of the physician was a sacred one," there was nothing mystical to his approach to medicine. Dr. Palmer enjoined his students to look at the human body in thoroughly materialistic and mechanistic ways: "The human body can be compared to a watch or an engine which have valves, wheels, pistons, cylinders etc.," and "when these get out of repair a mechanic is called in" who understands the problem.[6] The doctor is simply the mechanic of the body, and the body simply a machine, and if that was the case, religious meanings of the body were of no use in the treating of disease. During his medical education, Kellogg, in fact, imbibed deeply the idea that religion and medicine did not mix. In his graduation thesis for Bellevue Hospital, he wrote, "Certain it is, at least, that the numerous creeds and religious dogmas which have at various times obtained among mankind have been greatly influenced, if not wholly molded by the existing beliefs relating to disease and its causation. Religious teachers have ever found in the popular dread of disease a powerful means with which to enforce their doctrines, whether true or false. Quacks and charlatans have found a fertile field for their nefarious operations."[7] If this was indeed the case, then what did this imply about Seventh-day Adventist health reform, not to mention Seventh-day Adventism itself?

Safely back in the fold in 1876, Kellogg began the uncomfortable task of reconciling his skepticism with his boyhood faith. Due to Kellogg's close relationship to the Whites, especially Ellen White, who in many ways acted as a surrogate mother to him, Kellogg often felt considerable guilt over his inability to take all aspects of his Adventist faith at face value.[8] In 1879 he wrote her, "I know I have not that communion with Christ and that fullness of the divine spirit and influence that an active Christian ought to have," adding, "I know nothing of the emotional part of religion." And in 1882, he confessed, "Many times I have asked myself the question, What do I believe? Where am I? I have recognized the fact that it was only my early education that held me from becoming a skeptic." And five years later he wrote her, "I have theoretical faith, but am of such a doubting, suspicious nature that I cannot make a practical application of it."[9] During the General Conference meeting in 1888, and again after a severe illness in 1891, Kellogg seemed to experience religious awakenings, developments that greatly heartened Ellen White, but still his doubts continued.[10] Despite this, Kellogg never made the leap beyond faith to embrace wholly a materialistic worldview. The fact that he was a doctor—a man of science—made the problem acute, but instead of abandoning his boyhood faith altogether, he spent the rest of his life trying to harmonize science with religion and construct a theology that would allow him to honor both.

## HARMONY OF SCIENCE AND THE BIBLE

Shortly after becoming director of the Battle Creek Sanitarium in 1876, Kellogg felt compelled to reconcile some of his publicly professed Seventh-day Adventist beliefs with the growing materialism of science and medicine. At some point Kellogg had been accused by a fellow Adventist of holding "infidel sentiments." The Adventist leadership rejected the charge as "a great injustice" that "endangers his influence as physician-in-chief of the Sanitarium." At the 1878 General Conference in Battle Creek, a resolution was passed exonerating the doctor and inviting him to clarify his views by speaking to the assembled group on "the harmony of Science and the Sacred Scriptures."[11] He did so, and so pleased was Kellogg with the result that he expanded his talk into a short book entitled *Harmony of Science and the Bible on the Nature of the Soul and the Doctrine of the Resurrection,* published the following year.[12]

Kellogg began *Harmony of Science and the Bible* by arguing that there would be no conflict between religion and science if only Christians would not insist on literal readings of Holy Writ and not let their superstitious fear stand in the way of scientific, especially medical, progress. This theme, first expressed in his graduation thesis, would reappear again and again with much insistence in many of the doctor's public talks during the 1890s.[13] Kellogg also rejected "creeds, forms, and ceremonies" and defined religion simply "as the preservation of moral health; the keeping of one's self in harmony with the laws of God relating to our moral nature," adding the Christian physiological gloss that there was "no wide distinction between the laws of our moral and our physical natures."[14] Kellogg did not doubt that all of God's laws could be found in the Bible, but only if it was not read with dogmatic literalism. Conversely, Kellogg argued, scientists should not dogmatically insist on theories that are still only hypothetical, especially the three major evolutionary theories of the nebular formation of the solar system, uniformitarian geology, and organic evolution.[15] Having thus denied that science and religion were necessarily antagonistic, the doctor then went on to present an intricate thesis about the true nature of the human soul using analogies from biology, chemistry, and physics coupled with proof texts from the Bible.

# HARMONY

—— OF ——

# SCIENCE AND THE BIBLE

ON THE

## NATURE OF THE SOUL

AND THE

## DOCTRINE OF THE RESURRECTION.

—— BY ——

### J. H. KELLOGG, M. D.,

PROFESSOR OF PHYSICS IN BATTLE CREEK COLLEGE, MEM-
BER OF THE AMERICAN ASSOCIATION FOR THE AD-
VANCEMENT OF SCIENCE, AND THE AMERI-
CAN MICROSCOPICAL SOCIETY.

REVIEW AND HERALD
PUBLISHING ASSOCIATION,
BATTLE CREEK, MICH.
1879.

Title page of John Harvey Kellogg, *Harmony of Science and the Bible on the Nature of the Soul and the Doctrine of the Resurrection* (Battle Creek, MI: Review and Herald, 1879).

Kellogg constructed his "scientific" concept of the soul by assuming the truth of the physical resurrection of the body foretold by the Bible and by arguing for the doctrine of "soul sleep." While the physical resurrection was still a common belief among nineteenth-century Christians, Seventh-day Adventism was among a handful of American denominations to accept the doctrine of "soul sleep." Contra the table-rapping Spiritualists, Seventh-day Adventists rejected the idea that discarnate spirits could be active in the afterlife immediately after death. Rather, they believed that the souls of the dead existed in a state of unconsciousness like sleep and that souls regained consciousness only once resurrected ("reincarnated") after Christ's Second Coming. In part, the doctrine was accepted because if the soul could be conscious without a body, as the Spiritualists believed, then the resurrection of the physical body foretold in the Bible would be superfluous.[16] That the Bible could be in error on this point was simply inconceivable, so the "soul sleep" entailed by the necessity of physical resurrection must also be true. This established, Kellogg then mounted a "scientific" (that is, materialist) argument for how and why "soul sleep" occurs.

Given his outsized ego, it is probably no accident that Kellogg premised all his arguments in *Harmony of Science and the Bible* on the idea that the primary function of the human soul was to preserve an individual's identity for eternity. But how was this possible, Kellogg asked, considering that identity is expressed through consciousness and, as science has shown, consciousness is wholly dependent on the physical body, which, of course, disappears after death? Moreover, how is human identity maintained at all, considering that the body is constantly changing during its lifetime through growth, repair, and decay? The fact that the molecules of the body were completely replaced on a periodic basis was a boon for the idea that the reform of one's health was possible, but it posed a theological problem when it came to the bodily resurrection. The solution for Kellogg was to insist on the distinction between content and form, or, better, matter and pattern.[17] The body is made up of matter, which indeed disintegrates after death, but the unique pattern that organized the body during life, that is, the soul, is retained in heaven in the (perhaps metaphorical) book of life. The pattern, according to Kellogg, is "a perfect photograph of the individual, being an exact representation of the abstract organization which was once represented in matter."[18] Eventually, God will reincarnate each unique pattern with fresh matter at the time of the

Last Judgment. In the meantime, because each soul lacks a body and exists only as a stored pattern, it cannot be conscious, which explains why the souls of the dead must exist in a state of sleep until the general resurrection. To believe otherwise was to violate what is known scientifically about the biology of consciousness.

Kellogg later made more explicit the implications of his "scientific" theory of the soul for biologic living when he revisited it in an 1893 public Sanitarium lecture entitled "What Is the Soul?"[19] Here Kellogg attacked the notion found in many world religions, including Christianity, that the physical body was irrelevant to the soul and an impediment to its purity.[20] Not so, said Kellogg: the soul, which is simply the identifying principle of a person, can achieve consciousness and action only when equipped with a mind and brain in a physical body. Therefore, it is only in the incarnated state that an individual can develop the quality or character of one's soul. "Our characters," Kellogg reasoned, "are the result of the reaction of ourselves against our environment. . . . It is the education of our surroundings, and the surroundings that we create for ourselves, that make our characters. . . . In this way we are making our own souls, if you please. We are building our own characters, and these characters are our souls, and it is these characters that are to identify us in the world."[21] And because our souls will be "reincarnated" after death into a material existence much like the one on earth, the quality of our afterlife will be determined by how we choose to use both our minds and our bodies here and now. Both physical and moral defects, which according to Kellogg's biologic living are intimately related, will carry over from this life to the next.[22]

In a later document, Kellogg connected all of this to yet another of Adventism's distinctive doctrines, that of conditional immortality. Adventists believe that although all will be bodily resurrected at the Last Judgment regardless of whether they were wicked or righteous, only the righteous will be made immortal and survive for eternity. The wicked, on the other hand, despite their new bodies, will not be granted immortality and will suffer a second, permanent, death.[23] According to Kellogg, the reason the wicked will perish is "due to the fact that the soul gathers to itself an imperfect, a diseased[,] a sin-stricken body, a body which accords with the aspirations and character of the man, the purposes of the man during life[,] instead of the perfected body . . . which would please God."[24] Therefore, even though our earthly body is destroyed after death and we are provided with a new one, the treatment of our earthly body has an impact on the state of the body in the next. In fact, it contributes to our very salvation. The wicked will be given impure bodies to reflect the pattern of their impure earthly existence and thus will not be allowed to continue existing and are destined for annihilation. The virtuous, however, will be given pure resurrection bodies suited for the purity of heaven. They alone will be granted immortality and will live for eternity.

## KELLOGG'S THEOLOGY OF DIVINE IMMANENCE

In *Harmony of Science and the Bible,* Kellogg believed that he had successfully reconciled three key Adventist beliefs with scientific doctrine: bodily resurrection, "soul sleep," and conditional immortality. Yet science kept advancing, taking especially rapid strides during the last two decades of the nineteenth century. Kellogg continued to worry about the erosive effects of science on religion. In an 1887 address Kellogg, mindful of his own youthful struggles, now warned audiences that "too often the young, dazzled by the achievements of science, and perplexed by the apparent discrepancies between natural and revealed truth, are led to reject the simple revelation of inspiration, and to exalt beyond their real importance the *dicta* of men of science." Kellogg was especially concerned with "the wily but blasphemous sophistries of Ingersoll and his followers." In this address at least, Kellogg does not attempt to solve the problem, but simply falls back on a version of Pascal's wager: either scientific skepticism or Christianity may be true, but only Christianity, if true, will save you from sin in this life and get you into heaven in the next.[25]

Given the press of scientific change in the 1890s, though, Kellogg was forced to keep thinking and worrying about its impact not only for religion in general, but for his faith in particular. In his continuing efforts to reconstruct Adventist theology along scientific lines, the two aspects that Kellogg had the most trouble with were the Adventists' highly anthropomorphic conception of God localized in heaven and the relationship of this remote God with the material cosmos. This was especially acute for Kellogg in light of the naturalistic assumptions of modern evolutionary theory in cosmology, geology, and biology, which either presupposed the *deus otiosis* of deism or explained the cosmos in terms of completely mechanistic processes. According to Kellogg's later recollection (1897), "I was trying to believe in God and nature. I had two gods. But I could not go on thus. I could not see how God could be above nature, so I had taken the position that God was not above nature.... I believed that nature [was] almost equal with God."[26] Evolutionary theories, which most scientists had come to accept in the 1880s, had left Kellogg particularly "perplexed in my efforts to understand and reconcile the new views that were being brought to light with the Bible doctrines." Years later the doctor specifically cited his anxieties over the naturalistic evolutionary theories of German biologist Ernst Haeckel, "whom the whole scientific world then almost worshipped as an oracle," as he "had devised a highly seductive mechanistic theory of the origin of life and all natural phenomena."[27] In books such as *Monism as Connecting Religion and Science* (1895) and *The Riddle of the Universe* (1900), Haeckel had developed out of his evolutionary worldview an influential form of religious monism in which Nature was simply another name for an impersonal God.[28]

As he was wont to do, Kellogg confided his concerns to Ellen White, who, in an effort to help the doctor reject both deism and scientific materialism in favor of anthropomorphic theism, directed a personal testimony to him in 1882. In it she rejected the deistic or materialistic implications of evolutionary theory and posited a very close connection between God and nature. "Many express themselves," she wrote to Kellogg, "in a manner which would convey the idea that nature is distinct from the God of nature, having in and of itself its own limits and its own powers wherewith to work." Such people incorrectly conclude that a "vital power" inhered in nature "with which God himself cannot interfere." This position, however, was "false science," which made a "deity" of nature. The truth was that "God is perpetually working in nature":

> Nature in her work testifies of the intelligent presence and active agency of a Being who moves in all his works according to his will. It is not by an original power inherent in nature that year by year the earth produces its bounties, and the world keeps up its continual march around the sun. The hand of infinite power is perpetually guiding this planet. It is God's power momentarily exercised that keeps it in position in its rotations. The God of heaven is constantly at work. It is by his power that vegetation is caused to flourish, that every leaf appears and every flower blooms. It is not as the result of a mechanism, that, once set in motion, continues its work, that the pulse beats and breath follows breath. In God we live and have our being. Every breath, every throb of the heart, is the continual evidence of the power of an ever-present God.[29]

For Kellogg, Ellen White's testimony was indeed a revelation, a means by which "to escape from materialism and infidelity." Her testimony opened Kellogg's mind to the fact that he "was worshipping a false God that is called Nature, which because of this great error is personified and the word printed with a capital N." Although in hindsight White's solution to Kellogg's struggle with deism and materialism, that a sovereign God nevertheless micromanaged nature, seems fairly obvious, what is key to understand is that when Kellogg received the 1882 testimony, he apparently still had the utmost confidence in White's prophetic gifts.[30] What she enjoined him to believe, therefore, was not simply her opinion, but the absolute truth vouchsafed by God himself. In other words, revelation still trumped empirical science for Kellogg, and for this reason the doctor experienced intense joy upon receiving from White the divinely guaranteed "explanation" that "all the mysteries of life and all the wonders of nature is the presence of the great Creative Intelligence, the infinite personality, Jehovah."[31]

Kellogg would not have been Kellogg, however, if he had not made Ellen White's testimony his own. White's characterization of God's work in the cosmos was extremely vague, so Kellogg, still uncomfortable with an anthropomorphic God, took her imprecisely worded occasionalism as warrant for a theological position that deviated significantly from her understanding of God as inhabiting a particular space called heaven and controlling the cosmos through secondary causes.[32] Contemporary critics insisted on calling Kellogg's new theological position pantheism, that is, God and nature are one. Later, more precise critics would correctly label his position immanent theism or the doctrine of divine immanence (that is, God and nature are separate, but God is present in all of nature).[33] By whatever name it was labeled, Kellogg came to believe this conception of God as immanent in the world was the "great truth which harmonizes all correct religious views and principles—every truth that is essential to man's salvation harmonizes with one great central truth." What's more, the notion of God's immanence necessarily led one to understand "the great truth that God is in man."[34]

In what was perhaps one of the earliest public expressions of Kellogg's new theology of divine immanence—his 1893 talk "What Is the Soul?"—the doctor seemed to have completely resolved all his doubts about the relationship between God and nature and overcome the temptation to fall into materialism. Kellogg attacked "scientists . . . who are so blinded by the glare of modern scientific discoveries that they try to find some way in which the worlds could have made themselves; some means by which inanimate nature could have wrought these things out." He was particularly contemptuous of those who were continually promoting purely mechanical theories that "evolve everything from chaos." What they did not understand, said Kellogg, was that "matter is nothing but an expression of God. All the things we see around us are simply the expression of God's thought. All these wonderful forces that we see at work are simply expressions of God."[35] This is true especially of organic nature: "It is God that grows the plant; it does not grow itself; it is the divine power, which is in all things and in all matter [and] it is the same divine power working in my body that makes me what I am, and that makes you what you are."[36] Seven years later in *Shall We Slay to Eat?* Kellogg used his theology of divine immanence specifically to argue for vegetarianism: "No man who has a proper appreciation of what life is and what it means, and who is able to look out upon the great world of nature, and see in every object, animate and inanimate, an expression of divine intelligence,—not a God confined to some remote corner of the great universe of time and space, but a God actually present, living and working in every created thing,—certainly no such one can engage in the ruthless slaughter of innocent and helpless creatures for mere personal gratification."[37]

To strengthen his assertion of an immanent God, Kellogg frequently employed a series of four arguments that, for the doctor at least, proved "empirically" the truth of God's immanence.[38] First, Kellogg cited the unfathomable immensity of unseen cosmic forces, illustrated by the stupendous energy radiating from the sun and the immense force necessary for the precise rotation of the planets.[39] Kellogg inferred that because the ultimate nature of the invisible source of all this cosmic power, the power behind such things as gravity or the healing properties of certain medicines or even the origin of life itself, resisted scientific explanation, then this must point to some agency beyond the reach of the human mind.[40] In such cases Kellogg also employed his second favorite argument, the familiar reduction to first causes. According to a tale oft told by Kellogg, when he asked a young physician what he thought about the story of Jesus's curing the blind man by placing earth on his eyes, the young doctor responded that he would believe it were true if it could be demonstrated that the earth contained "curative properties." But then Kellogg asked, where do these curative properties ultimately come from, and how do they work? To this the young physician admitted that their ultimate power was "one of the mysteries of life. No one pretends to explain that." "You are entirely right," Kellogg replied, "and you must see that you have admitted that you are no better able to explain a miracle of healing performed by a lifeless bit of earth or a drug applied by the physician than I can explain the miracles wrought by the divine man who went about doing good two thousand years ago."[41] In both cases, therefore, it must be God's power at work. This was an argument Kellogg felt worked equally well on children by asking them, "How did that flower grow?"[42]

In his third argument Kellogg saw design inherent in the universe, especially in "this wonderful arrangement of the human body [where] we have evidence of design,—evidence of intelligent design."[43] Kellogg pointed to the extraordinary fine-tuning of the universe that makes life on earth possible: for example, the energy of the sun stored in grain and coal; the alternation of light and day, which allows for human beings to rest; and the temperateness of the planet, which, a few degrees more or less, would be uninhabitable.[44] And finally, echoing the nature mysticism made fashionable by the Transcendentalists and contemporary figures such as John Muir and John Burroughs, Kellogg simply exhorted his listeners to contemplate the vastness of the universe, the very awesomeness of which confirms the existence and omnipresence of God.[45] Apparently, in this last experience Kellogg not only found tangible proof of God's immanence, but also finally achieved something of the religious ecstasy he had always longed for.

### KELLOGG AT THE 1897 GENERAL CONFERENCE

The year 1897 represents a watershed for Kellogg in terms of his public advocacy of his new theology of divine immanence. The doctor made a point of addressing the General Conference of Seventh-day Adventists, which that year was meeting in Lincoln, Nebraska. Unlike his sanitarium lectures, this annual gathering of church leaders both lay and clerical was a golden opportunity for Kellogg to lay out the key ideas of his theology to a national Adventist audience. To this end Kellogg delivered a series of lectures entitled "God in Man."[46]

There was actually little that was new in these lectures, although he now developed some of the implications in radical directions. Kellogg repeated many of the same ideas, down to the identical examples and illustrations that he had used in his previous public talks at the sanitarium. He promoted the same nature mysticism emphasizing the immensity of the universe, the same meditation on cosmic powers such as gravitation and the light of the sun, the same design arguments, and the same emphasis on the mystery of the ultimate origin of life. All of this, of course, was in service of the most important aspect of divine immanence, the fact that God himself dwells in human beings. "What a wonderful thought," proclaimed Kellogg to his gathered Adventist brethren, "that this mighty God that keeps the whole universe in order, is in us!"[47] Indeed, the greatest aspect of God's immanence, the greatest miracle of all, was that God actually deigns to be the intelligence behind the so-called autonomic functions of the human body—that breath, heartbeat, digestion, muscular contraction, nervous system were all the continual work of God. Kellogg rhapsodized:

> When we look at the fact that man is the masterpiece of God; that when God made him, he pronounced him very good; that after he made everything else—the earth, the world, the animals, everything,—he said to his Son, Let us make man in our own image;—when we think of that, that God has taken clay and animated that clay, put into that clay his own self, put himself into it, so he has made in the mass of clay a god-like man, absolutely put divinity in the earth, and has given me a will, and has made himself the servant of that will, we see that God is man's servant.[48]

To say the least, Kellogg's conception of God as man's servant was a far cry from Ellen White's vision of God as sovereign monarch of the universe sitting on a throne in heaven. We can only wonder what the conference audience thought about it.

Yet "God as the servant of man" was not the only radical conclusion Kellogg derived from his theology of divine immanence: he also began to promote a radical perfectionism based on this conception of God. Kellogg told the conference audience that if human beings would only recognize the fact that God dwelt in them and worked with him by obeying both his physical and his moral laws, then they too could achieve in this life the physical and moral perfection of Jesus, for "the same divinity that was in Christ is in us, and is ever seeking to lead us to the same perfection which we see in Christ, to the attainment of which there can be no hindrance except our individual wills."[49] An emphasis on the quest for perfection itself was not unusual for Adventists of the time, but the idea that one could achieve it in this life because of the indwelling of God was. Moreover, the further implications Kellogg drew from his brand of perfectionism were now leading him to question, not defend, some key Adventist doctrines.

In a letter to Ellen White shortly after the Nebraska conference, Kellogg wrote that "those who meet the Lord when he comes will be above the power of disease as well as above the power of sin and . . . they will reach this condition by obedience to the truth," that is, biologic living. "It seems to me very clear," Kellogg continued, "that the sealing of God is a physical and moral change which takes place in a man as the result of truth and which shows in his very countenance that it is the seal of God, and that the mark of the beast is the mark of the work of the beast in the heart and it changes the body as well as the character and also shows in the countenance."[50] In other words, Satan's seal was simply the physical ugliness of an unhealthy body, whereas the seal that God places on human beings as an outward mark of their worthiness for salvation is physical health, if not physical beauty.[51] This, Kellogg argued, should be the true focus of Seventh-day Adventism, for "it seems to me our people have been wrong in regarding Sunday observance as the sole mark of the beast. . . . The mark of the beast . . . is simply the change in character and body that comes from the surrender of will to Satan."[52] Adventists, therefore, should not focus exclusively on observance of the Saturday Sabbath as the positive mark identifying the elect, but rather focus on the physical and moral perfection that comes from biologic living. This, for Kellogg, would be the true seal of the elect.[53]

Dr. Kellogg anticipated that many of his remarks to the conference in Nebraska would be controversial, so in the second of his four talks, which significantly was actually printed first in the Conference Bulletin, the doctor discussed his personal struggles with materialism and Ellen White's personal testimony to him in 1882, quoted above.[54] Armed with her imprimatur, the doctor apparently thought that his theological position would be above criticism. It was not. Some at the Nebraska conference were sympathetic to Kellogg, but the majority must have found it confusing that Seventh-day Adventism's most famous son should be expounding such novel and potentially heretical ideas. As one SDA minister wrote to Ellen White the following year, "With the swing that Dr. Kellogg has among so many of our young people, it seems to me that there is a wonderful danger in the teaching that he is promoting."[55] The public battle over Kellogg's new theology had now begun.

Writing from Australia, Ellen White dealt with the problem of Dr. Kellogg's theology of divine immanence in a special testimony read to the 1899 General Conference entitled "The True Relation of God and Nature." In the testimony neither Kellogg nor his ideas were ever mentioned directly, but it is clear he was her target. White began with the blunt statement that "since the fall of man[,] nature can not reveal a perfect knowledge of God; for sin has brought a blight upon it, and has intervened between nature and nature's God." In what is perhaps a direct dig at Dr. Kellogg, she observed further that "the most difficult and humiliating lesson that man has to learn, if he is kept by the power of God, is his own inefficiency, and the sure failure of his own efforts to read nature correctly. . . . Nature is not God, and never was God." White did not deny that "the Hand of God is continually guiding the globe in its continuous march . . . [and that] the physical organism . . . is under the supervision of God," but this is through secondary "laws which he has instituted [and which] are only his servants, through which he effects results." To call God the servant of man was simply blasphemous.[56]

In the same 1899 testimony, White also expressed concern for those, again presumably Dr. Kellogg, who neglected the importance of Christ in the economy of salvation: "Those who have not a knowledge of God by their acceptance of the revelation God has made himself in Christ, will obtain only an imperfect knowledge of God in nature." Without a true understanding of Christ, one is bound to become one of those "wise fools" who "foolishly deify nature and the laws of nature."[57] White's suspicion that Kellogg undervalued Jesus and his saving work actually went back several years. Since the early 1880s several prominent Adventists had attempted to steer the denomination away from a perceived "legalism," that is, a single-minded focus on behavior such as health reform, toward a position that balanced an emphasis on righteousness through works with righteousness through faith in Christ.[58] Back then White had been especially solicitous to convert Kellogg to this position, perhaps as a means to check what she already saw as his obsessive emphasis on health reform.[59] The 1899 testimony made it clear, though, that even at this late date, Kellogg had not yet gotten the message.

Undaunted by the 1899 testimony, Kellogg fired back at White in a sanitarium lecture later that year entitled "The Physical Basis of Faith." The language he used in this talk is psychologically revealing of his changing relationship with Ellen White. If a boy were to continue indefinitely to follow the guidance of his mother uncritically, Kellogg told his audience, this would "destroy his sense of logical integrity and logical honesty until by and by he got to the point where anything that came to him with good authority that he respected he would receive and believe even if his judgment and his instincts and his reason told him it was not true." "If we have reasoning faculties," Kellogg pointedly asserted, "it is because God gave them to us to use, and God never intended that man who has reasoning faculties, who is God-like, to believe blindly."[60] Moreover, if there was one thing God had given us the ability to understand, it was precisely his presence in nature, for it is through nature that we can know the very "Godhead of God."[61] Here Kellogg reiterated his four "empirical" arguments for God's immanence, but now he pushed these arguments to their logical conclusion: because God is perfectly knowable through nature, as any "savage tribe" can tell you, there was no need for the gospel or the Bible for salvation. Kellogg did not deny that salvation could be best achieved through knowledge of Christ, but he made it clear in this talk that those who are not Christians could still know God.[62] As he put it in a sanitarium lecture the previous year, "God does not ask whether [one] is a Christian or not, He does not ask what sect [one] belongs to, He only asks if we are in trouble, and if we are ready and willing to work in harmony with him."[63]

Having at a stroke called into question not only the revelations of Ellen White, but even the need for revelation in general, Kellogg then proceeded to draw further radical conclusions from the "empirical" fact of divine immanence. At one point in his talk, for example, Kellogg took his motto, "God is the servant of man," to extraordinary lengths:

> God said "You have made me serve with your sins" [Isa. 43:24]—so that even when a man sins God serves in him in his sin; when a man strikes a deadly murderous blow God serves in that blow,—he puts himself at our command and allows us to use him and even to abuse him and to make use of his power,—of Himself represented in us, not figuratively, in the way in which a man represents a country, but really, actually, for he made man in his own image, and then put himself in him.[64]

In other words, although God is not the author of sin, he is certainly its facilitator, and although this might seem unpalatable, apparently for Kellogg this was an inescapable corollary to his doctrine of divine immanence, the inevitable cost of a "scientifically" respectable theology.[65]

Yet another astonishing claim Kellogg made in the "The Physical Basis of Faith" was an extension of the radical perfectionism he had introduced to the General Conference in 1897. There, Kellogg had argued that the quest for physical perfection should be the sign of the millennial seal among Adventists, a sign more important than the Saturday Sabbath as a mark of the elect. In this talk Kellogg went further, arguing that physical perfection would potentially allow the elect to escape death. Indeed, if human beings were to eat the vegetarian diet of Adam and Eve in the Garden of Eden, then life could be extended indefinitely: "The only thing necessary for a man to live forever, is an abundance of life. If we had it all the time we might live forever." In animal foods, however, there is death instead of life, so for meat eaters, "the time will come when the death will preponderate over life, and then life disappears." Only in vegetable food is there "life and only life." If only human beings would restrict themselves to a vegetarian diet, then their lives would never end.[66]

Later, in a public talk in March 1901 to a class of American Medical Missionary College students, Kellogg returned to this idea of indefinite life, using not the example of Adam and Eve, but that of Jesus himself. Kellogg asserted that because Jesus never sinned, either morally *or* physiologically, his human life would have continued indefinitely if men had not killed him. This indeed was the true meaning of Christ's atonement: not his death on the cross or his entry into the heavenly sanctuary, but his exemplary life, demonstrating to mankind that spiritual and physical perfection, thus indefinite life, could be striven for by people on earth. After all, God was in them, just as he was in Jesus.[67] Earlier that month, in a talk to the General Conference outlining some of the same ideas, Kellogg was careful to qualify his perfectionism somewhat, cautioning, "There cannot be perfection in action or conduct until there had been sufficient light to make it possible," implying that such perfection would be achieved fully only by a future generation. Nevertheless, Kellogg did "believe there will come a time when sin, death, hurricanes, tornadoes and disease will not have power over the saved remnant, and that they will stand in the midst of these things, as did the Three Hebrew children unharmed in the midst of the fire, and then they will be ready for translation."[68] Ellen White, on the other hand, had always taught that such perfectionism was impossible and that only after Jesus had intervened during the tribulation would health and beauty be definitely restored to the remnant.[69]

But if Christ's exemplary moral and physiological life was the true purport of his atonement, what then did this mean for the Adventists' sanctuary doctrine of the atonement? In a lecture a month later entitled "Divine Healing," Kellogg answered this question in mocking terms that could not be misunderstood:

> Now, we have the doctrine of the Sanctuary. Many people have never really believed that, because it was so architectural. . . . Now the belief is almost entirely a material one. One sees three or four rooms set apart in Heaven or somewhere, and Christ walking back and forth from one room to another. This has been a perfectly terrible thing to believe. Two years ago it dawned upon me, when reading the 10th of Hebrews, that the Body was the Sanctuary. . . . And that is the whole message, the restoration of the Kingdom, Christ taking possession again, and the cleansing of the sanctuary—our bodies—so that Christ can work in us. . . . Now that doctrine is so simple and so beautiful that when I go out into the world with that doctrine, and tell them that man is upon such a different level—instead of being simply a clod of clay that dies and rots and goes down into the earth, he is a temple of the living God, he is the true tabernacle of God.[70]

Later, Kellogg would reiterate his rejection of the notion of a material sanctuary in heaven in a single pithy sentence: "The whole Sanctuary question is the question of our bodies, and of ourselves personally, and NOT A QUESTION OF ARCHITECTURE."[71]

By the end of 1901, in his quest to rationalize scientifically the religious basis of biologic living, John Harvey Kellogg had adopted a theology of divine immanence and a radical perfectionism that saw physical health and beauty as God's seal on his elect. Along the way the doctor had also questioned Ellen White's prophetic gifts,[72] while rejecting three of the most distinctive doctrines of Seventh-day Adventism: the anthropomorphic nature of God, the importance of the Saturday Sabbath, and the sanctuary doctrine of the atonement. This was a necessary step, said Kellogg, because previously Seventh-day Adventist doctrines were "not in a condition to present to the world." Happily, Kellogg believed, the theology of divine immanence had now changed all that:

> The time has come when our principles are at a point where we can meet any kind of opposition, and so can talk all our different doctrines, the diet question, the meat question, the dress question, they have all reached a point where they are in perfect harmony and have a scientific foundation that the world will recognize, and our religious

faith, our theological doctrines are all in harmony with it so that the time has come when the truth can go out into the world with a harmonious simplicity that intelligent people all over the world can recognize.[73]

Despite Kellogg's growing theological deviations during the 1890s, the Adventist leadership, including Ellen White, failed to move decisively to silence him or rebuke him directly in public. When, for example, recently named General Conference president Arthur G. Daniells heard Kellogg express some of his ideas, Daniells wrote in a classic understatement that he "didn't like the flavor" of them. But he did nothing more at the time.[74] Apparently, the fact that Kellogg was promoting his views to a limited audience primarily at the sanitarium or at conferences meant that it was not yet worth the risk of alienating America's most famous Adventist, especially as tensions over political issues were already running high. Within a year, however, both Daniells and White became much more proactive in their attempts to censure Kellogg, especially when they realized that the doctor aimed to publish his new ideas in a book targeted at the Adventist rank and file. The book would be called *The Living Temple*.

# 4

~

## The Living Temple

By the late 1890s Ellen White became deeply concerned about the growing worldliness of the Battle Creek Sanitarium, lamenting that it had "been perverted from its original design, until it resembles a grand hotel rather than an institution for the treatment of the sick."[1] White saw the concentration of so many of the church's major institutions in Battle Creek as threatening to become "like Jerusalem of old—a powerful center" beset with the sins of "pride, self-exaltation, neglect of the poor, and partiality to the wealthy." She began predicting privately that a great calamity was about to overtake the city due to what she saw as the widespread corruption of Adventism there. Later she would report that in a vision, she had seen "a sword of fire stretched out over Battle Creek."[2]

This calamity long predicted by Ellen White finally struck early in the morning of February 18, 1902. A fast-moving conflagration roared through the wooden frames of both the main sanitarium building and the hospital. Well-honed emergency procedures helped to evacuate safely all but one of the patients, but the two buildings were a total loss, with barely the foundations remaining. Some Adventists saw in this disaster the fulfillment of Ellen White's prophecy, but Dr. Kellogg, who was on his way to California when he got the news, rejected this interpretation and hurried back to Battle Creek to assure everyone that the sanitarium would rise again. Despite the outright opposition of some of the church leadership to rebuilding, and despite some hesitancy on the part of the city, Kellogg managed to wangle a three-year tax holiday for the sanitarium and then set about securing loans

Copyrighted 1902
by P. C. Peterson

Sanitarium fire on February 18, 1902.

and raising funds from Adventists and city boosters alike. Within three months an architect had been engaged, plans drawn up, and the cornerstone for the new sanitarium laid.[3]

In his speech at the cornerstone ceremony, Dr. Kellogg, reflecting his ongoing struggles with the church, reiterated his desire that the San remain "unbound by creed or sectarian shackles" and dedicated to a "religion greater, broader, and deeper than that of any sect which recognizes a formula as its creed, any synod, Sanhedrin, or hierarchy as its custodians or almoners." That "greater" religion would be "the Battle Creek Idea," a religion "in which science, philosophy, and the inspired Scriptures agree: namely, that man is a temple, controlled physically, mentally, and morally, if he will, by an indwelling Intelligence." And perhaps in a slap at Ellen White, Kellogg concluded by observing that the sanitarium represented to physicians and nurses around the world nothing less than did the "temple-city, Jerusalem," to the "ancient Israelite."[4] (A little later Kellogg took the Jerusalem metaphor even further,

Cornerstone-laying ceremony, May 12, 1902.

characterizing his role in the rebuilding as a latter-day Nehemiah.)[5] With this oratorical flourish, the rebuilding of the Battle Creek Sanitarium began in earnest.

Shortly after the sanitarium fire, Dr. Kellogg proposed a fund-raising drive that would enlist the entire Seventh-day Adventist membership to sell copies of his new book, *The Living Temple*. The book was originally meant to be the centerpiece of "the Forward Movement," "a special educational effort" approved by the 1901 General Conference Committee that was designed to create "a genuine revival of interest throughout the whole denomination in that phase of the gospel truth which relates to the body as the temple of the living God." Dr. Kellogg's book *The Living Temple,* which was to be ready in February 1902, was to "contain twenty-six chapters, thus providing one chapter as the basis for study each week during the six months" that the Forward Movement would run. "Viewing the body as the temple of the Holy Ghost,"

Kellogg's new book would give "instruction in the essential principles of anatomy and physiology as will enable one to apply intelligently in daily life those rational methods for the preservation of health and the cure of disease, which are based upon Biblical principles, and attested by long experience."[6]

In the end the Forward Movement never got off the ground, preempted by the trauma of the sanitarium's burning. Kellogg did complete *The Living Temple*, however, reportedly writing the entire book in the space of ten days with the help of a team of three stenographers.[7] The urgency was because Kellogg had decided to sell the book to raise funds for rebuilding the sanitarium in order to help defuse the concerns over its cost. Initially, conference president Arthur Daniells and the executive committee agreed to the scheme, but they specifically asked Kellogg to focus the work on physiology and health and to leave out his peculiar theological beliefs. Kellogg did not honor his pledge, and when the galleys of *The Living Temple* were made available to the executive committee, they, after some discussion, rejected the book project. Unwilling to be thwarted, Dr. Kellogg ordered five thousand copies of the work anyway from the Review and Herald Publishing Association—only to have the Review and Herald buildings burn to the ground in the second mysterious fire to hit Battle Creek within months. Kellogg nevertheless persisted in his efforts to get the book published and distributed through Adventist outlets, but he was blocked at every turn. In the end, only two thousand bound copies of *The Living Temple* were ever produced.[8]

## THE PANTHEISM CRISIS

*The Living Temple* contained few theological ideas that Kellogg had not already expressed in one way or another during the previous decade, although the book did present his theology of biologic living in its most complete form. And although most of its 568 pages are devoted to elementary discussions of human physiology and the cure of disease, theology pervades the volume and gives it a distinctly religious feel. In keeping with his lifelong theological project, Kellogg wrote in the preface that the book was designed to convince people that

> there is no conflict between true science and true religion, but that sound science cannot be irreligious nor true religion unphilosophical; that to be truly spiritual is to be in the highest sense natural; that man is not totally depraved and turned over to the

control of malignant agencies, but is a child of Heaven, a son of God, the image and representative of his Creator, placed in the world to stand as a ruler and a prince, to subjugate every force and every object to noble and divine purposes, and to work out an eternal and felicitous destiny through co-operation with the divine Spirit within him, which created him, which maintains him, which heals his diseases, which shares his griefs and sorrows and all his earthly experiences, and which is ever drawing him upward toward heavenly and supernal ideals, supplying both the incentive and the power requisite for attaining to the best in this life and in the life to come.[9]

The first chapter of *The Living Temple* begins with the by now familiar assertion that "God is the explanation of nature,—not a God outside nature, but in nature, manifesting himself through and in all the objects, movements, and various phenomena of the universe."[10] Indeed, "nature is simply a philosophical name of God."[11] For Kellogg, God was so immanent in living nature that every cell and microbe, every leaf and branch, was continually being created and sustained by the indwelling power of God.[12] In a few lines that really seemed to upset his Adventist critics, Kellogg elaborated that "there is present in the tree a power which creates and maintains it, a tree-maker in the tree, a flower-maker in the flower,—a divine architect who understands every law of proportion, an infinite artist who possesses a limitless power of expression in color and form; there is, in all the world about us, an infinite, divine, though invisible Presence, to which the unenlightened may be blind, but which is ever declaring itself by its ceaseless, beneficent activity."[13] As with trees and plants, so too the human body, for "God dwells in man[;] He is the life of man."[14] If, as the Bible tells us, God is light and light produces food, then by ingesting food we are ingesting the very power of God, his "Shekinah"; when digestion, referred to by Kellogg as "transfiguration," occurs, or the autonomic nervous system functions to power any of the organs, this is the action of God; and when the body heals itself from disease, this too is a manifestation of the power of God's personal presence in the human body.[15] Even human suffering is nothing less than God's voice calling on human beings to repent of their "physiological sins," and as such suffering should be considered a beneficent part of God's "ministry of pain."[16] Indeed, in view of the fact that all suffering and disease, including infectious disease, were largely self-induced in Kellogg's way of thinking, God's "ministry of pain" represented one of the highest examples of God's infinite mercy: even when we actively sinned, God came to our aid through pain.[17]

Elsewhere in *The Living Temple,* Kellogg reiterated his belief that God was the servant of man and inhabited the sinner and the believer alike, thus providing the power for the actions of both. The lesson to be drawn from this was that all that was necessary for human perfection, physical *and* spiritual, was simply to choose to live in harmony with God.[18] And because spiritual health presupposed physical health, the royal road to harmony with God was, of course, biologic living, which, since God lived in us, could be practiced by either the saint or the sinner. Kellogg completely rejected the notion that original sin would keep anyone from perfection, joking that "the total depravity which we often hear talked about is, half the time at least, nothing more nor less than total indigestion."[19]

One of the controversial aspects of Kellogg's developing theology that *The Living Temple* made clear was its decidedly non-Christocentric focus. Whereas "God" is mentioned one hundred times, "Jesus Christ" is mentioned only briefly, twelve times, and is treated as something of a peripheral character. Kellogg stated his belief in *The Living Temple* that part of Jesus's mission on earth was simply to give human beings a "tangible" object to worship, because the "conception of God as the All-Energy, the infinite Power, an all-pervading Presence, is too vast for the human mind to grasp."[20] In light of this, according to Kellogg, Jesus's miracles were simply designed to demonstrate the power of God operating everywhere in nature, a "view [that] does not belittle Christ or his power . . . but lifts the ordinary operations of nature to the same level."[21] Ultimately, Jesus's mission on earth was to allow one to recognize that "the great mind of nature is in essence like his own, only vastly transcending it; that the infinite personality is like his own personality."[22] This, of course, was simply a restatement of Kellogg's exemplary theory of Christ's atonement discussed in his previous talks, although the word *atonement* is never used in any sense in *The Living Temple.*

In view of Dr. Kellogg's persistent efforts to get *The Living Temple* into the hands of Seventh-day Adventists, Ellen White felt that she could no longer avoid confronting him publicly on his theological errors. The doctor and his allies attended a meeting of Adventist leaders in Washington, DC, later that year, apparently in an effort to explain Kellogg's ideas and gain control of the situation, but a letter arrived from White that put the "pro-Kellogg forces" on the defensive.[23] In it, White straightaway condemned the ideas of *The Living Temple,* as they did "not bear the indorsement [*sic*] of God" and were

THE

# Living Temple

By J. H. KELLOGG

"*Know ye not that your body is the temple of the Holy Ghost?*" *1 Cor. 6: 19*

𝔐

BATTLE CREEK, MICH., U. S. A.
**GOOD HEALTH PUBLISHING COMPANY**
1903

Title page of John Harvey Kellogg, *The Living Temple*
(Battle Creek, MI: Good Health, 1903).

nothing less than "a snare that the enemy has prepared for these last days," a "scientific deception" to distract the faithful from a correct appreciation of the meaning of the prophecies in the book of Revelation. This she knew to be the truth because she had had a vision of a divine "Instructor" who, holding up a copy of *The Living Temple,* condemned it as inspired by the Devil and filled with "vague, undefined" ideas "that even the writer himself does not comprehend."[24]

These were hard words, and soon the rift between Kellogg and White over *The Living Temple* became front-page news in Michigan, with the *Battle Creek Daily Journal* firmly taking "Rev." Kellogg's side.[25] Perhaps in response, writing a month later from her home in Elmshaven, California, White issued another public letter directed at Kellogg in which she characterized *The Living Temple* as "containing the alpha of a train of heresies . . . similar to those that I met in my first labors in connection with the cause in Maine, New Hampshire, Vermont, then in Boston, Roxbury, New Bedford, and other parts of Massachusetts." Apparently, White referred to her experiences after the Great Disappointment of 1844 when some Millerites interpreted the date to signify the arrival of Jesus as spirit in the souls of all true believers. Such "spiritualizers," as White called them, believing that they were now free of all sin, reputedly fell into an antinomian rejection of the Commandments—the omega of the "train of heresies." White feared that Dr. Kellogg and his supporters, "beguiled by beautiful, philosophical theories that are contrary to the truth," would inevitably fall into the same error through their "pantheism."[26] Such "spiritualistic" teachings, therefore, had to be stopped before they infected the entire church.

Because of the accusation of pantheism, White also accused Kellogg of preaching the impersonality of God, something Kellogg felt was a gross misunderstanding of his actual theological position. Perhaps part of the reason White made this accusation was that Kellogg did reject the idea of an anthropomorphic God.[27] Indeed, Kellogg joked that if we take literally the biblical descriptions of God as sitting above the circle of the earth, measuring out heaven with a span and holding the waters in the hollow of his hand, then God's body must have absurd dimensions. Obviously, such statements could be taken only as metaphors to assure us, according to Kellogg, that "God is a definite, real, personal being." Beyond that, discussions respecting the form of God are utterly unprofitable, and serve only to belittle our conceptions of him who is above all things, and hence not to be compared in form or size or glory or majesty with anything which man has ever seen or which it is within his power to conceive. In the presence of questions like these, we have only to acknowledge our foolishness and incapacity, and bow our heads with awe and reverence in the presence of a Personality, an Intelligent Being to the existence of which all nature bears definite and positive testimony, but which is far beyond our comprehension as are the bounds of space and time.[28]

This does not mean that God could not take on anthropomorphic form if he deemed it necessary: "The human mind is finite and cannot grasp infinity," but "this conception [does not] disagree with that of a special expression of God in some particular form or place," such as in the form of Jesus or "sitting on a throne in heaven, or dwelling in the temple at Jerusalem." However, anthropomorphism is a "special expression," not God's normal form.[29]

Although Kellogg did reject the idea of an anthropomorphic God, he was nevertheless particularly sensitive to defend himself against charges that he taught an *impersonal* God, a God who manifested no personality and did not take personal interest in his creatures. "Do you not believe in a personal, definite God?" Kellogg asked rhetorically in *The Living Temple,* replying, "Most certainly. An infinite, divine, personal being is essential to religion. Worship requires some one to love, to obey, to trust. Belief in a personal God is the very core of the Christian religion." Moreover, "The fact that God is so great that we cannot form a clear mental picture of his physical appearance need not lessen in our minds the reality of His personality."[30] Many years later Kellogg returned to this theme: "Personality does not mean a person, a man or a woman," for "the essence of personality is not form or shape, but it is the expression of will, of design, of a plan." We see this through God's handiwork in nature, Kellogg argued, in the design of the human body, in the body's ability to heal itself, as well as its autonomic functions. We also see it in the human and animal instinct to call for help in times of distress, which, according to Kellogg, was nothing less than the essence of prayer. Indeed, it is precisely the instinct of prayer that proves our Creator cares for us, for just as hunger implies the existence of food and thirst of water, so too the instinct of prayer demonstrates the reality of a personal God who must be there to help.[31] Such a conception of a personal God not only belied Ellen White's accusation of pantheism, but would also have clearly differentiated Kellogg's position from the impersonal monism of such naturalistic thinkers as Ernst Haeckel.

The following year, 1904, White, still concerned about the lingering dangers of *The Living Temple,* issued another testimony warning of Kellogg's "pantheism," his radical perfectionism, and his neglect of Jesus:

> The theory that God is an essence pervading all nature is received by many who profess to believe the Scriptures; but, however beautifully clothed, this theory is a most dangerous deception. It misrepresents God and is a dishonor to His greatness and majesty. And it surely tends not only to mislead, but to debase men. Darkness is its element, sensuality its sphere. The result of accepting it is separation from God. And to fallen human nature this means ruin. Our condition through sin is unnatural, and the power that restores us must be supernatural, else it has no value. There is but one power that can break the hold of evil from the hearts of men, and that is the power of God in Jesus Christ. Only through the blood of the Crucified One is there cleansing from sin. His grace alone can enable us to resist and subdue the tendencies of our fallen nature.

Kellogg's "spiritualistic" theories, according to White, would do away with any need for God's supernatural grace, for "if God is an essence pervading all nature, then He dwells in all men; and in order to attain holiness, man has only to develop the power within him." Thus, if Kellogg's theories were "followed to their logical conclusion," they threatened to do nothing less than "sweep away the whole Christian economy": "They do away with the necessity for the atonement and make man his own savior. These theories regarding God make His word of no effect, and those who accept them are in great danger of being led finally to look upon the whole Bible as a fiction. They may regard virtue as better than vice; but, having shut out God from His rightful position of sovereignty, they place their dependence upon human power, which, without God, is worthless. The unaided human will has no real power to resist and overcome evil."[32]

Ellen White's fear that Kellogg's "pantheistic" teachings might lead other Adventists astray was a very real possibility, as this was yet another period of great theological ferment within the church.[33] Either because of the influence of Kellogg or because the same influences that reached Kellogg reached them, a few other prominent Adventists also espoused "pantheistic" doctrines beginning in the 1890s.[34] For example, E. J. Waggoner, a popular Adventist physician and editor who had worked with Kellogg at the Battle Creek Sanitarium, published in 1894 a book that mirrored Kellogg's own nature mysticism. Entitled *The Gospel in Creation,* Waggoner's slim volume was a series of sermons encouraging meditation on the seven days of the world's creation as a means to better know the will of God. Waggoner would go on to promote notions of divine immanence much like Kellogg's at the 1897 General Conference, and at the 1899 General Conference Waggoner preached a form of perfectionism similar to the doctor's in which neither disease nor death would come to those who had achieved physical and moral holiness.[35] Still others, such as W. W. Prescott, a well-known Adventist biblical scholar, also accepted "pantheistic" teachings for a time, but ultimately rejected them under the correction of Ellen White and spoke out strongly against Kellogg at the 1904 Lake Union conference at Berrien Springs.[36] It was primarily Prescott's strong opposition to *The Living Temple* that prevented it from being published under the conference's auspices.[37] The staunchest supporters of Kellogg's theology were, understandably enough, his medical colleagues at the sanitarium (such as Dr. William Sadler and Dr. Charles Stewart), although these were not numerous. There is evidence that some rank-and-file Adventists accepted Kellogg's ideas, too, at least until they became so divisive after 1903.[38] From then on Kellogg's "pantheism," denounced by God through a testimony of Ellen White, carried within the denomination the stigma of a dangerous heresy.[39]

In the face of White's charges, Dr. Kellogg for his part claimed he was mystified by her attack on the book: "I dictated *The Living Temple,* many times with tears of gratitude in my eyes, that Mrs. White had sent me the light that had settled my faith and with a prayer in my heart that the book might prove as great a blessing by thousands of others as it had to me."[40] One can see why Kellogg could claim such confusion, for in the same year as the attempted publication of *The Living Temple,* Ellen White published *Education,* a long treatise on the elements of a true Christian curriculum.[41] In a chapter entitled "God in Nature," White reiterated her contention of God's control over all nature in terms that echoed her 1882 testimony, and Kellogg could easily point to passages such as this as evidence for her own ideas of divine immanence:

> The same power that upholds nature, is working also in man. The same great laws that guide alike the star and the atom control human life. The laws that govern the heart's action, regulating the flow of the current of life to the body, are the laws of the mighty Intelligence that has the jurisdiction of the soul. From Him all life proceeds. Only in harmony with Him can be found its true sphere of action. For all the objects of His creation the condition is the same—a life sustained by receiving the life of God, a life exercised in harmony with the Creator's will. To transgress His law, physical, mental, or moral, is to place one's self out of harmony with the universe, to introduce discord, anarchy, ruin.[42]

A close reading of *Education,* however, quickly reveals the very real differences between the two positions. In "God in Nature," White quickly tempered her approach to nature by pointing out that nature was fallen and that a study of nature reveals not only the power and influence of God, but the preponderant power and influence of the Devil as well: "Looking upon the evil manifest even in the natural world, all have the same sorrowful lesson to learn,—'An enemy has done this.'"[43] God may therefore act on nature through secondary causes, but nature itself is too corrupt for God's permanent presence in it. In *The Living Temple,* however, one looks in vain for any indication that Kellogg acknowledged any corruption in nature; indeed, for Kellogg natural evil seemingly did not exist and only moral evil was real.[44]

It is perhaps for this reason that Kellogg was so comfortable with God dwelling permanently in nature, and thus in the human body, because for him nature was perfect. In a lecture titled "General Diseases" from 1904, Kellogg reacted to an article that "said that the great fundamental error with the book 'Living Temple' was that it did not recognize the fact that man after he sinned, in sinning, perverted all the laws of nature." Kellogg would have none of this, rejecting it as the worst kind of "minister's philosophy." When human beings sin after the sin of Adam, Kellogg argued, "It is not God's law that is perverted; it is man that is perverted; it is man, man's will that is perverted, and through the perversion of his will, and the cultivation of wrong habits of life his body becomes perverted; but God's life can not be perverted, and the laws of man's being can not be perverted." Even after the fall, concluded Kellogg, "The laws of our being," the laws of nature, "are just as perfect as they ever were."[45]

## THE POSSIBLE SOURCES OF KELLOGG'S
## THEOLOGY OF DIVINE IMMANENCE

In responding to the attacks of Ellen White and others, Dr. Kellogg maintained that his beliefs had not changed, only evolved: "I have not abandoned any of the beliefs in which I was reared," he wrote in a letter to S. N. Haskell in 1904. "I see more in some things than some others do. *My study of science,* and especially of the things Sister White has written, have led me into somewhat larger views than I had when I was a boy."[46] It is hard to take such statements at face value, and one of the primary questions historians have asked about Kellogg's religious views is where they really came from. Although Kellogg himself traced them back to White's 1882 personal testimony, it is clear that Kellogg developed the details of his understanding of divine immanence gradually over the next two decades. Later Adventist historians have maintained that theological developments within the denomination led to Kellogg's "heresy." The argument runs that early Adventists were strongly Arian in their understanding of the Godhead. For them, God the father was eternal and uncreated, Jesus was his created son, and the Holy Spirit represented their combined "divine influence" and "the medium" by which "they have knowledge and power through all the universe, when not personally present."[47] Thus, although God and Jesus dwelled in heaven, their influence could still pervade the cosmos through the means of the Holy Spirit. It is possible that this older Adventist idea of God's pervasive influence over the universe did remain in the back of Kellogg's mind even as the denomination shifted to more orthodox Trinitarianism in the 1890s. However, this does not account for Kellogg's belief in God's *permanent personal* presence pervading and dwelling in *all* things in the cosmos.

Rather paradoxically, another explanation for Kellogg's theology essayed by Adventist historians points precisely to the Adventists' embrace of Trinitarianism as the root cause. In the 1890s, when Trinitarian ideas were first beginning to surface in the church, the idea of the personhood of the Holy Spirit, that the Spirit was not simply God's and Jesus's influence at work in the universe, but a coequal, personal manifestation of the Godhead, was also beginning to take root in certain Adventist circles. A few Adventists during the period took this in the direction of Pentecostalism and embraced speaking in tongues and faith healing as a sign of the Holy Spirit's active work in the souls of believers. Some Indiana brethren even taught that this would lead to spiritual and physical perfection, or what they called "holy flesh." Once "holy flesh" was achieved, they taught, a person would live until the Second Coming, however long it might be delayed.[48] A standard explanation by denominational historians of the origin of Kellogg's "pantheism" was that the doctor was influenced by the same Trinitarian excesses, and that although he rejected Pentecostalism, he nevertheless interpreted the personhood of the Holy Spirit as warrant for the doctrine of divine immanence.[49] Yet A. G. Daniells reported in 1903 that Kellogg fully accepted the personhood of the Holy Spirit only after the writing of *The Living Temple*. In fact, Kellogg reportedly told him that, "if he [Kellogg] had believed this [the personhood of the Holy Spirit] before writing the book [*The Living Temple*], he could have expressed his views without giving the wrong impression the book now gives."[50] It is not clear why this move would have shielded the doctor from criticism, since even Trinitarianism would not give warrant for his rejection of God's anthropomorphism. What is clear, though, is that Kellogg had embraced the doctrine of divine immanence well before he embraced Trinitarianism and the personhood of the Holy Spirit.[51]

So again, the question is, where did Kellogg's theology of divine immanence come from, if not from within his church? In addition to Ellen White, the one person that Kellogg himself did refer to most often as the authority for the doctrine of divine immanence was the English philosopher Herbert Spencer, whom the doctor cited precisely "because he is not a theologian" and therefore was presumably scientifically objective.[52] Spencer enjoyed quite a vogue during the Victorian Age, and his massive *System of Synthetic Philosophy* (1860–96), based on the notion that evolution was the fundamental law undergirding the entire universe, was a best seller in the United States.[53] Spencer's ideas were especially popular with modernist theologians and devout scientists who were desperately seeking some way to reconcile their faith with advances in modern science, especially evolution. Spencer assuaged their fears by confidently asserting that there was no conflict between science and religion. In a chapter from his *First Principles,* called simply "The Reconciliation," Spencer argued that "Common Sense asserts the existence of a reality; Objective Science proves that this reality cannot be what we think it; Subjective Science shows why we cannot think of it as it is, and yet are compelled to think of it as existing; and in this assertion of a Reality utterly inscrutable in nature, Religion finds an assertion essentially coinciding with her own." Therefore, "We are obliged to regard every phenomenon as a manifestation of some Power by which we are acted upon; though Omnipresence is unthinkable, yet, as experience discloses no bounds to the diffusion of phenomena, we are unable to think of limits to the presence of this Power; while the criticisms of Science teach us that this Power is Incomprehensible. And this consciousness of an Incomprehensible Power, called Omnipresent from inability to assign its limits, is just that consciousness on which Religion dwells. And so we arrive at the point where Religion and Science coalesce."[54]

The appeal of this kind of argument for Kellogg is obvious, and the doctor evidently knew the writings of Spencer well. During the 1880s and '90s,
Spencer was frequently quoted in Kellogg's *Good Health* as an expert on
everything from science to hygiene to education. More significantly, in several public talks, Kellogg supported his theology of divine immanence by
paraphrasing Spencer thus: "After we have explained all we can of natural
phenomenon, we are compelled to admit that back of everything and behind
everything there is an unknowable intelligence perpetually at work."[55] Kellogg used the mystery of gravitation and the seeming irreducible complexity
of the human body as particular illustrations of the Spencerian maxim.[56]
Unfortunately, Spencer never said exactly what Kellogg wanted him to say.
Although the philosopher did refer to the "Unknowable," he never quali-
fied this with "intelligence" or argued for intelligent design. Spencer in fact
argued against theistic understandings of the "Incomprehensible Power"
or "Unknowable."[57] Kellogg admitted as much in a talk entitled "Physical
Basis of Faith," observing that "the difference between Mr. Spencer and the
Christian is, that Mr. Spencer thinks this intelligence is an 'unknown and
unknowable' intelligence, while to the Christian this intelligence,—this infinite, ever-working intelligence IS known. This intelligence is unknown to
Mr. Spencer because he lacks that personal acquaintance with God which
comes from personal experience of living faith."[58]

    Kellogg, however, was not the only American to appropriate Spencer's
"Incomprehensible Power" and call it God: the nationally famous Congregationalist minister Henry Ward Beecher, for example, also made this move.[59]
Intriguingly, after 1903 when Kellogg's "pantheism" was discussed in the
pages of the *Review and Herald,* the editors of this Adventist journal routinely associated it with the so-called New Theology developed in the latter
half of the nineteenth century by American Protestant liberals, especially
Congregationalists.[60] Although called New Theology, the doctrine of divine
immanence actually had a long European pedigree before experiencing re-
surgence in the early nineteenth century among romantics reacting against
the remote God of Enlightenment deism. Among American romantics, the
doctrine had a decisive influence first on the Transcendentalists and Unitar-
ians, and then the Congregationalists beginning with Horace Bushnell.[61]
When, after the Civil War, Darwinian evolution became an unavoidable
issue among theological circles, many feared that God was becoming increas-

ingly marginalized, as more and more natural causes were being discovered behind events previously seen as miraculous. Theological radicals such as Henry Ward Beecher, John Fiske, Henry Drummond, Joseph Le Conte, and Aubrey Moore, all inspired by Herbert Spencer's notion of the "Incomprehensible Power," seized on the doctrine of divine immanence as a way of re-injecting God back into natural processes in such a way that theistic religion would not be seen as standing in the way of scientific progress.[62]

Although a Seventh-day Adventist, Kellogg was well aware of the "New Theology" as it developed. Kellogg had attended the sermons of Henry Ward Beecher when he was a medical student in New York in 1875, and he knew the writings of Henry Drummond, Joseph Cook, and Joseph Le Conte.[63] Moreover, in the "Literary Notices" section of *Good Health* (July 1884), the editor (presumably Kellogg) called attention to an article by Rev. George G. Lyon appearing in that month's issue of *Popular Science Monthly*.[64] Lyon's article, entitled "The New Theology," anticipated several of the points of Kellogg's theology of divine immanence. For example, Lyon wrote, "God is in man, living and moving of his own good pleasure; not beyond his reach nor without him, but in him and of him, and may be recognized in every stone and star.... The profound conviction of the Christian mind is, that the God who created, upholds the universe, and watches over and guides every movement of every atom day and night, and guards the every thought of every heart and gives them the impulse of their transforming energy[:] This is the divine in nature, and there could be no course of nature without it." What's more, Lyon, like Kellogg, also rejected total depravity and the need for Christ's atonement, boldly asserting the kind of perfectionism that Kellogg would espouse: "All the elements for the restoration from sin to righteousness," Lyon wrote, "are included in the provisions of Nature, and are sufficient when quickened and invigorated by the Divine Spirit" that dwells in every person, whether sinner or righteous, pagan or Christian. Lyon even anticipated Kellogg's "ministry of pain," "for suffering is not a penalty in token of [God's] disapproval, but a sign of mercy and reformation." Lyon concluded his article with a statement that must have really caught Kellogg's attention, as it harmonized completely with his own concerns: "One of the distinguishing characteristics of the New Theology," Lyon wrote, "is its respect for science, indicated by its efforts to put all its statements on a scientific basis and submit them in a scientific method, and to question the value or utility of any doctrine which does not

come under some general or harmonious law, or which cannot be scientifically presented." Even "the scientific dogma of the evolution of man from
monad through monkey, the New Theology is as ready to accept it as to reject
it, according to the evidence, for the divine immanence is constant, and is sufficient for every evolved condition without aid from or resort to unnatural or
supernatural supplementation to the uniformity of nature."[65] Such a willing
openness of religion to the modifications of science was something Kellogg
respected and made his own.

Yet another likely Congregationalist source of the doctrine of immanence
was Lyman Abbott, second pastor of the famous Plymouth Congregational
Church in Brooklyn and editor of the *Outlook,* one of the most influential
magazines in the country. Beginning in the 1890s, Abbott was the unques-
tioned champion of the doctrine of divine immanence as a means to reconcile religion and science, especially organic evolution.[66] Abbott was also
at least an acquaintance of Kellogg, although the record does not contain
enough evidence to make claims beyond that.[67] Abbott had embraced the
"New Theology" in the 1880s, writing in *A Study of Human Nature* (1885)
that "we perceive the Spirit of God behind all nature and immanent in all
nature."[68] Later, in his 1896 book, *The Evolution of Christianity,* Abbott's developing thought paralleled that of Kellogg: "In the spiritual, as in the physical," wrote Abbott, "God is the secret and source of life; phenomena, whether
material or spiritual, are the manifestations of his presence; but he manifests
himself in growth, not in stereotyped and stationary forms; and this growth
is from lower to higher, from simpler to more complex forms, according to
well defined and invariable laws, and by force resident in the growing object
itself." The unknown force that permeates all "is God—God in nature, God
in the Church, God in society, and God in the individual soul."[69]

In a later sermon published as *The Supernatural* (1899), Abbott would re-
state this idea with even more force: "God is in all of nature; all its forces are
the forces of God; all its laws are the methods of God; all its activities are the
activities of God." Indeed, "God is himself the life of life. All things are his
breath; literally, scientifically, absolutely, in him all things live and move and
have their being."[70] So impressed was Dr. Kellogg by this sermon that in an
issue of *Good Health,* he excerpted a passage on God's healing power in the
universe that would not have been out of place later in Kellogg's book *The
Living Temple.*[71] Conversely, we can detect the possible influence of Kellogg

on the later writings of Abbott. In a book entitled simply *The Temple* (1909), Abbott used the same verse from 1 Corinthians 6:91 that inspired Kellogg, and in the first chapter, "The Body," he wrote in terms that echoed Kellogg's biologic living: "The laws of health are the laws of God. Obedience to the laws of health is obedience to God. Disobedience to the laws of health is disobedience to God. To know what are the laws of health—of body and of spirit, of the individual and of society, of human life and of the world we live in—this is the sum of all knowledge. To obey those laws is the whole of religion."[72] Moreover, in a later chapter, "The Appetites," Abbott dwelled on themes that would do Kellogg proud: temperate living, a good diet based on "some acquaintance with the chemistry and the physics of the kitchen," not to mention the dangers of bolting one's food and the plague of dyspepsia.[73] Unfortunately, there is no direct reference to Kellogg in *The Temple*, but the congruence in themes and metaphors is striking to say the least.

Closer to home, Dr. Kellogg might well have encountered the doctrine of divine immanence from one of Battle Creek's most celebrated nineteenth-century ministers, the Reverend Reed Stuart of the Independent Congregational Church.[74] Stuart began his pastorate as a Presbyterian, but his decidedly modernist and liberal theological views, strongly influenced "by the writings of such men as Darwin and Huxley, Emerson and Thoreau," eventually led him into the Congregationalist Church.[75] His erudite but accessible sermons were highly popular not only with his congregation, but with the general public as well, and occasionally they were reprinted in their entirety in the local press. Thus, we find on the front page of the October 11, 1884, edition of the *Battle Creek Weekly Moon* the complete text of Stuart's sermon "God in the Soul."[76] Framing his remarks as a response to both materialist science and dogmatic religion, Stuart laid out a defense of mankind's spiritual nature by arguing for the doctrine of divine immanence: God's presence "appears in many shapes but it is the same;—in nature it is strength, in history it is purpose, in religion it is inspiration, in the soul it is truth; and planets, nations, persons, are its agents and administrators." We know this not only from the intelligent design of the material universe, Stuart continued, but also from the aesthetic and moral intuitions that flow forth from the human soul. Indeed, the human "soul is the cup into which God has poured His choicest wine of His being[;] It is the highest form of Deity on earth."

Stuart was acutely aware that the doctrine he was preaching had "been stamped as heretical by the learned Doctors of Divinity" under the label of "Pantheism." Yet, according to Stuart, it was precisely "those who have been called pantheists . . . who have saved religion from the death coil of ecclesiasticism and theology." In fact, every religious reformer from the Buddha, Plato, and Jesus to Saint Francis, Fox, and Emerson have all "taught the immanence of God" as the only means to "man's highest health and sanity." Again, there is no direct evidence that Kellogg knew Stuart personally, but considering the fact that his "pantheistic" ideas were available to all to read on the front page of a leading local newspaper, it seems highly unlikely that the doctor was not familiar with them.[77]

Finally, it must also be said that family influences may have been a factor in the doctor's theological development. A tantalizing possibility is that Kellogg was inspired by his older half brother Merritt G. Kellogg to adopt the idea of divine immanence. Merritt claimed that it was he who suggested it to his brother while they were both students at Trall's Hygeio-Therapeutic College. In an unsigned mimeographed statement with the dateline "Battle Creek, Michigan, October 13, 1916," Merritt related that he had confided to his younger brother that through his study of chemistry, he had concluded that atomic structure was due to "intelligent activity" and that in fact this "intelligent activity" permeated all the universe, whether living or dead. John Harvey reportedly rejected this notion at first.

> Many years later, however, he informed me that after duly considering the matter, he had decided that I had the right view. "But," he said, "atoms and molecules of matter, the plants, the vegetables, and the growth of animals are not because matter itself is intelligent, but because there is a guiding mind that is using matter as its instrument. That mind is God," said my brother. "It is God's intelligence that is operating and guiding everything that exists, and, inasmuch as the forces that produce and exhibit the activities of matter are not applied from without the thing acting, but are within it, it must be that God by some of his attributes, exists in and acts through every form of matter."[78]

According to this statement, then, John Harvey was originally inspired by Merritt's speculations about "active intelligence" in matter and at some unspecified later date transformed this into his immanent theism. Unfortunately, Merritt does not specify the date when John Harvey formulated his immanent theology, nor did Kellogg ever refer to Merritt's theological speculations at Trall's Hygeio-Therapeutic College.

Another, more likely, family source for the theology of divine immanence available to Kellogg was his wife, Ella Eaton Kellogg. When Kellogg married Ella Eaton in 1879, he was marrying outside of the faith, as she was a devoted Seventh-Day Baptist. The early Seventh-day Adventists had adopted the Saturday Sabbath through the influence of the Seventh-Day Baptists, and at first the two groups enjoyed cordial relations. However, as Seventh-day Adventists developed their theology in more rigidly sectarian directions, relations broke down and Adventists became more creedal in nature.[79] Seventh-Day Baptists, on the other hand, were fiercely congregational in polity, and so, beyond the Saturday Sabbath, they saw no reason for a fixed creed. In fact, the modernist wing of the denomination, centered on Alfred University in upstate New York, had already charted a very liberal course by the time of the Civil War.[80] Ella Eaton, born and raised in the shadow of Alfred University, attended that institution from 1869 to 1872. Here, according to her later reminiscences, she fell under the influence of the university's president, Rev. Jonathan Allen, and was also personally mentored by Rev. A. H. Lewis, a professor of theology.[81] Both Allen and Lewis saw no conflict between science and religion, believing that science illuminated God's order in the universe. Allen expressly adopted an immanent theology as the most logical explanation of God's relationship to his creation, calling this his "Bethel Theory of the Universe."[82] In an 1882 baccalaureate sermon President Allen defined his "bethelistic doctrine" as "apprehend[ing] the universe as the living temple of God." As such, God pervades everything, including human beings: "Every soul was created expressly to be the 'temple of the living God,'" and "humanity is the highest earthly organ of the divine life and manifestation—created for a constant in-living and intercourse of the divine with the human."[83]

Ella Eaton Kellogg could not have helped but be steeped in this theology during her years as a student at Alfred, and even after graduation and her removal to Battle Creek, she maintained close ties to her mentors. In 1895 A. H. Lewis and his wife attended the sanitarium and were guests in the Kellogg home (in addition to being a personal friend, Lewis was a leader in the national purity movement, as were the Kelloggs).[84] It was during this visit, according to the recollections of Adventist Arthur L. White, that "Lewis talked his pantheistic views, which did not fall on deaf ears."[85] It is entirely possible that if Kellogg did get his doctrine of divine immanence from Seventh-Day Baptist sources, his wife or her mentor Lewis from Alfred was the conduit.[86]

Considering that during this period the modernist "New Theology" of divine immanence was "in the air," so to speak, it is impossible to say definitively where Kellogg first encountered this idea. It may well have come through the cumulative influence of the several sources detailed above. The important conclusion to be reached, however, is that although Kellogg would remain sectarian in his emphasis on biologic living, the immanent theology behind it actually brought him closer to the liberal theological mainstream in America. Kellogg never called himself a modernist, but both his theology and his nondenominational ecclesiology bore all the modernist hallmarks. Amateur theologian that he was, this was probably not a conscious process. Driven by his desire to reconcile science with religion, Kellogg naturally gravitated in this direction, and, indeed, he always claimed that his study of biology forced him to accept the truth of divine immanence.[87] Importantly, though, it is clear that, however he came by it, Kellogg wanted Seventh-day Adventism to move in the direction of his modernist theology and ecclesiology, and for those who wished to stand by the "old landmarks," it is no wonder why he was perceived as a threat to the church.

## THE IMPACT OF *THE LIVING TEMPLE*

Despite all the criticism coming from Ellen White and the Adventist leadership, Kellogg attempted in 1904 to republish *The Living Temple* under a new title, *The Miracle of Life*.[88] It differed little from the original except that it bore a new preface in which Kellogg defended himself against accusations of heterodoxy. "New religions are hatching almost daily," but the "author has no sympathy with such movements, and in this work has not sought to present any new theory or philosophy, but only elucidate the old and established truths of Christianity as they are exemplified in and applicable to the human body." Indeed, *The Miracle of Life* was intended to be "a protection against the flood of mysticism, which, under the name of theosophy, pantheism, so-called Christian science, metaphysics, and various other guises, is deluging the world."[89] Such claims did not convince the Adventist leadership, however, and, although his book was heavily advertised in *Good Health*, Kellogg ap-

Dr. John Harvey Kellogg doing calisthenics with Chinese diplomat
Wu Tingfang at the Battle Creek Sanitarium, ca. 1905.

parently made as little headway distributing *The Miracle of Life* to Adventists
as he had with *The Living Temple*.[90]

Because of its limited circulation, *The Living Temple* had little impact outside of Seventh-day Adventism. Mary Foote Henderson, one of Kellogg's
most ardent disciples outside of the church, quoted it in her own health reform tome, *The Aristocracy of Health* (1904), and the book also impressed the
Chinese diplomat Wu Tingfang, who sought to introduce biologic living to
China.[91] Perhaps because of Wu's interest, Kellogg paid to have the volume
translated into Chinese. Interestingly, the translator, Rev. M. C. Wilcox, a
Methodist, felt bound to explain in the preface that although Dr. Kellogg
"rightly believes in the divine immanence, i.e., that the Supreme Being . . .
dwells in all things, including the human body and manifold functions," "the
Supreme Being" nevertheless "is regarded as separate from all that is created."
This was something Wilcox felt he needed to stress, because "some might
infer from a few of the statements in the book that the Supreme Being and 'all

things' are one in the same which is not the author's meaning."[92] Apparently, even in Chinese translation, there were continuing worries that the doctor's theology might be misconstrued as pantheism.

Beyond these two conspicuous examples, the book met with silence outside of the Seventh-day Adventist Church. Within the Seventh-day Adventist Church, however, its impact was profound, albeit overwhelmingly negative. In the final analysis Ellen White ascribed Kellogg's theological deviations to his theological naïveté, his flawed character, and his naked ambition.[93] She believed that Kellogg opportunistically interpreted her 1882 testimony the way he did because it allowed him to lobby for a greater emphasis on biologic living within the church. Kellogg, she felt, was blithely unaware of the theological consequences when he first proposed his new ideas.[94] However, the fact that Kellogg persisted in his heretical beliefs despite her admonitions and even went as far as to publish them in *The Living Temple* could only be ascribed to the fact that the doctor "was under the influence of satanic agencies."[95]

In 1904 White wrote a letter from Nashville, Tennessee, entitled "Warning against Deceptive Teaching," in which she recounted a vision she had in which Dr. Kellogg (not identified by name but referred to as "the one who has stood for many years as the leader in our medical work") enthusiastically presented his "scientific theories which are akin to pantheism" to a large meeting in Berrien Springs. White's angel told her that "evil angels had taken captive the mind of" Dr. Kellogg and that he was "under [their] spiritualistic education." She was then "bidden to warn our people on no account to send their children to Battle Creek to receive an education, because these delusive, scientific theories would be presented in the most seducing forms." Moreover, she was "to tell our ministers to enter into no discussion over these theories, but to let them alone," because "when engaged in discussion over these theories, their advocates will take words spoken to oppose them, and will make them appear to mean the very opposite of that which the speaker intended them to mean." Even with such warnings, White was told that "some in the medical missionary work, who have been wavering, will yield up the faith, and give heed to seducing spirits and doctrines of devils." But if they do, too bad for them: "Let the world go into spiritualism, into theosophy, into pantheism, if they choose," White wrote. "We are to have nothing to do with this deceptive branch of Satan's work." From then on, Kellogg became for

White the new watchword for heresy and Battle Creek Sanitarium nothing less than a nest of heretics.[96]

Beyond simply ratcheting up tensions between Dr. Kellogg and the church, *The Living Temple* contributed to the theological conservatism growing within the church during the period, and some within the tradition point to the "Pantheism Crisis" as one of the primary reasons the Seventh-day Adventist Church became increasingly and deliberately wedded to its traditional biblical literalism after the turn of the century. Eventually, the denomination would align itself with the Fundamentalist movement in the first decades of the twentieth century as a means of resisting the kind of theological modernism Kellogg represented, an alignment that would last until the 1960s. Even today, however, *The Living Temple* lives on in the history and folklore of the Seventh-day Adventist Church as an example of theologizing gone desperately wrong.[97]

# 5

⌒

## Dr. Kellogg's Break with the
## Seventh-day Adventist Church

May 31, 1903, was a gala day for Battle Creek. A little more than a year after the fire that had destroyed the original sanitarium building, thousands of people were drawn to the dedication ceremonies of the rebuilt Battle Creek Sanitarium. In its new incarnation the sanitarium boasted a graceful Italian Renaissance building six stories high and the length of three and half football fields. Everything was bigger and grander than before: more guest rooms, a bigger gymnasium, a bigger palm garden, a state-of-the-art operating theater, more hydrotherapy rooms, a grander dining room, and seeming miles of open-air loggias and porches where patients were required to take the air. Some twenty thousand barrels of Portland cement and seven hundred tons of structural steel went into the construction of the building, making it, according to the front-page story in the *Battle Creek Morning Inquirer*, "Strictly Fire-proof" (the paper went on to report that a huge bonfire was kindled in the basement of the main building to test this claim).

The new San was not quite completely finished when a large speaker's stand, "festooned and ablaze with flags and bunting," was erected on the steps of the new main entrance. Hundreds of chairs were set out to accommodate the anticipated throng, which by two thirty that afternoon had already occupied every available seat. Accompanied by the marches of the Germania brass band and greeted with the "tumultuous applause" of the crowd, the dedication ceremonies were opened with scores of matrons and nurses parading in military precision to a special section reserved for them on either side of the speaker's platform. Once seated, the audience settled

Bird's-eye View of Sanitarium, Battle Creek, Mich.

New sanitarium, ca. 1903.

in for oratory from nine speakers, including politicians, professors, business leaders, doctors, and one minister. Dr. Kellogg would give the keynote of the festivities, followed by a benediction by the San's longtime chaplain, Lycurgus McCoy.[1]

Several themes—patriotism, civic pride, public service, natural healing—unified the day's speeches, but one theme, the sanitarium's continuing religious mission, was woven throughout. In a brief address elder A. T. Jones succinctly outlined the rudiments of Christian physiology on which the "Battle Creek Idea" was based. "In the beginning," intoned Elder Jones, "God 'made man upright,' a temple of health." But man sinned, and with sin came disease; but God did not intend for man to be ill, so he sent first Moses and then Christ himself to "redeem the [body] from desecration." Unfortunately, the first Christians missed the point of Christ's coming, and the early church, by denying the body through damaging asceticism, violated God's purposes. Happily, though, God "has a church still in the world, and he intends that that church shall make known the gift of God's saving health to all people and all nations" through the agency of "this grand Temple of Health."[2] Major H. E. Johnson, the governor's representative, observed that "to heal the sick, to restore strength to the weak, to bring back joy to the joyless, is next to creation. It is the work of man made in the image of God, none more Christ-like, none more merciful." Yet others spoke of Dr. Kellogg as a "revelation of a new type of man" and of the sanitarium's "consecrated" employees as "'minute-men' and women for God" guided by "the principle of the Father-hood of God and the Brotherhood of Man, and the completeness of human existence in the life through the teachings of Jesus Christ." Dr. Kellogg, when he rose to spoke, was modest about his achievements, giving all the credit to "kind Providence." "Human hands have not built this building," said the doctor. "No human brain has been able to conceive the things necessary for the construction of this building. . . . [Therefore,] we present this building to you,—not as our work, but as God's work."[3] After the dedication ceremonies were completed at the sanitarium, they continued later that evening at the Seventh-day Adventist Battle Creek Tabernacle with an interdenominational slate of local ministers who continued to extol the San's mission of spreading the gospel of health.[4]

As with the old San, Dr. Kellogg insisted that a "quiet, unobtrusive reli-gious atmosphere" be maintained at the new sanitarium.[5] He achieved this by insisting that the staff set the example. In a manual entitled *Principles of the Battle Creek Sanitarium* published after the rebuilding, workers were admonished that "the Sanitarium, and the various enterprises connected with it, have been planted by Divine Providence for the work of the gospel, including the representation and promulgation of important reforms in rela-tion to diet, dress, temperance, and other matters pertaining to the healthful care of the body." With this in mind, if an employee was "not in harmony with these reforms, his influence [was] against, rather than for, the work" and he therefore had no business remaining connected to the Sanitarium ("'He that is not with me is against me,'" quotes the manual, "'and he that gathereth not with me scattereth.' Luke 11:23"). For those who accepted the awesome task of being "God's stewards," strict canons of biblical behavior were expected: honesty, fidelity, sincerity, singleness of purpose, and a lack of covetousness (especially in terms of salary). More specifically, workers at the sanitarium were to take it as a "most sacred obligation" to promote healthful dress and the Edenic diet ("Due respect for this feature of the work will lead to the adoption and enthusiastic support of thoroughgoing vegetarian principles, and of all other features of the advanced light which Providence has given on this important theme"). Each of the workers was to consider him- or herself as a medical missionary in training, "always on duty, and responsible to God and his fellow workers for the influence he may exert by work, act, or attitude." Indeed, "The aid of all is asked in . . . checking any spirit of unfaithfulness or disloyalty, however it may be manifested." Any "conduct unbecoming a Christian" would be grounds for "separation from the work."[6] The institution might be nonsectarian, but that emphatically did not mean that its mission was not a religious one. To make this clear, Kellogg had emblazoned in stained glass above the San's front desk a verse from Deuteronomy 30:20 referring to the vivifying power of the Lord: "He is thy life."[7]

Remarkably, a scant fifteen months after it burned, the Battle Creek Sanitarium reopened its doors for business. Within two months operations at the sanitarium were back to normal, its lavishly decorated rooms and marble halls packed to overflowing with guests.[8] The next few years would see the San reach its apogee and achieve the height of its national fame, and in 1907 Kellogg would inaugurate a splashy house organ, the *Battle Creek Idea*, to promote the San even more widely. Behind the scenes, however, tensions between Kellogg and the Adventist leadership had reached the breaking point. Controversy over *The Living Temple* and its "pantheism" continued to escalate, with Kellogg's allies and his enemies becoming more polarized by the day. Kellogg still believed that he was in a strong position and could exert his influence at will, but he would soon meet his match when the new president of the Seventh-day Adventist General Conference, Arthur G. Daniells, finally decided enough was enough.

### THE BREAK

Kellogg had been at odds with just about every General Conference president since the 1880s, but his conflict with conference president Arthur G. Daniells became especially bitter.[9] Daniells was an able administrator who found Kellogg overbearing, but was willing to work with him, at least in public, to foster the medical work of the denomination. In 1902, however, much to Kellogg's frustration, Daniells enforced a no-debt policy, thereby blocking Kellogg's attempt to create a sanitarium in England.[10] The ensuing row, coupled with Daniells's discovery of Kellogg's skepticism of Ellen White's prophetic gifts, made Daniells an implacable foe, more determined than ever to bring the medical work under denominational control. Kellogg, for his part, tried to engineer Daniells's ouster from the General Conference Executive Committee. When this failed Daniells rallied his own supporters at the General Conference to pass a resolution declaring that Adventist institutions must be owned by church members and administered directly through one of the agencies of the General Conference. Kellogg in turn retaliated by dissolving the International Medical Missionary and Benevolent Association in 1905, but not before transferring its assets to the sanitarium, leaving only its debts to the General Conference (the following year Kellogg would create a nonprofit, the American Medical Missionary Board, to administer the transferred IMMBA funds).[11] As galling as this was, it did allow Daniells to create a formal medical division that was clearly subordinate to the General Conference, much to the disgust of Kellogg.[12] Theological conflicts coupled with tit-for-tat power politics had created an untenable situation between Kellogg and the denomination's leadership.[13] The years 1905 and 1906 saw continued sniping and political maneuverings by Kellogg and Daniells, creating an atmosphere that was becoming increasingly poisonous and damaging to both the sanitarium and the denomination.[14]

Finally, in 1907 Dr. Kellogg was asked by the Battle Creek Seventh-day Adventist Church to resign from the congregation (the Battle Creek church had already separated itself from the sanitarium in January 1906).[15] Kellogg refused to do so, demanding instead a public heresy trial, which the church was loath to grant.[16] The closest he ever came to such a trial was on October 7 of that year, when two elders from the church, George Amadon and A. C. Bourdeau, paid a visit to the doctor at his home to ask him what he would do if he were dropped from the church rolls. The result was a wide-ranging interview that lasted from 8:20 in the morning to 4:30 in the afternoon. Recorded by two of Kellogg's stenographers, the interview fills seventy-four pages of single-spaced type on legal paper.[17]

After some preliminary chitchat, Kellogg completely dominated the interview from the first, vigorously defending *The Living Temple* against charges of pantheism. "If I were a pantheist," Kellogg exclaimed, "I would be out worshipping the sun. How can a man be a pantheist and do what I am trying to do," "hold[ing] up things here in the Sanitarium"?[18] Claiming quite rightly that the ideas in the book were the same that he and others had presented before at the General Conferences and at various camp meetings, Kellogg further asked why no one had objected then, and now that the charges were being made, why was not an investigatory committee being formed to settle the question once and for all? Most of all, why had Ellen White not objected to the book even after it was placed in her hands, and why did Kellogg find out about her criticisms only through the letter presented at the 1903 meeting in Washington, DC? Without really giving his interlocutors a chance to answer, Kellogg stated his conclusion to this last question: although he admired Ellen White as a woman of God, some within the denomination, specifically W. W. Prescott, Willie C. White (the prophetess's son), and conference president Arthur G. Daniells, had all manipulated her and her testimonies in order to destroy Kellogg and wrest the medical work away from him. As Kellogg may have intended, once the issue of the legitimacy of White's testimonies was brought up, all serious discussion of his theology was left by the wayside. The bulk of the remaining interview was given over to the doctor's detailed anecdotes to prove White's history of plagiarism and fraud in order to bolster his claim that the charges against his theology were trumped up as part of a long-standing "conspiracy" by "the preachers" to destroy him personally and gain control of the medical missionary work.[19] Given Kellogg's loquacious defense of himself at the interview, it is no wonder the Battle Creek elders declined to put the doctor on public trial.[20]

The fact that Kellogg wanted to focus on politics while the elders wished to talk theology begs the question, what, indeed, was the real issue in the "Pantheism Crisis": theology or power? The answer, despite Kellogg's public protestations, is clearly that the two issues were indissolubly linked. For all his protestations that he honored Seventh-day Adventism's sectarian distinctiveness, it is clear that Kellogg wished to take the denomination in the modernist direction of nondenominational medical missionary work. As Kellogg put it in the interview, his goal all along had been "to make the whole Seventh-day Adventist people a denomination of medical missionaries working . . . to make it the great Good Samaritan organization of the world."[21] To do so, Kellogg knew that he had to de-emphasize the role of doctrine in the denomination, and what doctrine there was needed to be elastic enough to accommodate the rapid changes in science and medicine. This meant abandoning biblical literalism and adopting a theology of immanence more in line with his scientific and medical training.[22] Institutional control and theology, therefore, went together, as perhaps Ellen White and other conservative

Adventist leaders intuited only too well.[23] Far from being trumped up as Kellogg maintained, the charges against his theology were simply a convenient but powerful indictment of his modernist agenda for the denomination as a whole.

A little more than a month after his marathon interview with Amadon and Bourdeau, Dr. Kellogg was disfellowshipped at a meeting at the tabernacle after being charged with failing to support the local church, disrespect for "the gifts now manifest in the church," and conspiring to "overthrow the work for which this church existed." The vote for his dismissal was unanimous. Dr. Kellogg made no effort to avoid it.[24] If remaining a Seventh-day Adventist, he said, "compelled [him] to be a hypocrite, a schemer, a manipulator, and a party to things that are base and corrupt, I would prefer to be cast out."[25] Ever after, Kellogg defended both his actions and his faith in biologic living: "This truth is worth more to me than any position which the Seventh-day Adventist people can offer to me, or anyone else."[26] No matter how dependent he was on Adventist resources to run his various sanitarium enterprises (and the future would show just how dependent he was), Kellogg said he felt duty bound to make the sacrifice for what he regarded as religious truth. From then on, Kellogg declared, he and all those working at the Battle Creek Sanitarium would be "independents" who did "not belong to any church."[27] "If the Seventh-day Adventist organization cannot tolerate me no other could," said Kellogg in the interview, "I propose to stand alone for the Lord, to stand for the truth alone when I have to . . . , and if we cannot do it co-operating with the Seventh-day Adventist people, we will co-operate with all the Christian people we can everywhere."[28] Kellogg never did join another church, and in later years his good friend Rev. Carleton Brooks Miller of Battle Creek's Independent Congregational Church characterized Kellogg as "like Lincoln," "independent of sect or creed."[29]

Kellogg's break with the church effectively spelled the loss of the sanitarium to the Seventh-day Adventist Church. Kellogg had adroitly used the rechartering of the Battle Creek Sanitarium in 1897 to consolidate his control over the institution by using a provision in the charter to purge church leaders from the sanitarium association. With the doctor's disfellowshipment, almost all denominational control or influence over the institution was lost.[30] Although detrimental to the denomination, the severing of ties to the Battle

Creek Sanitarium must have come as something of a relief to Ellen White. For years she had been counseling against the concentration of Adventist institutions in Battle Creek, which she said had become too worldly and commercial.[31] In light of this, the February 5, 1901, issue of the *Review and Herald* announced that a bureau of information was being formed to help "those desiring to move out of Battle Creek."[32] To escape the corruption of city life, Battle Creek College had already been moved to rural Berrien Springs in 1901. Renamed the Emmanuel Missionary College, it would later grow into Andrews University. This move was followed two years later by the removal of the General Conference and the Review and Herald Publishing Association to Takoma Park, Maryland, just outside Washington, DC. Kellogg had long relied on a large supply of Adventists who were willing to staff his enterprises at minimum (or below minimum) wages; he was therefore much against the exodus of Seventh-day Adventist institutions from Battle Creek.[33] Perhaps to forestall the complaints of Kellogg and other Adventists with strong ties and property investments in Battle Creek, the General Conference move was initiated a scant month after Takoma Park was chosen, and only ten days before the move was it announced to the public in the *Review and Herald*.[34] From then on Ellen White counseled that all Seventh-day Adventists should leave Battle Creek.[35]

Meanwhile, in line with White's wishes, the Seventh-day Adventist Church had begun developing a series of smaller sanitariums throughout the United States and abroad in places such as Australia and Denmark.[36] The biggest and most successful of these institutions was established in Loma Linda, California, in 1906. The Loma Linda Medical Center was destined to outstrip by far the Battle Creek Sanitarium in both size and importance, becoming the new center for the church's worldwide medical missionary enterprises and the anchor for an international chain of Adventist hospitals and medical schools. Envying its success, Dr. Kellogg would attempt to establish ties with this facility over the years, but to no avail. The church leadership remained wary of ever again letting the charismatic heretic have any role in the denomination's medical work.[37] And so, with Kellogg's disfellowshipping from the church in 1907, the nearly half-century era of Seventh-day Adventism as the dominant sectarian force in Battle Creek came to a definitive end.

## KELLOGG AND THE MIND CURE

Dr. Kellogg had always been fascinated with religious traditions other than Seventh-day Adventism, and although he never joined another church after his break with the Seventh-day Advents, he retained a lively interest in other religions, especially if they advocated health reform. Apparently, his interests along this line grew after the turn of the century in an effort to demonstrate that the health reform was not unique to Seventh-day Adventists.[38] Kellogg, for example, explored the health teachings of such movements as the Shakers, the Salvation Army, and Leo Tolstoy's Christian socialism; after the San's rebuilding, Kellogg now located the origin of the sanitarium not in the Western Health Reform Institute, but in the Transcendentalists' Brook Farm.[39] Especially interesting to him was Mormonism, the doctor having read the Book of Mormon in his youth. In 1898, while passing through Salt Lake City on a tour of sanitariums, Kellogg was asked to address an assembly at the Mormon Tabernacle. There he spoke about Joseph Smith's revelation enjoining vegetarianism and how Mormon dietary practice dovetailed with his own (afterward he was treated to "a regular Sanitarium dinner" with "no meat upon the table"). From then on he kept in contact with leaders from both the Salt Lake City and the Missouri Mormons concerning health reform.[40]

Swedenborgianism, too, gained the doctor's attention. Kellogg was well aware that Sylvester Graham had been influenced in his vegetarianism by the teachings of Rev. William Metcalfe of the Philadelphia Bible Christian Church, an offshoot of the Swedenborgian New Church. Kellogg was a friend of Rev. Henry S. Clubb, who for many years was pastor of that Philadelphia church and, as president of the Vegetarian Society of America, an occasional visitor to the sanitarium, where he lectured on Swedenborg and vegetarianism in 1909.[41] In the early 1920s founder of the *Wall Street Journal* and frequent sanitarium guest C. W. Barron sent all thirty-two volumes of *Swedenborg's Works* for inclusion in the sanitarium's library, which Kellogg gratefully accepted. Barron was an ardent New Churchman, writing long articles on Swedenborg's theology that Kellogg admired ("Thanking you very much for an opportunity to read this interesting manuscript, which presents another evidence of the marvelous insight into the secrets of existence which Swedenborg seems to have obtained"). Kellogg later told Barron that Swedenborg "was certainly an astonishing genius," and if he were alive today, no doubt "he would be an advocate of biologic life," shunning meat and supporting Prohibition. As late as 1928 Barron was still sending Kellogg Swedenborgian literature, with Kellogg promising to conduct a "fair study of Swedenborg" as soon as his work allowed.[42]

There was one religious tradition with a pervasive emphasis on healing that seems to have exercised an especially strong, but equivocal, influence on Kellogg: New Thought. In 1902 Kellogg wrote a brief sermon entitled "In Tune with the Infinite," which he published in *Good Health* and the *Life Boat* and then reprinted in *The Living Temple* the following year.[43] In it Kellogg told his readers that "the human body . . . represents an instrument, a harp of a million strings, at which two players preside, the one human, the other divine; the one fallible, erring, the other infallible, unerring. When these two players move in harmony, the song of life is sweet and melodious, a symphony; when the human player strikes even one discordant note, the harmony is broken, the melody is spoiled." In light of this fact, "The one thing needful for success, for happiness in life, is to live in harmony with God, to keep 'in tune with the Infinite.'" This phrase, which he always placed in quotes, became a favorite of Kellogg's, and although he never identified the author, most of his readers would have instantly recognized it as the title of Ralph Waldo Trine's 1897 best seller of the same name. It is curious that Kellogg never acknowledged its source, although he knew Trine's works firsthand.[44] Perhaps Kellogg's reticence to identify Trine was due to the fact that he was one of the most popular and successful promoters of a strain of American spiritual healing called New Thought, a tradition that derived from an amalgam of Emersonian Transcendentalism, mesmerism, and the "mind cure" pioneered by Phineas P. Quimby. In the 1870s and 1880s, the New Thought movement coalesced around a coterie of Quimby's students such as Warren Felt Evans, Myrtle and Charles Fillmore, and Julius and Annetta Dresser, whose son, Horatio, would become a leading New Thought spokesman. Broadly speaking, New Thought proponents, who sometimes styled themselves as "metaphysical physicians" or "mind curists," believed that physical or mental distress was caused by erroneous beliefs blocking the influx of divine or cosmic energy. Such traditions had long been off limits to Seventh-day Adventists. Ellen White, who had long been suspicious of "electric physicians" and "magnetic healers" as simply another form of Spiritualism, saw the so-called mind-cure science as more of the same, if not "Satan's masterpiece." To put oneself under the power of a mind curist, she believed, was tantamount to putting oneself in the hands of the Devil.[45]

Dr. Kellogg, on the other hand, was apparently of two minds about New Thought. He acknowledged that of all "curative agents which may be brought to bear upon the body, the mind undoubtedly ranks among the first," and for this reason the "magnetic manipulator, the clairvoyant, the mesmerist, the patent medicine peddler, or the metaphysical healer" may all be able to heal psychosomatic or "functional" ailments.[46] Kellogg had been convinced of this during his medical school days after a stint in the laboratory of George M. Beard, later famous as the discoverer of "neurasthenia."[47] However, just as with faith healing, most metaphysical healers went too far, Kellogg complained, by claiming that all diseases, functional *and* organic, could be cured through the power of the mind. As such, Kellogg warned, "These various popular humbugs are well calculated to serve as foolometers to test the length, breadth, and thickness of the foolishness of the nineteenth century," a "modern fetich" even more useless than homeopathy.[48] Kellogg ridiculed such metaphysical practitioners as Warren Felt Evans, whose book *Primitive Mind-Cure: The Nature and Power of Faith* (1885) was filled with both "bad grammar" and "bad philosophy" (Kellogg was especially incensed that Evans identified "Emerson, Alcott, and Thoreau, and the other Transcendentalists of New England," as precursors of this kind of New Thought, but of course, historically Evans was correct).[49] Even worse for Kellogg were those metaphysical practitioners who promised absent cures. Kellogg joked that anyone so sensitive that they could be cured over the distance of several miles by a mind curist would also have to be "protected from such coarse and powerful agents as starlight and moonshine, terrestrial magnetism and such like forces."[50] Ironically, in light of his own problems with *The Living Temple*, Kellogg further excoriated the New Thought movement on theological grounds because it had appropriated the "mysticisms of the Veddas" and was clearly a species of pantheism.[51]

Yet there were elements of New Thought that Kellogg obviously found extremely attractive. Trine's *In Tune with the Infinite* is a case in point. Trine's language of living in harmony with God's natural laws and his exhortation that one must "recognize, working through you, the same Infinite Power that creates and governs all things in the universe, the same Infinite Power that governs the endless systems of worlds in space," must have struck a chord with Kellogg, as similar statements appear in *The Living Temple*.[52] Just as importantly, although Trine believed in the omnipotence of thought, he nevertheless recognized that the body still needed light, fresh air, rest, exercise, and good food in order to be healthy, and he also taught that by fixing the mind on higher things, "*excesses* in eating and drinking, as well as all others, naturally and of their own accord fall away."[53] Trine was at pains to teach that, in addition to negative thinking, "bad food, bad drink, or bad air makes bad blood; that bad blood makes bad tissue, and that bad flesh makes bad morals."[54] Neither Kellogg nor the Christian physiologists could have said it better themselves. In fact, Kellogg published in *Good Health* in 1900 a long extract from *In Tune with the Infinite* (identifying Trine but not the source), headed "The Effect of Thought on the Body," in which Trine succinctly set forth his balanced approach to mental healing.[55]

For his part Kellogg had long recognized what we would today call "the power of positive thinking" on maintaining bodily health, which Trine articulated so well.[56] Kellogg was also much in accord with Trine's emphasis on the importance of sleep and dreams as conduits to the "infinite intelligence" in order to solve problems or make decisions (indeed, Kellogg maintained that he solved the problem of flaked cereals precisely in this manner). Moreover, both believed that all new ideas ultimately come directly from the mind of God.[57] In passages such as the following, it is easy to detect the direct influence of Trine on Kellogg:

> Sometimes we get near enough to God so that we can think his thoughts, and then we think aright. Every true and right thought is a divine thought, no matter who thinks it; and the only way we are led astray is by the human will being set in operation to pervert ideas and construct them into wrong thoughts. . . . The thing we need to do, is to have our brains "in tune with the Infinite," and then we can think God's thoughts all the time, and then our thoughts will be God's thoughts.[58]

In the final analysis, although it was dangerous for Kellogg to align himself too openly with Trine, especially after the doctor was charged with pantheism in 1903, Trine nevertheless represented for Kellogg a New Thought moderate whom one might respect, one who purveyed the best of the tradition without, in Trine's words, falling prey to the "many absurd and foolish things" that have been claimed in the name of New Thought.[59]

There was, however, another New Thought thinker whose impeccable credentials as a physiologist made him easy for Kellogg to acknowledge: Horace Fletcher, the man William James singled out in *Varieties of Religious Experience* as a harbinger of "healthy-mindedness."[60] Fletcher, successful businessman, world traveler, painter, sportsman, and sometime leader of Chinese pirates, had been converted to New Thought in the 1890s, quickly producing two books on the subject: *Menticulture; or, The A-B-C of True Living* (1895) and *Happiness as Found in Forethought Minus Fearthought* (1897). In *Menticulture* Fletcher proposed that the "germs" of fear and worry have kept humanity from perfection, but the mind could be emancipated from fear and worry through a simple process of will. Once this was done, humanity would "switch the Divine Spark (which is the energy of man) on to the wires that connect with motors belted to good acts, and good thoughts, and worthy appreciation, and to cut out the circuits of worry and anger and their branch lines entirely, leaving them to rust and decay through disuse."[61] In his follow-up to *Menticulture, Happiness as Found in Forethought Minus Fearthought,* Fletcher expanded on the idea of mental emancipation, primarily by coding it into a wealth of New Thought neologisms, making the actual practice of his system even more vague. Fear, worry, and all other destructive emotions now fell under the category of "Fearthought," which was to be replaced by "Forethought," defined as *"the logical, trustful, hopeful, Christian, and therefore stimulating, consideration of the future."* This would lead to "DIVINE SELECTION," the ability of mankind to modify *"the brute law of the 'survival of the fittest, or strongest,' by cultivating harmonic conditions favoring growth and producing happiness."* If only people would obey "God's Higher Law of Harmony," eschewing the past in favor of living in the "Now-Field," cultivating "Spiritual cerebration" (that is, directed dreaming), and eliminating the root of all Fearthought (that is, the fear of death), through "intelligent, persistent counter-suggestion," "Forethought" could be achieved. Despite his penchant for jargon, many must have been sold on Fletcher's method of mind cure, as both books became modest best sellers, going into multiple editions.[62]

Importantly, Fletcher, like Trine, never denied the importance of bodily health and went even further in integrating physiology into his system of New Thought.[63] Fletcher thus came to the attention of Kellogg not only through his New Thought writings, but also because he believed that the

highest "menticulture" could be obtained only if that bane of American existence—indigestion—were avoided absolutely. Fletcher hit upon the idea that
to avoid indigestion, food should be chewed for prolonged periods of time,
at least until all hint of flavor had disappeared, after which the natural swal-
lowing reflex would suck the food into the body. By predigesting food in the
mouth, the body would be able to extract more nutrition more efficiently
from smaller portions, leading to weight loss and smaller, less foul-smelling
feces. When people objected to the time it took to eat a meal in this way,
the "Great Masticator" replied, "With All Eternity ahead of me, cannot I
afford at least $\frac{1}{48}$ of my time for careful feeding of my body[?]" "The key to
good digestion," Fletcher concluded, was through chewing, "and the sooner
mankind comes to realize this important truth the quicker will come the
millennium of nutrition normality."[64]

Kellogg was an early and enthusiastic convert to Fletcher's system.
Fletcher himself called it "Physiologic Optimism," but Kellogg coined the
term *Fletcherism.* Soon a large sign commanding guests to "Fletcherize!"
was posted in the sanitarium dining room and a "chewing song" composed
to promote Fletcherism among the San's guests.[65] So potent was his system,
Fletcher claimed, that individuals would add decades to their lives and no
longer need doctors except as educators in correct health practices. And
because "man is more susceptible to evolutionary influence than any of the
animal kind," it also meant an elevation in the race "towards higher and
higher supermanhood."[66] These were sentiments Kellogg could agree with.
From his first visit to the sanitarium in 1902 until his death in 1919, the jovial
Fletcher became a favorite guest. His physiological ideas were promoted
in articles in *Good Health* and the *Battle Creek Idea,* his New Thought and
physiology books were sold through Kellogg's Modern Medicine Publishing Company, and Fletcher himself for a time became a coeditor of *Good
Health.*[67] Fletcher returned the compliment by giving a glowing encomium
to Kellogg and the Battle Creek Sanitarium in his book *The New Glutton* and
by handing out copies of the doctor's *The Living Temple* to friends (although
he chided Kellogg for using biblical evidence for health reform, as "scientific
minds" would be "shocked").[68]

Under the influence of Trine and Fletcher, Dr. Kellogg became more insistent on the power of positivity. The cover of *Good Health* for March 1915,
for example, carried an aphoristic editorial signed by the doctor with the

"Fletcherize" sign in Battle Creek Sanitarium dining room, ca. 1908.

headline "Optimism: Look Upward and Outward and Cheer Up!" "'Fear-thought' is a destructive force," Kellogg thundered; it is the "ugly offspring of pessimism and cowardice," "an enemy" and "false prophet." The only sure cure for "Fear-thought" was "Optimism": "Look no longer downwards, but turn your face toward the eternal sky," for "the Infinite Power that made you is hovering about you with healing in His wings."[69]

Such themes can be seen most conspicuously in Kellogg's book *Neurasthenia*, first published in 1915 and revised the following year. Neurasthenia, or "nervous exhaustion," was the brainchild of Kellogg's onetime mentor Dr. George Beard, who believed it to be a new form of disease brought on by urban, industrial living. Kellogg was skeptical that neurasthenia was a discrete disease, although he did believe it was indeed a common symptom of many different diseases, most of which were organic in nature and all of which could be cured through biologic living. Certain psychic states, however, such as worry, fear, and depression, could themselves cause neurasthenia, and thus these psychic states needed to be addressed directly if neurasthenic symptoms were to be overcome. Accordingly, an entire chapter of *Neurasthenia* was given over to a discussion of worry, which Kellogg maintained could be cured by a combination of biologic living, diverting hobbies, and forcing "one's mind into optimistic channels of thought . . . by reading optimistic authors or talking to optimistic people." In stubborn cases, however, one must not be tempted by such newfangled therapies as Freudian psychoanalysis, but rather resort to the "most effective of all remedies," religion, especially the "Christian faith," which is "the greatest of all panaceas for mental maladies of all sorts." However, what Kellogg recommended was not the Christianity of those of "melancholy piety" whose "creed is neurasthenic" and whose religion nothing but "a reformed sort of pessimism" (read: Seventh-day Adventism?), but rather an optimistic Christianity of light and joy.

Kellogg listed as specimens of this kind of religiosity a dozen or so psalms that, when "committed to memory and frequently repeated . . . will become fixed in the subconscious" and, serving as countersuggestions, "will exercise a molding influence" and "serve as a potent remedy for . . . fear and worry and 'fear thought.'" Such use of the psalms as countersuggestions was simply prayer systematized and made efficient.[70] Of course, Kellogg warned, this could not be simply a mechanical exercise, but must be accompanied with a belief in the immanence of God, for the "great Power, which made us and keeps us in life, is an inexhaustible source of strength upon which the weakened neurasthenic may draw for help; a Power which is ever ready to minister to the 'mind diseased.'" In other words, all we have to do in the end for either physical or psychological health is to "'live in tune with the infinite.'"[71]

The influence of the New Thought of both Trine and Fletcher in Kellogg's prescriptions is obvious in *Neurasthenia*. Kellogg had long taken an interest in developments in psychology and sought to make it a component of biologic living, but he was put off by the hypnotic method of Charcot and the sexual theories of his student Freud.[72] In the approaches of Trine and Fletcher, however, Kellogg found an approach to mental healing that took into account not only the spirit but also the body, and, what's more, the metaphysical aspects of their systems were based on a Christian physiological insistence on obeying God's natural laws and coincided nicely with Kellogg's own theology of divine immanence.

Of course, there was mind cure and then there was "mind cure," and Kellogg was always careful not to be identified with the latter. In the middle of *Neurasthenia,* Kellogg paused to deliver a chapter-long harangue against two Boston-based "mind-cure" traditions for which he had grave doubts: the Emmanuel Movement and Christian Science.[73] The Emmanuel Movement, started in 1906 by the Reverend Elwood Worcester of the Emmanuel Episcopal Church, had spread to several other cities and been emulated by a half-dozen other Protestant denominations.[74] Trained in both psychology and higher criticism of the Bible, Worcester initially started the program because he had become convinced that he could revive Jesus's healing ministry by integrating a spiritually informed psychotherapy into his church's social outreach. To that end Worcester created a cooperative endeavor that brought together physicians and clergy dedicated to curing the functional nervous diseases of the down-and-out of Boston through lectures, moral exhortation, and the use of a variety of forms of mental suggestion. Dr. Kellogg was initially intrigued by newspaper reports of the tremendous success of this program of religiously inspired healing, and for a time he even contemplated introducing it into the Battle Creek Sanitarium for people in need of "suggestive therapeutics."[75] A visit to Boston in 1907, however, quickly disabused him of the wisdom of this idea. Not only did Kellogg get the impression that the Emmanuel Movement was largely a personality cult centering on Dr. Worcester, who catered to "lone women" in need of "coddling," but he also discovered that hypnotism was widely used as a therapeutic tool. Kellogg, who had studied hypnotism under Dr. Charcot of Paris in the 1880s, was "convinced that it was not a good thing," because, like mesmeric healing or any other form of the mind cure that necessitated putting one's mind under the control of another, it involved the weakening of one's will. In the end, Kellogg concluded, the Emmanuel Movement was "a religio-scientific substitute for both scientific medicine and the good, old-fashioned Bible religion" and was nothing but "a more or less orthodox rival of Christian Science . . . with a foundation not much better."[76]

As may be surmised from this characterization of the Emmanuel Movement, Kellogg's opinion of Christian Science was not high. Like New

Thought, Christian Science was developed by one of the students of Quimby, Mary Baker Eddy, but Eddy developed her "mind cure" in ways very different from New Thought, imbuing it with an absolute idealism that denied the reality of matter. Eddy detailed her system, which she called Christian Science, in *Science and Health,* originally published in 1875, but going through several revised editions in subsequent years. Attracting followers, Eddy established the Church of Christ, Scientist, in 1879, over which she exercised rigid control, and the Massachusetts Metaphysical College two years later. Christian Science enjoyed quite a vogue during the 1890s and the first two decades of the twentieth century, during which time it was one of the fastest-growing new religions in America.[77]

John Harvey Kellogg was well aware of the growth of Christian Science early on, reprinting in *Good Health* in 1888 an article entitled "The 'Christian Science' Delusion" and commenting himself on the new religion in the journal a year later. Kellogg saw Christian Science as an affront to everything he had worked for in hygienic reform. Quoting from *Science and Health,* Kellogg attacked such statements as "Physiology is anti-Christian," "Nothing hygienic can exceed the healing power of mind," and "The so-called laws of health are simply laws of mortal belief." These, he said, were the absurd ravings of "this school of fanatics" and their fraudulent and mercenary leader, Mary Baker Eddy. Kellogg was especially indignant that Eddy singled out massage, hydropathy, and regimens of diet, exercise, and fresh air as idolatrous. For Kellogg, Eddy's ideas would be risible if it were not for the fact that her "professional 'faith healers'" were successfully preying on "the credulity of the public," leading many of them to an early grave.[78] Christian Scientists during this time were increasingly being charged with violating medical licensing laws, which Kellogg steadfastly supported but which the general public seemed unwilling to enforce in court.[79] Perhaps because of this, Kellogg was not above running articles with sensational titles such as "Killed by Christian Science" and "Another Victim of Christian Science," the second of which dealt with the inflammatory subject of the death of a child under the care of a Christian Science practitioner.[80]

After the turn of the century, in the face of the survival and growth of Christian Science and perhaps due to his own equivocal engagement in New Thought, Dr. Kellogg was forced to admit in an article entitled "The Menti-cure" that Christian Science could not be all "humbug," as "no ab-

Dr. Kellogg conducting a question-box lecture at the
Battle Creek Sanitarium, ca. 1920s.

solute humbug could for years so hold the confidence of many thousands
of intelligent men and women as so-called 'Christian Science' has done."[81]
Nevertheless, Kellogg was always concerned to differentiate biologic living from Christian Science. Perhaps in response to an anonymous query
submitted to one of his question-box lectures that had the temerity to ask
how the doctor reconciled his belief in God with the need for a special diet
considering that Christian Science doctrine on this point was obviously "one
step in advance of yours,"[82] Kellogg delivered a series of lectures beginning
in 1907 attacking Christian Science as both "unchristian" and "unscientific."
Subsequently published serially in the *Medical Missionary* and *Battle Creek
Idea*, these lectures deployed all the arguments, scientific, theological, and
ethical, that the doctor had ever developed against Christian Science over
the previous twenty years. Kellogg's personal criticism of Mary Baker Eddy
reached a crescendo in these pieces. On the scientific side, Kellogg charged,
she denied the value of basic hygiene, of medical research, of the rigorous

training of doctors and nurses, of the body itself. On the religious side, she denied the Bible; the reality of evil, sin, and death; the importance of Christ's atonement; his Second Coming; even God as a personal being. Under her authoritarian rule, Christian Science was little more than a venial cult designed to make money and not, as a truly Christian institution would, to help the poor for free. Perhaps displacing his feelings about Ellen White onto Mary Baker Eddy, Kellogg was particularly incensed by her claims to divine inspiration and healing miracles.[83] When Eddy died late in 1910, Dr. Kellogg rather gleefully asked on the front page of the January 1911 edition of *Good Health*, "Has the vital element of this new cult died with the passing of Mrs. Eddy?" "Time only will determine," Kellogg mused, but "whatever is not true must sooner or later die; and the sooner the better."[84]

Until at least the 1920s Christian Science functioned as an effective whipping boy for Dr. Kellogg, just as Spiritualism had functioned for Ellen White.[85] By contrasting biologic living to Christian Science, Kellogg was able to defend against those who would confuse the two as similar theological systems.[86] Moreover, by comparing his own system with a decidedly unorthodox healing system, Kellogg was able to highlight the features of biologic living in such a way that, although not making it seem completely orthodox either theologically or medically, at least made it seem more orthodox by comparison. Strategically, therefore, Christian Science played an important role for Kellogg, allowing him through his attacks on the tradition both to fend off continuing accusations of pantheism from his Adventist critics and at the same time to protect his professional bona fides in the medical world, hence the separate chapter in *Neurasthenia*.

### C. W. POST AND LA VITA INN

There is a curious companion to the story of Kellogg and Christian Science that points up the popularity of various forms of mental healing in Battle Creek during the latter half of the nineteenth century, a popularity that in an indirect way would have a major impact on the doctor and his sanitarium. In 1895 Mrs. Agnes Chester, a Battle Creek Christian Science practitioner, was charged with practicing medicine without a license after serving as a midwife.[87] Chester was tried twice, the first trial ending in a hung jury and the second with acquittal. This was not an unusual outcome, for at this time

C. W. Post. *Courtesy of Willard Library Historical Images of Battle Creek Collection.*

juries in Michigan were quite reluctant to convict any alternative healer for violating licensing laws, for reasons of both free trade and freedom of religion.[88] One of the witnesses called to help her make both arguments was C. W. Post, a businessman and sometime mental healer who was then on his way to becoming Battle Creek's first breakfast-cereal magnate.[89]

Post came from Texas in 1890 to be treated for nervous prostration and general ill health at the Battle Creek Sanitarium. He stayed nine months, but he grew dissatisfied with the treatment he received from Kellogg, whom he found insufferably autocratic. He also hated the vegetarian diet. At some point during his stay, Post's wife introduced him to a local Christian Science practitioner, Elizabeth Gregory, who in turn introduced him to Mary Baker Eddy's *Science and Health.* Post, who left the care of the San to move into Gregory's home, began to thrive under her treatment, and the more he studied Christian Science, the more he became convinced that matter was unimportant and that disease consisted in wrong thinking, hence his willingness to be a character witness for Agnes Chester in court. Post, however, never embraced the Christian Science label, and although his beliefs in fact came to resemble more the New Thought of Ralph Waldo Trine and Horatio Dresser, he rejected the New Thought label as well.[90] Nevertheless, as he developed his thinking on the subject, much of both traditions made their way into his thinking, a fact reflected in the technical vocabulary he adopted to express his emerging worldview.

Although raised a Congregationalist and prone to quote the Bible,[91] Post came to reject traditional Christianity and all the "driftwood of creeds, dogmas, and orthodox statements" in favor of a vision of a personal yet nonanthropomorphic God who pervaded the universe and was found immanent in man. Not a true Christian Scientist, Post conceded that matter was real but negligible, and taking an idea prominent in New Thought, Post taught that God's universe was in the process of evolution away from the material toward spiritual perfection. In fact, according to Post, the biological evolution of man as described by Darwin, Spencer, and Haeckel was simply a way station on mankind's inevitable progress toward spiritual "unfoldment" and the achievement of perfection, signaled by the eventual superseding of the physical body, disparagingly called the "mud doll" by Post. Evil, therefore, did not exist in the universe, nor did disease, and even while one was still encumbered by the "mud doll," all one had to do to escape was to "turn from the world of illusion to the world of eternal realities." This was done by rejecting "mortal mind" in favor of the "Law of Harmony," which would allow for the "inflow" of the "Universal Divine Mind."[92] Based on this idea, Post devised a system of healing outlined in *The Modern Practice: Natural Suggestion; or, Scientia Vitae,* a book without chapters that for 160 pages alternates between exhortations toward the "Higher Life" and the "mental suggestion treatments" necessary to achieve it.[93]

Seeking to institutionalize Scientia Vitae, Post bought a twenty-six-acre farm on the eastern outskirts of Battle Creek (the Cliffs Addition), incorporating it in 1892 as a sanitarium under the name La Vita Inn. Here he employed a staff of two other mental healers, Elizabeth Gregory and a young onetime Seventh-day Adventist named Jacob Beilhart. Beilhart, who had met Post while working at the Battle Creek Sanitarium, was one of the two helpers fired by Dr. Kellogg for faith healing in 1892. Post had apparently been impressed by his faith-healing nurse and invited him to become a partner in the new enterprise. Soon, under the genial care of these three, miraculous cures were being reported at the inn, not least among those patients who were despaired of at "a prominent sanitarium," the location of which Post declined to give, because "it is not our purpose to cast the slightest reproach on any physician, hospital, or sanitarium, who, while they fail in a great many cases, do honestly what they can for the alleviation of human distress." Despite this professed discretion, it was obvious that Post harbored a distinct antipathy toward Kellogg and all "vegetarian cranks." After his stay in the sanitarium, Post announced that he was "not required to screw himself all out of shape by trying to follow a lot of ridiculous laws which Moses or some other mesmerized individuals declare were made by God." Indeed, Post intended La Vita Inn to be something of an "anti–Battle Creek Sanitarium." It was not fortuitous that with Scientia Vitae one could eat whatever and as much as one wanted. Beef steaks, bacon, and biscuits were encouraged, as there was no need at La Vita Inn "for a course in dieting, hot water, Graham bread, bran mush, and various forms of nonsense that often go under the name of hygiene." Drugs, however, such as opiates, alcohol, tobacco, and caffeine, were strongly discouraged, although after a stay at La Vita Inn, the need for such substances was said to vanish even for the hardened addict, yet another miracle of the Scientia Vitae system. The only thing definitively banned at La Vita Inn was "Materia Medica," that is, "the pills and pellets" of so-called medicinal drugs.[94]

Despite its liberal dietary rules and more relaxed environment, La Vita Inn never caught on and was never a serious competitor to the San. Moreover, domestic turmoil ensued when Beilhart discovered that Post had fathered a child with Beilhart's wife, causing the onetime faith healer to decamp to form a long-lived religious commune based on a blend of Christianity, Theosophy, and free love, called the Spirit Fruit Society.[95] At this point Post lost interest in mental healing and turned his active mind to another project: the marketing of health foods, specifically a coffee substitute originally called Monk's Brew but renamed Postum (1895), a breakfast cereal called Grape Nuts (1897), and a type of cornflake originally called Elijah's Manna but renamed Post Toasties (1908) due to customer consternation over the perceived irreverence of the original name. Although these products were in fact imitations of similar foods Dr. Kellogg had been selling through his modest mail-order company, Sanitas, it was Post's genius with marketing (sharpened, he said, by study of Christian Science and the mental therapeutics of Charcot) that allowed him to reach a mass market and become Battle Creek's first cereal millionaire. In his pamphlet *The Road to Wellville,* included with every jar of Postum or box of cereal, Post asserted that along with positive thinking to access the divine mind, a steady diet of Grape Nuts and Postum would bring one closer to the "Power of all Life" and make one into "the perfect man or woman the Creator intended." It was an uphill battle at first, but eventually thousands, and then millions, were convinced that Post's cereals would do just that. A new mass industry was born.[96]

Post's success set off a cereal boom in Battle Creek that lasted from about 1900 to 1905, a boom "comparable to a Texas oil strike or the Florida real estate boom of the 1920s." "Battle Creek," observed one contemporary wag, "has twenty-one thousand people, all of whom are engaged in the manufacture of breakfast foods." More than a hundred such food companies formed in Battle Creek, although very few of them survived to turn a profit.[97] Reportedly, when informed of Post's intention of marketing a version of Kellogg's Minute Brew commercially, Kellogg was complacent, saying that the more people that were making it, the more people would use it.[98] However, when Post made millions and was followed by numerous imitators, Kellogg was none too happy: "By ingenious advertising, much after the method of medical quacks, some of these concerns have built up large business interests and have waxed rich by their ill-gotten gains. One party in particular has made some millions by the sale of a cheap mixture of bran and molasses." Kellogg resented the fact that "the prestige of Battle Creek as a health center has made this an attractive place for the operations of ... pretentious and predatory ... food charlatans ... [all] at the expense of the Battle Creek Sanitarium."[99]

The success of C. W. Post and Battle Creek's other cereal entrepreneurs during the late 1890s was also not lost on John Harvey Kellogg's brother Will K. Kellogg. The younger Kellogg chafed at the doctor's unwillingness to capitalize on the success of their food inventions.[100] For twenty-five years taciturn Will K. had worked as John Harvey's right-hand man, called upon to do jobs, both big and small, at all hours of the day or night. In addition to functioning as the sanitarium's business manager, Will K. supervised John Harvey's food experiments, managed the thirty-odd individual businesses started by Dr. Kellogg, and acted as John Harvey's personal secretary.

Will K. was eight years younger than his famous brother, who, according to Will K.'s biographer, "had always assumed authority over his brother, even in boyhood."[101] In Will K.'s own bitter assessment, he was little more than "J. H.'s flunkey." The truth of this assessment is no better illustrated by the fact that when Dr. Kellogg took up the bicycling fad in the 1890s, a familiar sight was Will K. trotting alongside, taking memos as the doctor pedaled around and around the sanitarium's circular drive.[102] Underpaid and underappreciated, Will K. developed a growing resentment toward his older brother over the years. Finally, in 1902 Will K. had made up his mind to quit his brother and make his own way in the world. Six months later, though, the sanitarium burned to the ground, and Will K. felt duty bound to help rebuild the institution. He was drawn back in.

When Will K. Kellogg finally did leave the sanitarium and broke free of his brother's orbit in 1907, he stepped into the role he was destined to play, captain of industry.[103] Despite Post's head start, Will K. sensed what the industry could become. Back in the late 1890s, when John Harvey had set up the Sanitas Food Company to market the growing range of sanitarium food products, Will K. naturally became its manager. However, in this case he received a quarter of the profits of the new company instead of drawing a salary. This incentive led Will K. to experiment with new methods of marketing, which quickly paid off in increased sales. John Harvey was not happy with this turn of affairs, as he believed that commercial success in this line would lead to unfavorable publicity and harm both the San's mission and the doctor's professional standing (one of the reasons Will K.'s signature began appearing on Sanitas packages was to distance the doctor from this business). Nevertheless, Will K. had learned valuable lessons, and when he was given the opportunity to buy the rights to cornflakes from his brother in 1906, he did not hesitate to start the Battle Creek Toasted Corn Flake Company. Relations between the brothers soon soured over the marketing of cornflakes and other cereal products, eventually degenerating into a drawn-out legal battle over the right to use the family name, a battle eventually won by Will K.[104]

Although his first several years as a businessman were financially precarious, Will K. Kellogg's twenty-five years' experience as a business manager paid off. Through the creative and lavish use of advertising and (from the consumer's point of view at least) a superior product (Will K. had added

Will K. Kellogg attentively taking dictation at the side
of his brother, Dr. John Harvey Kellogg, ca. 1900.

salt, sugar, and malt to enhance the flavor), Kellogg's cornflakes eventually became a multimillion-dollar brand and, in an irony that would have pleased John Harvey's younger brother, the principal reason we remember the Kellogg name today. So profitable did the cornflake business become that Will K. spent much of the last twenty-six years of his life giving his money away through the W. K. Kellogg Foundation set up for that purpose.[105]

Interestingly, Will. K. Kellogg represents an extreme trend in the secularization of the health reform movement, moving from Ellen White with her millennial commitments to John Harvey Kellogg with his "scientific" modernism through C. W. Post and his variation on New Thought. It is as though Will K. Kellogg was the one-generation personification of the Weberian transition from the Protestant ethic to the spirit of capitalism. Will K. was raised in the same devout Adventist environment as his brother, but religion seems to have been less of a concern for him. He attended the Seventh-day Adventist Church growing up, although with what seriousness is impossible to tell (one story has young Will K. inscribing the name "Bob Ingersoll" in the church register as a prank). He also married within the church. However, when Will K. was disfellowshipped at the same time as his brother in 1907, he, like his brother, did not protest, saying, "The fact that I have not attended church for the past twenty-seven years would certainly indicate that the people did the proper thing to let me out." Nevertheless, Will K. maintained good relations with many of his old Adventist friends (occasionally taking their side in their battles against his brother John Harvey), continued to observe the Saturday Sabbath, and for years tried to maintain a vegetarian diet. He also continued to pray on a regular basis, read the Bible, and "believed in a higher intelligence" ("Doubtless," his biographer observes, apparently without irony, "his God had the same attributes that he had: neatness, efficiency, justice and intermittent compassion"). But Will K. never "pretend[ed] to extreme piety" and would rarely discuss religious matters. Thus, despite the fact that his biographer described him as a "deeply religious man who seldom went to church," it might be better said that business, and then philanthropy, became the younger Kellogg's true religion.[106]

# 6

~❧~

## Dr. Kellogg and Race Betterment

Despite John Harvey Kellogg's very public spat with his brother over the cereal business, the reputation of the Battle Creek Sanitarium continued to grow, attracting even more of the rich and famous to its doors in the 1910s and '20s. Other rival sanitariums had arisen in town to challenge the San's dominance, such as Dr. Phelps's across the street and, of course, La Vita Inn, but these could not compete and closed their doors after a couple of years.[1] In 1907 Bernarr Macfadden, famous for his advocacy of a muscular America, decided to compete with the Battle Creek Sanitarium by establishing one of his "healthatoriums" in Dr. Phelps's elegant fieldstone building.[2] Two years later he was out of business, and Kellogg simply absorbed his facility lock, stock, and barrel. Business was good at the San.

Dr. Kellogg, now a portly gentleman sporting a natty Van Dyke moustache and chin whiskers, continued to be a familiar figure bustling around town, instantly recognizable in his trademark white suit, adopted because it allowed the body to absorb more sunlight, especially the ultraviolet rays that Kellogg believed were a particularly "precious source of light and energy."[3] Not one to brood over troubles, past or present, Dr. Kellogg maintained the confidence and drive that had characterized him as a youth. He basked in his now international fame; none other than Leo Tolstoy himself was an appreciative reader of *Good Health,* and Kellogg maintained an active correspondence with a number of prominent European physicians and scientists, including the Russian physiologist Ivan Pavlov, who would set up a small research facility at the sanitarium.[4]

The break with the Seventh-day Adventist Church posed major institutional and financial challenges for the Battle Creek Sanitarium and its allied enterprises.[5] Although Kellogg predicted other Christians would flock to his medical school, the rupture with the Seventh-day Adventist Church led to the gradual erosion of enrollments at the American Medical Missionary College; this and the unfavorable Flexner report led to its closing in 1910. This was a blow, but Dr. Kellogg remained optimistic that at some point he would be able to reorganize the college and reopen its doors again.[6]

Meanwhile, Dr. Kellogg continued his evolution as a religious thinker, shedding during this time most, but not all, of his remaining Seventh-day Adventist beliefs, perhaps spurred by the fact that Ellen White passed away in 1915.[7] Back in 1907, when Kellogg was confronted directly by the church elders about his beliefs at the marathon interview, he had reasserted his conception of God as an immanent presence and his denial of God's anthropomorphic nature, and he was also clear that he rejected the infallibility of White's testimonies (Kellogg's public skepticism of the testimonies, in fact, led in part to Daniells's insistence that their acceptance be a test of orthodoxy within the church).[8] However, the doctor did carefully affirm his continuing belief in some key Adventist doctrines: literal premillennialism, the Saturday Sabbath, "soul sleep," even the sanctuary doctrine of the atonement, although this last with qualifications.[9] After the 1907 interview the latter two doctrines would disappear almost completely from Kellogg's writings, but he would hold on to the Saturday Sabbath and apocalypticism a little longer.

Since even after the break most of Kellogg's sanitarium staff still consisted of Seventh-day Adventists, the doctor continued having the institution observe the Saturday Sabbath.[10] Eventually, however, the issue of the Saturday Sabbath became a point of contention. Although Sunday services and Sunday Bible study based on the International Sunday School Lessons were available to both employees and guests,[11] non-Adventist employees found the Saturday Sabbath onerous for a variety of reasons. For example, in 1909 Dr. Kellogg attempted to recruit William M. Danner, chairman of the Evangelical Alliance of Greater Boston, to come to Battle Creek to be a salesman for the sanitarium's breakfast foods. Danner declined the offer, citing the old complaint that at the sanitarium there were "two Sundays in one week" and, according to what he heard from one of the employees, "*no Sunday* for the most part to all connected with the place who do not fall in to the Saturday

Dr. John Harvey Kellogg and his surgical team, ca. 1910.

observance." Moreover, "since Sunday Sabbath is the American Sabbath,"
Danner felt that "the unsettling influence of Saturday observance" on his
family and himself "would be a real menace to my happiness and efficiency."[12]
Other patients at the institution objected to the Saturday Sabbath because
they did not wish surgical operations on Sundays, while still others, such as
Upton Sinclair, who visited the San in 1907, found the whole Sabbath question simply odd. "So here is a million dollar establishment," wrote Sinclair in
*The Profits of Religion,* "with a thousand or two patients and employees, and
on Friday at sundown the silence of death settles upon the place, and stays
settled until sundown of Saturday, when everything comes suddenly to life
again, and there is a little celebration, like Easter or New Year's, with what I
used to call 'sterilized dancing'—the men pairing with men and the women
with women."[13] It was clear that the practice of a Saturday Sabbath was growing irksome to many of Kellogg's guests and employees.

In 1909, in an address to the sanitarium's employees, Kellogg reiterated his firmness in enforcing observance of a Saturday Sabbath while at the same time trying to maintain the institution's policy of nonsectarianism: "Here is a non-sectarian institution, an undenominational institution, and all denominations are represented here, and we must find some way of holding up our spiritual life and our religious life, and at the same time allowing freedom of conscience and freedom of worship—to worship God according to the dictates of our own consciences, but without pride or sectarian discussion." However, having said this, Kellogg went on to insist on the Saturday Sabbath, ostensibly not for any sectarian reason, but simply because Saturday observance was historically correct ("Nobody of intelligence who understands the history of the thing would question that the Saturday Sabbath is the Sabbath"). Other than that, Kellogg concluded, the choice of a day was ultimately arbitrary, and some day must be picked, because it was the observance of the Sabbath that differentiated Christians from heathens.[14] It is hard to say how far this mollified anyone in the audience, but Kellogg was in a bind as long as he was dependent on workers who were predominantly Seventh-day Adventists. It is notable that in subsequent years when the number of Adventists coming to the sanitarium either as patients or as workers dropped, Kellogg began to downplay the Saturday Sabbath. Perhaps, too, because his pious Sabbatarian wife died in 1920, Kellogg now felt comfortable allowing "quiet" recreational activities on Saturdays, and by the mid-1930s, "Saturday observance at the Sanitarium was largely perfunctory."[15] It is not clear whether this diminution of the importance of the Saturday Sabbath reflected changed attitudes on the part of Kellogg or was simply due to the fact that by this time the doctor was devoting more and more time to a branch sanitarium he had established in 1930 in Miami, Florida. In any case, by the 1930s the atmosphere at the Battle Creek Sanitarium was largely secular, and although Kellogg complained of this, apparently the Saturday Sabbath was not the central issue.[16]

Of all Seventh-day Adventist doctrines, Kellogg retained its apocalyptic worldview the longest, albeit in increasingly naturalistic forms. When asked at the 1907 interview if he believed in literal premillennialism, Kellogg readily assented, and at least until World War I statements in his publications frequently expressed a literal belief in the premillennial doctrine of the Second Coming of Christ, albeit always with a biologic living spin.[17] In a typical statement from 1906, Kellogg asserted, "The evidences that this world's history is drawing to a close are so many and so conclusive that no room is left to doubt or question the meaning of the prophetic vision which has stood a warning to the world during so many generations." However, "The only hope for the saving of even a few from the approaching ruin is through intelligent, consistent medical missionary work, based upon the foundation of a return to natural, simple habits of life, the recognition of the natural order which God established in Eden as the divine order."[18] In other words, the remnant would be saved not by belief in the Saturday Sabbath or any other Adventist doctrine, but through the practice of biologic living. But what then would be the character of the coming apocalypse? Would it be some supernatural intervention that would cause the calamity before the Second Coming, as the book of Revelation foretold, or would the tribulation at the end have some more naturalistic cause? Increasingly, as he distanced himself from church, Dr. Kellogg opted for the latter, with "race degeneration" emerging as his master apocalyptic narrative.[19]

## RACE DEGENERATION

Although Dr. Kellogg remained conflicted about the Darwinian hypothesis of the origin of species to the end of his life,[20] it is clear that he accepted early on the idea that species, even the human species, were mutable. Dr. Kellogg long taught that ever since the abandonment of the Edenic "bill of fare" (that is, the vegetarian diet enjoined in Genesis 1:29), mankind had begun a slide toward wholesale degeneration. Human degeneration through flesh eating, which began in earnest after the flood, manifested itself by shorter and shorter life spans: according to the Bible, Adam, Methuselah, and Noah lived to be nearly a thousand years old, while Noah's descendants lived increasingly shorter periods.[21] This was because, according to Kellogg, flesh eating had accelerated human beings' susceptibility to the noxious effects of germs, which he believed was the true cause of premature old age and death.[22]

Such ideas about degeneration and decreasing longevity through failure to abide by the laws of life did not originate with Kellogg, but were prominent in the ranks of antebellum Christian physiologists such as Sylvester Graham, William Alcott, and Elizabeth Blackwell.[23] "Who ever imagined," wrote Blackwell in 1852, "Adam suffering from dyspepsia, or Eve in a fit of hysterics. The thought shocks us—our Eden becomes a hospital."[24] Such diseases were the result of man's fall. Sylvester Graham taught that "God created our first parents perfectly beautiful" and that the present ugliness of the human race was a sign of its degeneration after the expulsion from the Garden of Eden.[25] The plausibility of the biblical account of human degeneration for the Christian physiologists was bolstered by three widespread beliefs about human heredity in the nineteenth century. The first was the inheritability of certain diseases (or the propensity to contract that disease, such as tuberculosis, cancer, heart disease, gout). The second was the belief that certain negative character traits that led to disease (for example, intemperance or excessive sexual desire) were also subject to hereditary descent.[26] The third belief was the related concept of the heritability of "acquired characteristics," called "Lamarckianism," after the early-nineteenth-century French naturalist Jean-Baptiste Lamarck. This belief supplied a mechanism by which the health and moral character of children were the result of individual actions of the parents, so that if a parent either improved or impaired him- or herself through virtuous or immoral practices, the child would consequently experience better or worse character and health.[27] For the Christian physiologists, chief among these detrimental practices were alcohol and tobacco consumption and sexual overindulgence, all of which, according to Alcott, could result in disease and debility in offspring to the "third and fourth generation."[28] The logical inference from such Lamarckian thinking, given humanity's degraded condition, was that human beings had been making sinful rather than virtuous choices for a long time.

Importantly, the Christian physiologists never equated heredity with destiny.[29] "Few persons are so much affected by inheritance," wrote William Alcott in his *Laws of Health* (1857), "as to render their condition one of misery." One had only to "obey the whole physical and moral code" and more often than not, life will "be a blessing."[30] What's more, if a person endeavored to improve her character and health before conceiving children, the children would benefit by a superior hereditary endowment. Thus, although the degeneration of the human race was a plain fact to the Christian physiologists, this was never seen as a pessimistic doctrine. The good news was that the degenerative processes could be stopped if only men and women would follow the laws of health; indeed, given the rapid effects of Lamarckian inheritance of acquired characteristics, the doleful effects of race degeneration going all the way back to the fall could be completely reversed after a few generations. Eventually, human beings could even once again achieve those tremendously long life spans enjoyed back in the Garden of Eden. This was a thrilling prospect to William Alcott: "Whose heart does not beat high at the bare possibility of becoming the progenitor of a world, as it were, of pure, healthy, and greatly elevated beings—a race worthy of emerging from the fall—and estamping on it a species of immortality?"[31]

Dr. Kellogg accepted many of the ideas of human heredity as propounded by the Christian physiologists. Kellogg probably first encountered the Christian physiologists' teachings on heredity through an article on the subject by Horace Mann reprinted in the Whites' *Health: or, How to Live*.[32] He probably encountered them again during his education at Trall's and through his own reading of Alcott, Graham, and Blackwell. As early as the late 1880s, heredity became a prominent theme in Kellogg's writings. In his *Plain Facts for Old and Young*, Kellogg quoted approvingly Dr. Oliver Wendell Holmes's opinion that "each of us is only the footing up of a double column of figures that goes back to the first pair. Every unit tells, and some of them are *plus* and some *minus*." Mostly "minus," according to Kellogg, for human beings were nothing less than the product of "six thousand years of transgression."[33]

Key to Kellogg's understanding of heredity, as it was for the Christian physiologists, was Lamarckianism: "The physician whose eyes have been enlightened," he wrote in an 1894 talk, "sees in much of the conduct of human beings which is charged to individual depravity, in the nervousness, wrongheadedness, weakness of will, and over mastering propensities, the hereditary results of whiskey drinking, tobacco smoking, selfindulgent [*sic*] fathers; or tea drinking, corset wearing, fashion enslaved mothers."[34] Articles reinforcing this idea became commonplace in *Good Health* in the 1880s and '90s.[35] Such things as alcohol, tobacco, caffeine, and constricting clothing, as well as a meat diet, were truly "race poisons," as their detrimental effects were not limited to the individual who consumed them, but were transmitted to that person's offspring as well. In a *Good Health* editorial from 1910 entitled simply "Race Poisons," Kellogg asserted that "the effects of . . . wholesale poisoning are apparent in every civilized land in the obvious race degeneracy which is taking place."[36]

Given his Lamarckianism, Kellogg shared the Christian physiologists' conviction that God had not intended heredity necessarily to determine one's destiny. "Although a terrible incubus of degenerating tendencies may have been inherited from earthly parents," wrote Kellogg, "the great Father of all men . . . has provided a way by which through repentance (change of mind) and obedience, we may be re-created, restored, and lifted above the thraldom of disease and sin."[37] Thus, "the man who has inherited a feeble constitution, by sowing the seeds of health may build up vigor and strength. The man born with a predisposition to consumption may so develop his lungs and his vital resistance as to be less susceptible to this disease than is an ordinary man."[38] According to Kellogg, the Bible tells us that such improvement was possible even for those whose hereditary deficit went back several generations, for despite "several centuries' exposure to the debasing and degenerating influences of Egypt, the children of Israel, under the leadership of Moses, given a schooling in obedience while wandering forty years in the wilderness," were "delivered from leprosy and plagues, and various other maladies which afflicted the Egyptians" and "healed from the hereditary tendencies which they might have acquired from their environment."[39] Thus, by making an effort toward personal health reform, one not only improved one's own welfare, but, given the Lamarckian assumptions behind this optimism, would improve the welfare of one's offspring as well.[40]

Over time Kellogg would modify his Lamarckianism, but he never doubted that to some degree acquired characteristics could be inherited.[41] To adopt a hard hereditarian position that rejected the possibility of acquired characteristics, a position vigorously promoted by the German evolutionist August Weismann,[42] would make nonsense of Kellogg's perfectionist insistence that heredity could be continuously improved through biologic living. Lamarckianism was just too important for the plausibility of biologic living for it ever to be abandoned.[43] Even when Kellogg recognized the experimental proof of Mendelianism, the inheritance of some biological traits through discrete, apparently unchanging, genes, he still attempted to use it as an argument for inheritance of acquired characteristics: for example, in a 1910 article in *Good Health* entitled "Mendel's Law of Heredity and Race Degeneration."[44] Seven years later a book review in *Good Health* praised W. E. Castle (famous for his early work on fruit flies) precisely because Castle warned that the current state of genetics did not warrant a hard hereditarianism.[45] It must be said, however, that Kellogg was not alone in his tenacious advocacy of Lamarckianism even well into the first decades of the twentieth century, for many other scientists could not bring themselves to embrace what some called "scientific Calvinism."[46]

Ultimately, Kellogg, like the Christian physiologists, believed that race degeneration, though very real, was not inevitable if only each human being would come to understand that heredity concerned not the individual but the race.[47] The problem was how to instill such "race consciousness" and begin the practical process of improving the race. Achieving race consciousness and slowing the rate of race degeneration, Kellogg recognized, would be a long-term project, one that would require nothing less than "radical reform in the habits and characters of individuals, as [perhaps] nothing short of a temporal millennium would be able to effect."[48] Unfortunately, by the turn of the century, it seemed increasingly clear to Kellogg that there was not time to await the arrival of the "temporal millennium" because a racial catastrophe of apocalyptic proportions loomed on the horizon.

### BIOLOGICAL APOCALYPSE

Like many other Americans of his class, Kellogg came to fear that the United States as a nation was experiencing a rapid acceleration of race degeneration. By this time the list of inheritable maladies and social ills had expanded from simply physical infirmities to include criminality, pauperism, and "feeble-mindedness," a catchall term for a variety of mental deficiencies. What's more, a growing body of statistics seemed to indicate that the rate at which these maladies were occurring was accelerating. Like many of his contemporaries, Kellogg traced this lamentable increase to recent improvements in public health, an idea he may have first encountered in Herbert Spencer's *Study of Sociology* (1873).[49] In an address to the Michigan Board of Health in 1881, Kellogg stated that "public hygiene alone would really tend to the deterioration of the race by the reversion of the process described by Mr. Darwin as 'survival of the fittest,' by keeping alive the weak and the feeble, and so securing the survival of the least fit, as a result of which the race would be deteriorated by heredity, and intermarriage of the strong by the weak."[50]

Spurred by his work in the national purity movement, Kellogg again expressed his growing alarm over race degeneration in a speech before the Civic, Hygienic, and Philanthropic Conference held in Battle Creek in October 1897. Kellogg's speech received national attention, including an article in the *New York Times*.[51] It was soon published as a series of articles in *Good Health*, entitled "Are We a Dying Race?"[52] The answer Kellogg gave to that question was an emphatic yes: "Not withstanding our marvelous accumulations of wealth and wisdom, we are certainly going down physically to race extinction." As evidence of this fact, Kellogg argued that the average number of people reaching one hundred had actually been decreasing in the past two hundred years. Although modern human beings had never enjoyed the stupendously long lives of the biblical patriarchs, nevertheless, up until the advent of effective medicine and sanitary reforms, Kellogg claimed that the average number of centenarians was much higher than it was in his day. Part of this decline was due to the greater availability of such race poisons as bad diet, alcohol, and tobacco, but part of it, too, was due to advances in public sanitation, which led to a situation where the weak survived and reproduced, thus diminishing the "constitutional vigor of the race."[53]

Kellogg's concern over "race vigor" reflected another fear that had become common in America after the turn of the century: "race suicide." First articulated by sociologist Edward A. Ross in 1901 and popularized by President Theodore Roosevelt thereafter, race suicide was the idea that by limiting the size of their families through contraception and other means, middle- and upper-class white Americans were being outbred by "inferior races," that is, southern and eastern Europeans, African Americans, and especially Asians. The inevitable result, according to Ross, would be that white Americans would "shrink to a superior caste able perhaps by virtue of its genius, its organization, and its vantage of position to retain for a while its hold on government, education, finance, and the direction of industry, but hopelessly beaten and displaced as a race." It would then be only a matter of time before white Americans even as a superior caste would "wither away before the heavily influx of a prolific race from the orient." Kellogg, who was a friend of Ross and later an acquaintance of Roosevelt, accepted this idea, reporting the president's remarks on race suicide with approval and providing statistics in *Good Health* to prove its reality in the United States.[54] Along these lines Kellogg had earlier written against "criminal abortion," especially "in New England," the hearth of white America, "where families of eight and nine were formerly exceedingly common," but now, due to abortion, "the average number of persons to a family is scarcely more than three among the native born population." "At this rate," warned Kellogg, "it is evident that this monstrous vice threatens to exterminate the race if nothing is done to check its ravages."[55]

Lurking behind the concern over race suicide was the long-standing myth that the white race was destined to play a leading—if not messianic role—in world history. Kellogg, a proud descendant of New England Puritans, took this belief seriously.[56] For example, when Josiah Strong published *Our Country* in 1886, now recognized as the premier statement of white racial messianism in the late nineteenth century, a laudatory review appeared in *Good Health,* recommending it as "worthy of an attentive and candid perusal." "This is a really forcible work," wrote the reviewer, perhaps Kellogg himself, "the chief purpose of which ... is to emphasize the importance of the United States as a Christianizing agency in the world. While many may disagree with the conclusions drawn from the facts presented, it cannot but be conceded that the author has brought together a vast number of useful and potent facts, and that he correctly forecasts the future as to the dangers threatened by certain growing influences among the social elements of this country."[57]

One of the dire things that Strong predicted was that the "Anglo-Saxon" race was in danger of being weakened by intermarriage with "lesser races" and was thus in danger of losing the energy and will to fulfill its global civilizing and Christianizing mission. That this level of degeneracy had not yet happened was due, according to Kellogg, to the continued "importation of the robust and hardy peasantry of Germany and Scandinavia, whose simple habits have thus prevented any marked degree of physical decadence."[58] However, given the white race's accelerating degeneracy due to unbiologic living coupled with the decline in the birthrate, it was only a matter of time before it would indeed fail. "That the Anglo Saxon race is degenerating is a fact too patent a fact to be denied any longer," proclaimed an editorial in *Modern Medicine* in 1901.[59] And in a *Good Health* article from 1904 entitled "Deterioration in Great Britain," Kellogg wrote, "Even a casual visitor to London must be struck with the great number of inferior, deteriorated looking people whom he meets upon the streets. This great center of civilization seems also a center of human degeneracy."[60] Even in the United States, there were some regions, principally the South, where people who were the descendants of "Anglo Saxon stock, which has been called the 'flower of the race,'" have degenerated alarmingly into "indolence, shiftlessness, and poverty."[61]

To avoid race suicide, Kellogg believed that the white race must turn to biologic living, produce more and healthier children, and avoid "race mixture." "Marriage between widely different races is unadvisable," Kellogg had written in 1881. "While there is no moral precept directly involved in marriage between widely different nations, as between whites and blacks and Indians, experience shows that such marriages are not only not conducive to happiness, but are detrimental to the offspring," adding, "It has been proven beyond room for questions that mulattoes are not so long-lived as either blacks or whites."[62] Kellogg had long held a version of what would come to be called scientific racism, one of the more unsavory offshoots of Darwinian thinking.[63] According to so-called scientific racists, humanity is divided into biologically distinct races that form a hierarchy, with the white race at the top. What's more, scientific racism posited the notion that the mental and physical endowments of each race were fixed by heredity and that intermarriage between races led to the degeneration of the superior race. Apparently, Kellogg's scientific racism originated with a crude form of climatic determinism that he believed created a racial gap "between people living in cold climates and those living in warm climates": "We see the difference," Kellogg explained. "The people living in temperate climates are vigorous people— they rule the world," adding, "This is what gives the people of England the dominance over the people of India; a few Englishman [sic] are able to rule millions of Hindoos."[64]

That such racist ideas exercised a tenacious hold over Dr. Kellogg is indicated in an editorial from a 1914 edition of Good Health, entitled "A Foolish Experiment."[65] Here Kellogg detailed the work of "a certain Dr. Schultz" who was attempting "to breed a new race" by creating a closed community consisting of a variety of different races—"a Swede, an Indian girl, an English boy, a negro girl, an Eskimo baby, a Hawaiian boy, a young Spaniard and a Porto Rican"—all in hopes that they would "intermarry and by continuing to intermarry during several generations create a race with universal qualities." Although "the folly of such an experiment is so evident that it is hard to believe that any intelligent person would seriously undertake to carry out so impractical a scheme," Kellogg made it clear that creating a race that "will combine the special advantages of the white [race] with the peculiar abilities of the native" was biologically impossible. Such a universal type simply could not be achieved by this kind of process, and, indeed, a universal race was unnecessary, because "there may be many types of perfect man, each adapted to his own sphere of activity and his own environment." This was a classic argument of scientific racism: that all races could achieve a kind of perfection within their own sphere of activity, although for all but the pure white race this sphere would always be limited.[66] Four years later Kellogg reiterated the biological necessity of maintaining racial purity. An article in a 1917 issue of *Good Health* congratulated the Scandinavian people on the fact that they "have been fortunate in their freedom from race mixtures and have given us abundant evidence in recent science, art, literature and exploration that the daring spirit of the Vikings is still at home in the land of the Midnight sun."[67] God may have created mankind as one, but Kellogg believed that subsequent exposure to climatic extremes had created subspecies, which, though all equally worthy in the sight of God, were nevertheless biologically incompatible and intellectually unequal.

Kellogg's scientific racism coupled with his Christian missionary universalism created some strange attitudes, especially when it came to African Americans, whose uplift he championed. Kellogg had always retained good relations with Battle Creek's black population, and it was well known in the folklore of the town that Kellogg had given heroic attention to Sojourner Truth in her last illness.[68] Kellogg, moreover, rejected the exclusion or segregation of blacks at the Battle Creek Sanitarium or at any of its schools or educational programs, and some sixty-seven African American doctors and nurses graduated from the sanitarium's schools in the twenty years before 1917, many of whom remained on staff. Kellogg was also an enthusiastic supporter of the Seventh-day Adventist Church's mission to southern blacks, and in 1899, when church officials were debating the most effective and politically safe approach to their evangelization, Kellogg argued that the color line should simply be ignored. To this end, he helped support an African American orphanage in Chattanooga, Tennessee, under the charge of Mrs. A. S. Steele, who was given leave by Kellogg to solicit donations at the Battle Creek Sanitarium. In later years Kellogg welcomed into his home seven African American girls from Steele's institution for training in biologic living and arranged for the placement of thirty of her orphans in the Haskell Home, an orphanage that Kellogg had founded in 1894.[69] And finally, Kellogg personally invited Booker T. Washington to be a guest at the sanitarium in 1910, a visit covered extensively in the *Battle Creek Idea*.[70] Yet as much as he admired certain individuals, Kellogg's opinion of the potential for African Americans as a race was not high: "The intellectual inferiority of the negro male to the European male is universally acknowledged," he wrote in 1902.[71] And six years later, in an article entitled "The Degeneration of the Negro," Kellogg reported on a paper he had heard at the National Conference of Charities and Corrections that predicted that "the negro will ultimately become extinct." Kellogg apparently agreed with the paper's conclusion that "the causes of the degeneration of the negro were clearly shown to be chiefly the outgrowth of immorality, and . . . that no degree of education and no mere sanitary or social measures could possibly save the negro from degeneracy and extinction."[72] Although "biologic living" may save a remnant of the white race, for blacks, apparently, there was little hope.

In Kellogg's mind, as in the minds of many Americans after World War I, the great competitor that threatened to outstrip the white race for the struggle of global supremacy was Asia. In many respects Kellogg admired the Chinese and Japanese, not least because of the prevalence of vegetarianism among them. Kellogg was good friends with the Chinese diplomat Wu Tingfang and encouraged his efforts to spread biologic living to China.[73] Yet such a friendship did not keep Kellogg from fearing the rise of "the yellow races," a fear that rose in pitch in the last decades of his life. In a talk from 1938 Kellogg wrote, "The white race is going down and . . . in 25 or 30 years from now the yellow races will rule the world."[74] Unlike the civilized races of the West, the populations of "Japan and China are increasing rapidly and are going to increase very rapidly in the next few hundred years because they have been able to survive and maintain their numbers notwithstanding they have no protection from insanitary conditions and no public health laws to amount to anything." The inevitable result was that "they will pretty soon have control of the world," and "the white races will be enslaved by them." Eight years earlier Kellogg had written a friend that he had become aware of an "increasing prejudice among the Orientals to Christian philosophy, largely due, no doubt, to the arrogant attitude of the missionaries." "It looks to me," Kellogg noted ruefully, "as though Christian civilization is going to be superseded within a century or two by a new civilization based on heathen philosophy instead of Christian." The only bright spot for Kellogg was that once Asians ascended to power, they, too, would be overwhelmed by the race poisons that were destroying whites and eventually go extinct. The best that could be hoped for white Christian civilization, then, was "the survival of a remnant of people who recognize the situation and are determined to do what they can to prevent it and save the human race."[75]

But how could this remnant be created? Kellogg was loath to advocate the abandonment of sanitary reforms to allow the "natural law of selection" to function, because, despite the tenor of some of his remarks, it was against his Christian conscience to advocate in any way killing the weak.[76] "The genius of Christianity," he wrote, "is not the dominance of the strong, but the protection of the weak: he is greatest who serves most. Here seems to be two principles at war with each other,—a principle in the natural world tending to the weeding out of the feeble and weakly, and the principle in the spiritual world demanding the sacrifice of the strong for the weak. If to be perfectly natural is to be truly spiritual, as the writer believes, there ought to be some way of reconciling these conflicting principles."[77] Kellogg's primary solution to this dilemma was to step up efforts at promoting biologic living and to increase the urgency of his call for Americans to voluntarily "return to Nature."[78] But like many others in the last decades of the nineteenth century and the first decades of the twentieth, Dr. Kellogg also began to see more authoritarian remedies as necessary if the white race were to be preserved.[79]

As far back as his 1881 sex manual, *Plain Facts,* the doctor wrote that although he was "not prepared to offer a plan" for saving the race from degeneration, it was nevertheless "very clearly important that something should be done in this direction."[80] A little more than a decade later, in a talk entitled "The Medical Profession" (1894) delivered to the Ann Arbor Students' Christian Association, Kellogg predicted that "the medical sanitarian of the future will not be satisfied with human beings as they are, but will seek to make them better by insisting upon the application to the human race of some of the principles which the stock-breeder has long practiced with wonderful success in improving the species." This, however, would mean employing harsh negative sanctions: "The marriage of consumptives, inebriates, and persons suffering from grave general defects, will be prohibited by law. Possibly this will extend to moral defects as well."[81] In his 1897 talk "Are We a Dying Race?" Kellogg used the analogy of stockbreeding again in order to raise the possibility of marriage restrictions imposed by the state. Even more conspicuously, Dr. Kellogg in 1898 championed the idea that each community should convene a medical board to examine all the youth of the community and grade them on a scale of 1 to 3, 1 being the best hereditary stock "physically, mentally, and morally." Only those of the same class would be allowed to marry, with the 1s creating "an aristocracy of health." Such a class of people, of course, would also be an "aristocracy of Christian manhood and womanhood," believing that "the body is the temple of the Holy Ghost" and understanding that "the laws which govern the healthful performance of the bodily functions are as much the laws of God as those of the Decalogue." Kellogg admitted that the scheme was "Utopian,"[82] but nevertheless asserted that "the time for 'selective action' has come" in order "to take that 'longer step' toward the 'golden age, millennium, heaven, etc.'"[83] For Kellogg, "selective action" would involve a comprehensive plan to control the breeding of human beings, a plan that he would soon tout under a label now gaining popular currency in the United States: eugenics.

### KELLOGG AND EUGENICS

Led by his concerns over race degeneration and his fascination for cutting-edge science, John Harvey Kellogg would devote the last thirty years of his long life to the then developing "science" of eugenics, the attempt to improve humanity by understanding and systematically controlling human heredity.[84] Francis Galton, a cousin of Charles Darwin, began advocating controlled human breeding in the 1860s, coining the term *eugenics* in his 1883 *Inquiries into the Human Faculty*. Advances in genetics and demography provided a practical scientific foundation for Galton's ideas, which took off in both the United States and Britain after the turn of the century. In America especially eugenics attracted considerable support among white middle-class professionals who saw it as a bulwark against the "degenerating" tide of foreign immigration and the growth of the African American population. Thus began an era of well-funded eugenics research, which included large-scale demographic data collection and the drafting of legislation at both the state and the federal levels concerning marriage laws, immigration restrictions, and compulsory sterilization of "mental defectives" and other "undesirables." National organizations, too, were founded, such as the American Breeders Association (1903), the Eugenics Record Office (ERO, 1910), and the Eugenics Research Association (1923). These groups in turn published a variety of scientific and popular journals and newsletters that made eugenic ideas a topic of keen interest in the mainstream press. Moreover, the promotion of eugenics did not remain the province of scientists and academics, but was taken up as well by a variety of social reformers, progressive politicians, and many among the clergy. During its heyday in the 1910s to the 1930s, eugenics became little less than an American national obsession.[85]

Despite having promulgated hereditarian ideas beginning in the 1880s, Kellogg nevertheless did not immediately come out in public support of eugenics when it began to emerge as a national movement in the late 1890s. Kellogg's biographer speculates that because of eugenics' close association with Darwinism, Kellogg's public support of eugenics would have exacerbated his difficulties with the Adventist leadership at this time.[86] This undoubtedly was true, but other factors were at play as well. It should be pointed out that the earliest promoters of directed human breeding in the United States were religious and social radicals such as John Humphrey Noyes, leader of the Oneida Perfectionists, and the feminist Spiritualist Victoria Woodhull (it is interesting to note that when Kellogg first came out in favor of a eugenics-like program, he referred to it using Noyes's term, *stirpiculture*).[87] Fear of association with such "free love" radicals may have made Kellogg cautious of embracing eugenics, as it did others. The WCTU, for example, despite its Department of Heredity, shied away from explicit programs designed to achieve a "higher type of manhood or womanhood," considering them too radical for their rank and file.[88]

There were other inhibiting factors that were at least as important as fear of being associated with social radicals. Until the 1890s Kellogg held fast to the softer hereditarianism of the Christian physiologists. Around the turn of the century, however, Kellogg, without ever abandoning Lamarckianism, adopted a somewhat harder hereditarian stance, probably because the advancing scientific consensus was hard to ignore. However, according to Richard Schwarz, there may also have been very personal reasons for the shift. John Harvey and Ella Eaton Kellogg had no children, so in 1891 the Kelloggs announced that they would begin taking in needy children as a foster family. Eventually, the Kelloggs welcomed into their home forty-two children who came from a variety of socioeconomic backgrounds, including some of exceptional poverty. In one pathetic instance, Kellogg, after reading a newspaper account of a five-year-old found chewing on a discarded candle at the side of his dead mother in a tenement house, made arrangements for

Dr. and Mrs. Kellogg with adopted children at the Kellogg residence, ca. 1900.

the child to be brought to him immediately. In addition to fulfilling Kellogg's desire to have children, this large foster family of orphans was an excellent way of testing his theories of the power of biologic living to overcome even the most impoverished environments and hereditary dispositions. In most cases this seemed to work. The majority of the Kelloggs' foster children went on to live productive lives and retained happy and grateful memories of their upbringing. A few, however, were spectacular failures. When asked to find "the most miserable child in Chicago," one of Kellogg's associates brought him "Huldah's kid," the abandoned son of a prostitute who was found living on the streets and eating garbage. Despite Kellogg's best efforts, George (as the child was named) was a bitter disappointment, eventually becoming an alcoholic drifter not above cadging money from Kellogg at inconvenient moments. Other of Kellogg's foster children from similar backgrounds also failed to thrive, leading the doctor to believe that heredity had a far more powerful hold over these children than he had thought. Later, friends of Kellogg reported that "it was this set of circumstances more than any other which aroused Kellogg's interest in the eugenics movement."[89]

Throughout the first decade of the twentieth century, Dr. Kellogg continued to trumpet the theme of accelerating race degeneracy and the need to take swift action to counteract it. If America failed to do so, Kellogg warned, the consequences could be "the final extinction of the nation, perhaps of a whole human family."[90] Ever since he first articulated the theme in his 1897 "Are We a Dying Race?" the specter of "race extinction" haunted Kellogg, and the phrase appeared with increasing frequency in *Good Health*.[91] Kellogg acknowledged that he was "sometimes ridiculed as a calamity howler," but "the awful fact" was that "the human race, especially the civilized portion of it," was "rapidly sliding down the hill of physical deterioration toward race extinction."[92] As Kellogg drew away from the Seventh-day Adventists and their literal apocalypticism, his biological apocalypticism intensified.

Kellogg was probably first emboldened to embrace eugenics through his friendship with Irving Fisher, a nationally famous economist from Yale who was an early and unabashed proponent of eugenics. Fisher was also a frequent visitor to the San after having read about it in Mary F. Henderson's book *The Aristocracy of Health* in 1904.[93] As an economist, Fisher stressed the link between good health and increased economic productivity, and he thus sought the most efficient ways to maintain the health of America's workforce. Part of this could be accomplished through individual health awareness and greater attention to public health, but eventually Fisher came to see eugenics ("scientific humaniculture") as the best means to ensure the health of the "American race."[94] In 1906 Fisher was elected by the American Association for the Advancement of Science to serve as president of the Committee of One Hundred, the goal of which was to lobby for a national health policy, if not a cabinet-level secretary of health. Fisher was a strong voice for eugenics within the committee, and eugenics formed the centerpiece for his *Report on National Vitality: Its Wastes and Conservation* (1909), written at the behest of the National Conservation Commission set up by President Theodore Roosevelt. Fisher, of course, was careful to invoke Roosevelt's fear of "race suicide" as a reason for the urgency of a national eugenics program.[95] Later in 1925 Fisher would spearhead the creation of the American Eugenics Society, one of the foremost organizations for the promotion of eugenics.[96] When in residence at the San, Fisher frequently spoke to sanitarium audiences, and articles by Fisher began appearing in *Good Health* in 1905.[97] Two years later Fisher asked Kellogg to serve on the Committee of One Hundred, and *Good Health* soon became one of the vehicles for the dissemination of the committee's work.[98] It was most likely through Fisher and the committee that Kellogg was introduced to the wider eugenics movement and began to make contacts with its leading personalities.

One such personality was Charles B. Davenport, director of the Carnegie Institution's Station for Experimental Evolution at Cold Springs Harbor on Long Island, New York. Trained as a zoologist, Davenport had become deeply interested in eugenics in the 1890s through the work of Galton and his school of biometricians, and he soon came to see genetics "as the one great hope of the human race; its savior from imbecility, poverty, disease, immorality." As one of the earliest American converts to Mendelian genetics upon its rediscovery around the turn of the century, Davenport was convinced that most if not all traits, including social traits, were hereditary and could easily be determined by simple Mendelian ratios. In 1910 Davenport managed to secure a large bequest from Mary Harriman, widow of the railroad magnate E. H. Harriman, to create the Eugenics Record Office, which was later incorporated into Cold Springs Harbor. Davenport dedicated the ERO to eugenics research and promotion, and with the help of his right-hand man, Harry H. Laughlin, he made it into the most important center for eugenics research in the United States.[99]

Kellogg evinced a keen interest in Davenport's work. In March 1911 the doctor reprinted in *Good Health* an article by Davenport entitled "Euthenics and Eugenics: A Study of the Relative Influence of Heredity and Environment upon Life," which, surprisingly, stated in no uncertain terms that eugenics was vastly more important than "euthenics" (that is, environmental and health reform).[100] Despite this, Kellogg made direct contact with him the following year when, as a member of the Michigan Board of Health, he requested a worker from the Eugenics Record Office be sent to help with eugenics education in Michigan, which Davenport was happy to do. Kellogg also requested that Davenport sponsor his membership in the American Breeders Association, which Davenport also did.[101] For the rest of his life Kellogg would remain in close contact with Davenport and the ERO, and both men worked tirelessly for the promotion of a national eugenics program, motivated in part by their shared concern with the survival of the white race.

Indeed, it was Charles B. Davenport who convinced Madison Grant, author of *The Passing of the Great Race,* the bible of scientific racists and a book Kellogg admired, to visit the sanitarium for his arthritis in 1923.[102] Grant, as a consequence of his scientific racism, had became a nationally important promoter of eugenics through a series of International Eugenics Conferences beginning in 1912, which Kellogg helped to fund.[103]

Kellogg for the first time used the word *eugenics* in a 1910 editorial in the *Battle Creek Idea,* entitled "A New Introduction of an Old Term."[104] "In medical, hygienic, and philanthropic circles and literature," Kellogg wrote, "one cannot have failed to notice the recent reappearance of an old word, one which has done service in the old days of Greece when personal heroism and prowess was the pride and hope of the nation": *eugenics.* Kellogg felt that revival of this word, with all its historic associations with successful warriors of the past, was especially timely, for "never before did so much depend upon the understanding and practice of the science and art of race development as now," since the implementation of eugenics has become "not merely a question of race superiority, but of self-preservation." Coded into this statement was a theme—the urgency of preserving a remnant of the white race in the face of imminent extinction through a combination of eugenics and euthenics—that Kellogg would now sound with increasing stridency. There then followed in the editorial another eugenics theme that Kellogg would also repeat for the rest of his life: it was the "solemn obligation" of parents to their offspring that they be "well born" through the "science of eugenics," which would do for the human species what "the vulgar breeding of cattle and horses" had done for domestic animals.

In addition to an emphasis on "positive eugenics," that is, the encouragement of the fit to reproduce, the doctor also advocated more coercive measures or "negative eugenics" to make sure the unfit did not. As early as 1881 Kellogg had hinted that sterilization of the unfit might be an expedient solution to "race degeneration" by ending his discussion of the negative effects of heredity with a brief discussion of castration.[105] Elsewhere, Kellogg had also spoken in favor of a law introduced in Indiana in 1881 to prevent the marriage of the unfit, decrying the fact that "popular blindness to ... the laws of heredity ... should have been so great as to have made no demand for an action of this kind sooner." Kellogg would long remain a supporter of the Indiana law, referring with approval to its provisions for the sterilization of criminals and warmly welcoming as an honored guest to the sanitarium Dr. J. M. Hurty, the secretary of the Indiana Board of Health who spearheaded the law.[106] Moreover, in an address to the Connecticut State Conference of Charities and Correction in April 1911 (an address subsequently published in the *New York Medical Journal* and then as a U.S. Senate document at the behest of Senator Townsend of Michigan), Kellogg made it clear that as part of a national eugenics program urgently needed to forestall the extinction of the human race, "laws and sanctions" must be established that "will check the operation of heredity in the multiplication of the unfit."[107]

When Kellogg was reappointed to the Michigan Board of Health that year, he vigorously promoted a coercive eugenics agenda to the governor and state legislature, including laws to require physical examinations before marriage and marriage restrictions placed on those found to be unfit. It is probably not coincidental then that during Dr. Kellogg's term on the board, the Michigan Legislature proposed Public Act (PA) 34:1913, "an act to authorize the sterilization of mentally defective persons."[108] Back in 1897 Michigan had been the first state in the nation to attempt a sterilization law, calling for the castration of criminals and "degenerates," but it failed to pass constitutional muster. Meanwhile, several other states did pass such legislation, and by 1913 Michigan legislators were ready to reintroduce a sterilization law. Indicating the degree of public support that the bill now enjoyed, PA 34:1913 passed with overwhelming support in both houses.[109] It is not known how much direct lobbying Kellogg did to get this law passed, but it is clear that he supported it, as he did other states' sterilization laws as they were passed.[110] Considering how effective the procedure was, Kellogg wrote at one point, "one can only wonder why sterilization of the unfit . . . meets with any opposition whatever."[111] Thus, although Kellogg might have wished that eugenics could succeed through individual effort, he, along with many eugenics reformers, believed that those without the will to comply would nevertheless have to be forced into compliance by the authority of the state. By 1919 Kellogg was warning of the "perils of personal liberty" when it came to the successful implementation of eugenics.[112]

There were limits, however, to how far Kellogg was willing to go with negative eugenics. In 1915 Dr. Harry J. Haiselden, a Chicago physician at the German-American Hospital in Chicago, refused to intervene to save the life of a severely deformed infant on eugenics grounds. Apparently, this was a common practice with Dr. Haiselden, but in this instance his actions resulted in a coroner's inquest and a call for his indictment by the Illinois attorney general. Haiselden, who enjoyed wide popular and medical support for his stance, was never convicted on any charges, and, indeed, two years later he starred in a silent movie called *The Black Stork*, dramatizing his willingness to withhold treatment from defective babies.[113] John Harvey Kellogg, though, was not one of Haiselden's supporters. In a signed *Good Health* editorial addressing the "Haiselden case" entitled "Testing Eugenics," Kellogg asked, "If we admit the right of parents or physicians, or of any body of persons, to take a human life when no crime has been committed or attempted, where will we stop?" Although Kellogg was willing to have the state intervene to prevent "undesirables" from reproducing, he was insistent that the "ideals, moral standards and sanctions developed by civilization" demand that "the very highest respect should be paid for human life, and especially that the strongest safeguards be thrown about the defenseless life of infancy." Although killing defective infants was something that the ancient Greeks did, "no enlightened community" should allow it today.[114]

## THE RACE BETTERMENT CONFERENCES

By 1914 Dr. Kellogg decided it was time to step out on the national stage as a promoter of the eugenics movement. He did so by sponsoring the First Race Betterment Conference at the Battle Creek Sanitarium. Kellogg got the idea for a national conference from Rev. Newell Dwight Hillis, who had succeeded Lyman Abbott as the pastor of Brooklyn's Plymouth Congregational Church.[115] Newell was intensely interested in a scientifically based social gospel, which he set forth in his book *The Influence of Christ on Modern Life* (1900). Long concerned with problems of heredity and purity, Hillis had launched a "eugenics crusade" in New York City and was on the Expert Advisory Committee of Charles Davenport's Eugenics Record Office at Cold Spring Harbor. Believing that eugenics should be the centerpiece of the social gospel, Hillis found Dr. Kellogg to be of like mind.[116] Together they recruited a raft of eugenics luminaries, including Irving Fisher and Charles B. Davenport, to help them put together a program.[117]

The First Race Betterment Conference met over a week in January at the Battle Creek Sanitarium. The *Proceedings*, published later that year in a thick

Vegetarian banquet at the First Race Betterment Conference.

volume of 625 pages, listed some 406 delegates, doctors, dentists, scientists, academics, social reformers, politicians and government officials, and clergy who attended the five-day event, which featured papers, exhibits, movies, and "physical and mental perfection contests" for boys and girls, as well as a "Better Baby" contest.[118] The papers, which combined euthenics with eugenics, were wide ranging, with sections on statistics, hygiene, purity reforms, child rearing, and, of course, eugenics and immigration. Covered extensively in the press, the conference was national news for weeks after.[119]

Kellogg was a constant presence throughout the conference, using it as a bully pulpit to promote a grandiose vision of eugenics "with a euthenic, 'biologic living,' twist" (the fact that the two always went together in Kellogg's mind was the reason he preferred the term *race betterment* to simply *eugenics*).[120] In a paper entitled "Needed—a New Human Race," Kellogg asserted that by means of an "intimate study of the laws of eugenics and euthenics," the human race can confront "the exterminating cosmic forces to which every living creature is amenable." Indeed, "We possess knowledge enough of euthenics and eugenics to create a new race within a century if the known

# PROCEEDINGS

OF THE

# First National Conference on Race Betterment

January 8, 9, 10, 11, 12, 1914

## BATTLE CREEK, MICHIGAN

PUBLISHED BY THE RACE BETTERMENT FOUNDATION

EDITED BY THE SECRETARY

"To be a good animal is the first requisite to
success in life, and to be a Nation of good animals
is the first condition of national prosperity."
—*Herbert Spencer.*

Title page from *Proceedings of the First National
Conference on Race Betterment* (Battle Creek, MI:
Race Betterment Foundation, 1914).

principles of healthful living and scientific breeding were put into actual practice."[121] All it would take to create a "thoroughbred" race, Kellogg sanguinely predicted, was a program of "physiologic and biologic righteousness" maintained over four generations. Not only would such a program create an "aristocracy of health," but the nation that adopted such a program first would achieve global supremacy.[122] To achieve this goal the doctor lobbied hard for the creation of a national eugenics registry "to accomplish for human beings, the same marvelous transformations, and, to evolve the same betterments that have been and still being accomplished for pigs and cattle." Such a registry would not only be the basis for charting "human pedigrees," but also "provide better knowledge of the influence of environment on germ plasm [genetic material], particularly as regards inheritance of acquired characteristics." It might also serve as a blue book for those looking for eugenically suitable mates.[123]

The enthusiasm generated at the First Race Betterment Conference led Kellogg to change the name of his nonprofit American Medical Missionary Board to the Race Betterment Foundation.[124] This signaled a major shift in its priorities away from medical missionary work toward a focus on education for the public on the benefits of eugenics as the doctor conceived it. As Kellogg put it, the new name "more broadly and comprehensively expressed [the foundation's] aim, objects and purposes and the work that it was doing for the betterment and the improvement of mankind in every relation of life than did the former name, for as we all recognize, the word 'Missionary' was becoming confined to a limited scope of religious activities only."[125] In an article in the *Medical Missionary* announcing the name change (as well as the termination of the journal itself), Kellogg argued that although medical missionary work had now been "recognized as an integral and essential feature of evangelistic effort," it was clear that the "whole race is fatally sick" and that "earnest and active efforts" were needed "to stay the destructive forces that are work" and heed the "cry that precedes a most appalling calamity." Kellogg disclaimed any loss of interest in the medical missionary work, but noted that the change from the American Medical Missionary Board to the Race Betterment Foundation "indicates the direction which our principal efforts are to take for the present."[126] Despite his protestations, Kellogg did gradually lose interest in medical missionary work, such that by 1930 he was characterizing Christian missionaries as "arrogant" and their work a failure. Indeed, Kellogg believed that missionaries should now focus completely on "the improvement of the physical and social conditions of the natives instead of making the main effort the destruction of their faith in the old religions which have been handed down to them through thousands of years."[127]

The first task of the Race Betterment Foundation was to plan a follow-up meeting in 1915. For strategic reasons it was decided to hold the meeting in San Francisco at the upcoming Panama-Pacific Exposition. The fair organizers were excited by the idea, even setting aside the week of the conference as "Race Betterment Week."[128] Again, the conference was a success and press coverage extensive.[129] Kellogg renewed his promotion of the eugenics registry, which had indeed been started in conjunction with Davenport's Eugenics Record Office at Cold Spring Harbor earlier that year.[130] "The world needs a new aristocracy," Kellogg repeated, "not an artificial blue blooded aristocracy created by wealth or official authority, but a real aristocracy made up of Apollos and Venuses and their fortunate progeny." It was now time for greater government involvement, even if this would necessitate that "we divest ourselves of a lot of unwholesome sentiment in relation to personal liberty." Kellogg called for the creation of a vast health bureaucracy, essentially turning the nation into a vast sanitarium so that education in biologic living could be brought to "every civilized community" by "health missionaries." This would mark, Kellogg predicted, "the beginning of a new and glorified human race" that "far down in the future will have so mastered the forces of nature that disease and degeneracy will have been eliminated." "Hospitals and prisons will no longer be needed," Kellogg prophesied in clearly millennial tones, "and the golden age will have been restored as the crowning result of human achievement and obedience to biologic law."[131] Some of the more extreme positions of his paper generated negative reactions in the press, but Kellogg relished the controversy: "One newspaper," noted Kellogg, said that he was "trying to make the United States into a great stock farm, by breeding for human efficiency," to which the doctor puckishly replied, "I wish we had the power to do that very thing," because "it certainly would be a great deal better than to have the United States a great stock farm, breeding mongrels—which we are doing now."[132]

As an adjunct to the Second Race Betterment Conference, the Race Betterment Foundation created a Race Betterment Pavilion for the Panama-

Pacific's Palace of Education in order to showcase advances in eugenics knowledge. According to A. E. Hamilton of the Eugenics Record Office, writing in quasi-biblical language for *Good Health,* the pavilion was designed to be "a warning, a program, and a prophecy": "It is the voice of a new physiological morality crying in the wilderness of ignorance, indifference and neglect, to make straight the way of coming generations by our more rational attention to the way we live and move and have our being here and now."[133] To that end the pavilion featured a series of displays divided between "Race Degeneracy" (complete with warnings of Anglo-Saxon race suicide) and "Race Betterment," which included a poster stating the lofty goals for Kellogg's foundation: "to create a new and superior race thru Euthenics, or personal and public hygiene and Eugenics, or race hygiene."[134] In addition to the pavilion, the Race Betterment Foundation sponsored a "Morality Masque" entitled *Redemption,* which attracted some five thousand people to the Civic Auditorium in Oakland.[135] The "Morality Masque," which has the distinction of being "the single largest theatrical production mounted by the American eugenics movement," was an elaborate allegory of the eugenic salvation of mankind through the agency of an "Unseen Spirit," perhaps a symbol of Kellogg's immanent God, although it is hard to tell how much input Kellogg had on the pageant.[136]

Due to the outbreak of World War I and other setbacks, it was not until 1928 that the Third Race Betterment Conference was organized, this time back at the sanitarium in Battle Creek. In addition to eugenics, the conference again reflected Kellogg's capacious understanding of "Race Betterment," including papers on "Personal and Public Hygiene, Industrial Sanitary Science, Rural Hygiene, Child Hygiene, Nutrition, Bacteriology, Chemistry, Physiology, Physics, Medicine, Education and Scientific Research." Like the previous conferences, this one had something of a carnival atmosphere: over the five days of the conference, in addition to the paper sessions and exhibits (one of which demonstrated Mendelian ratios using stuffed guinea pigs fastened to a panel), conference-goers were entertained with square dancing organized under the auspices of the industrialist Henry Ford and serenades from a local child septet known as the Seven Vivacious Vegetarians. It should also be noted that the Third Race Betterment Conference attracted contributions from a larger number of sterilization proponents, scientific racists, and anti-immigrant nativists than previous conferences.

Race Betterment Pavilion. *Courtesy of Willard Library Historical Images of Battle Creek Collection.*

This included a paper by E. A. Ross, the originator of the concept of "race suicide." A conference highlight was the "Fitter Family Contest," with prizes awarded to the fittest families of Battle Creek.[137] In addressing the contest winners, who were presented with a bronze medal showing a eugenically fit family with the motto taken from Psalm 16 ("Yea, I have a goodly heritage"), Dr. Kellogg told parents that, like a prizewinning horse, their prizewinning offspring deserved special treatment, including medical checkups every six months in order "to inspire" them to take "care of this masterpiece of God that they have been given—their bodies."[138] While somewhat less well attended than the previous two conferences (the *Proceedings* claimed that twenty-five hundred people on average attended the evening sessions), the third was counted a success, generating more than 450,000 lines of copy in the nation's press.[139] Plans for a Fourth Race Betterment Conference were immediately begun.

### THE RELIGION OF EUGENICS

Although Kellogg meant for his Race Betterment Foundation to be a secular organization, this did not mean that he intended eugenics to be devoid of a spiritual focus. At the end of his paper for the 1928 Race Betterment Conference, Dr. Kellogg renewed a call he had been making since at least 1914: "Eugenics, race hygiene as suggested by Galton, and euthenics, individual hygiene, must be made a religion, or rather a supplement to all other religions."[140] Kellogg was not alone in the national eugenics movement in calling for such a religion, and in fact there developed by the 1920s at least four different visions of what such a religion should look like. Some, such as G. Stanley Hall, the famous psychologist and early eugenics promoter, believed that eugenics was "latent in our Scriptures" and that it was "simply a legitimate new interpretation of our Christianity." Indeed, for Hall, Jesus was "the best unipersonal exemplar of the race idea, the true superman."[141] Eugenics, therefore, was simply the true meaning of the Gospels and thus completely compatible with the churches as they now existed. At the other end of the spectrum were atheists such as Charles B. Davenport, who believed that the moral power of religion should be harnessed to promote eugenics, although he had little use for its mythological or symbolic side. In a talk for the Battle Creek Sanitarium's Golden Jubilee celebration in 1916, entitled "Eugenics as Religion," Davenport contended that through eugenics, human beings who were predisposed to be moral through genetic endowment would become preponderant in society and the amoral bred out. After this, religion would fade away, as the fear of punishment in an afterlife would no longer be needed to make people moral.[142]

Even more radical visions of the religion of eugenics arose—for example, that of Dr. Kellogg's friend Dr. Aldred Scott Warthin, the well-known director of the Pathology Laboratory of the University of Michigan from 1903 until 1931.[143] Warthin presented his ideas in a remarkable paper at the Third Race Betterment Conference called "A Biologic Philosophy or Religion a

Necessary Foundation for Race Betterment."[144] Here Warthin argued that
it was time to do away with Christianity with its "sentimentalisms" such
as a belief in God or the immorality of the soul and recognize the "divinity" of "evolution." "If there is anything divine in this Universe," preached
Warthin, it was the living "protoplasm" and that which gives rise to it, the
"immortal germ plasm" (that is, the genetic material). In his proposed "religion of life," Warthin defined sin as any act that would either prevent the
transmission of the best germ plasm or facilitate the survival of "low par"
germ plasm. The "old religions" held out the possibility that such sins might
be forgiven, but "forgiveness of sins has done more harm, biologically, than
almost any other thing in the human race." For this reason, Warthin concluded, "old faiths, old superstitions, old beliefs, old emotions must then pass
away" to be replaced "by a new faith, a new biology."

For many in the eugenics movement, both Davenport's atheism and Warthin's mystical monism were too radical to be attractive options, nor was
there much interest in simply a eugenics reading of traditional Christianity.
Christian clergy were indeed welcomed and encouraged to join the national
eugenics movement, but only those of a modernist bent who were willing to
have their religion accommodate the advances of science were seen as valuable partners in the work.[145] As one writer for the "Eugenics and the Church"
column in the American Eugenics Association's journal, *Eugenics,* wrote,
"The kind of person who is supremely concerned with the physical reappearance of Christ next Thursday at 9:15 AM cannot be expected to be greatly
interested [in eugenics] nor the one who is concerned with the technicalities
of ecclesiastical millenery, or with the fine points of metaphysics."[146] Another
writer to the same journal contended that "the job of the preacher is to tune
the soul of man to the new universe" by "harmonizing science and religion,"
and in the process he will transition his flock "from a personal, loving but
Jealous God . . . to a Reason, a Logos, a Something so vast there is no word
to serve as a sign or symbol, an all-pervasive intelligence . . . of which we are
surely a part."[147] In other words, what was needed was a theology of divine
immanence that would satisfy mankind's desire for theism, perhaps paying
lip service to traditional Christian symbols, but ultimately abstract enough
not to stand in the way of the advance of science.

A number of eugenicists—for example, biologist Edwin Conklin and
surgeon Alexis Carrel—wrote books exploring this fourth option,[148] but one

of the most popular authors along this line was Albert E. Wiggam, journalist, popular speaker, and one of the most effective publicists for eugenics in the country at this time.[149] Importantly, Wiggam was also a close friend of Dr. Kellogg, probably first meeting the doctor when Wiggam was a featured speaker at the 1912 Battle Creek Chautauqua, of which Kellogg was an ardent supporter.[150] Kellogg and Wiggam soon became fast friends and lifelong correspondents, with Wiggam penning an article about the doctor for the *American Magazine* entitled "The Most Remarkable Man I Have Ever Known." It seems that both men were very fond of one another, sharing the same interests and passions, including the reconciliation of religion and science and a desire to promote eugenics on a national scale.

In 1922 Wiggam published a book entitled *The New Decalogue of Science*. It went on to become a national best seller. Wiggam's book called for the replacement of traditional Christianity with the new religion of biology, with eugenics as its centerpiece. Addressing a fictitious "Statesman," Wiggam reminded him that God had once revealed himself through the Ten Commandments, the Golden Rule, and the Sermon on the Mount, revelations the Statesman had very conspicuously failed to live up to. This was not so surprising, however, because only recently had God revealed that which was necessary to carry out his earlier ethical injunctions: science. Now, Wiggam wrote, "instead of using tables of stone, burning bushes, prophecies and dreams to reveal His will, He has given men the microscope, the spectroscope, the telescope, the chemist's test tube and the statistician's curve in order for men to make their own revelations." Indeed, "If His will is ever to be done on earth as it is in Heaven, it will be done through the instrumentalities of science." In fact, if either Christ or Moses were alive today, he "would be the first to perceive that a new Ten Commandments must be added to those on the tables of stone, that a new moral and spiritual dispensation must emerge from the modern Mount Sinai—the laboratory of science."[151]

Wiggam stressed the urgency of ushering in this new scientific dispensation, arguing that a variety of evils threatened to lead civilization to "Armageddon" if mankind did not religiously and ethically evolve. Many of these ills were rooted in the current economic system, in industry, in art, in government, in war, and in education. Accordingly, much of *The New Decalogue* is devoted to Wiggam's "scientific" prescriptions in these areas. However, chief among the evils threatening civilization was the now familiar claim of the degeneration of the "advanced races" due to the misguided and indiscriminate application of the Golden Rule through medicine, hygiene, and sanitation that allowed the unfit to survive. What was needed, then, was for the Golden Rule to be reestablished "upon a sound biological basis," a new moral code that was "not a personal nor tribal nor immediate morality, but a planetary, cosmic, generational, protoplasmic ethics that alone will make men really righteous." Such a moral code would recognize the "eternity of protoplasm" and be based on "the duty of eugenics," which is the "method ordained of God and seated in natural law for securing better parents for our children, in order that they may be born more richly endowed, mentally, morally and physically for the human struggle." Indeed, "Had Jesus been among us [today], he would have been president of the First Eugenics Conference," where "He would have cried: 'A new commandment I give unto you—the biological Golden Rule, the completed Golden Rule of science[:] *Do unto both the born and the unborn as you would have both the born and the unborn do unto you.*'" "This, and only this," Wiggam concluded, "is the final reconciliation of science and the Bible. Science came not to destroy the great ethical essence of the Bible but to fulfill it. It is the only thing that can fulfill it. And eugenics, which is simply conscious, intelligent organic evolution, furnishes the final program for the completed Christianization of mankind."[152] Unfortunately, the obstacles to such a new religion in this country were the Catholic Church and Protestant Fundamentalists such as Billy Sunday and William Jennings Bryan, all of whom rejected the religion of naturalism. Wiggam understood why this must be so, as the coming naturalistic religion would have to abandon "a personal God," as well as "heaven, immortality, and supernaturalism." However, properly educated, mankind would warm to the new faith as "a joyous, stimulating, dynamic philosophy of life which enables men to live by a clear light of reason, which illuminates and guides their emotions, instead of groping, as the masses have always done, in the blind darkness of dogmatic faith." Indeed, Wiggam's scientific faith means we no longer have to be "afraid of God":

> The scientist has accepted both Him and His universe and has quit trying, as the Fundamentalist does, to put him outside of His universe and build one of his own. . . . The significant and beautiful thing is that [with science] we know we are working in utter harmony with "that high, unknown purpose of the world which we call God." Whatever

God is, we know he is the immanent genius of things. . . . And the scientist gazing through his microscope, his telescope, his spectroscope and into his test tube can say with a faith born of a knowledge which the old prophets did not have, "I have sought after God and I have *begun* to find him."[153]

For decades Kellogg himself had been groping for precisely such a theology of divine immanence that thoroughly divinized biology while at the same time not completely abandoning the ethics of the old faith. As Kellogg put it in a 1914 editorial, "The world needs a new religion," not "a religion greater than Christianity, but such an amplification of the present conception of Christian principles as will make the demands of physical righteousness a part of the greater Decalogue."[154] Wiggam did exactly this, and by making eugenics the centerpiece of that "greater Decalogue," he articulated just the kind of religion of eugenics that Kellogg had been calling for. In anticipation of the publication of *The New Decalogue of Science*, therefore, *Good Health* reprinted almost in its entirety the original article from the magazine *Century* on which the book was based, and an excerpt focusing on Jesus the eugenicist appeared shortly after.[155] Two years later *Good Health* was still touting this "wonderful book," and Kellogg would extol Wiggam as the man who understood the necessity to "extend the Golden Rule . . . to fit a broader vision that modern research has opened to us" in eugenics. From then on Kellogg would see it as his mission to promote "new ethical standards, a new conscience, a broader religion, a code of ethics that will place the canons of biological law alongside those of the Decalogue, that will make man's responsibility to the human race—those who are to come after him, as well as those with whom he comes in contact—the ruling influence of his conduct."[156] Perhaps under the influence of Wiggam's scientific religion, Kellogg in the mid-1930s began to question the reality of heaven and the immortality of the soul, and by 1940 even the long-cherished idea of a personal God came into question for the doctor.[157]

Armed with this new "broader religion," Kellogg would continue throughout the 1930s to promote this religious vision of eugenics through the Race Betterment Foundation, although by this point Dr. Kellogg was in his eighties and beginning to decline physically.[158] In 1936 the Race Betterment Foundation received a large bequest from the estate of Mary F. Henderson, and Dr. Kellogg decided to resurrect his idea for a biologic remnant by creating an organization he called an "Aristocracy of Health." This organization was

Miami-Battle Creek    Miami Springs, Florida

The Miami–Battle Creek Sanitarium, ca. 1930.

designed to bring together "a small group of earnest devotees of health and eugenics" to form the nucleus for the evolution of "a superior race of man."[159] Launched with great fanfare in the pages of *Good Health*, it met with little, if any, success. Kellogg, nevertheless, kept up the fight to promote race betterment. In 1939 Kellogg hosted the Nobel Prize–winning surgeon Dr. Alexis Carrel at the Miami–Battle Creek Sanitarium, where together they discussed Carrel's mystical vision of race betterment as presented in his 1935 best seller, *Man, the Unknown*.[160] Kellogg was keen to attract Carrel permanently to the Race Betterment Foundation, and after their visit Kellogg wrote Carrel a rapturous letter: "I consider myself most fortunate in having had the opportunity to converse with you and to learn more of the great philosophical truths which you have expounded in your work 'Man the Unknown.'" Kellogg was especially "pleased" that Dr. Carrel had laid "so much stress upon the spiritual phase of human betterment," pledging that he would "make every effort to present to the people rational practical ideas about [Carrel's] 'new way' which must be followed if even a small fraction of the human race is to be saved from extinction and developed into a superior type of *homo sapiens.*" Indeed, in order to save "Christian civilization" and "the white races," Kellogg told Carrel that he was already "laying plans for activity and development in the work of the Race Betterment Foundation, which I trust will contribute something of the knowledge of the new way of life which is needed."[161] Unfortunately for Kellogg, however, Carrel decided to return to France and threw in his lot with the Vichy government, which was then undertaking race-betterment schemes of its own.

Despite these setbacks and despite his advancing age, Kellogg never gave up his promotion of race betterment, based as it was on his firm faith that God, "working through eugenics and the marvelous germ plasm, may save the race and even improve it." Indeed, in 1940, in one of his last published statements promoting the Race Betterment Foundation, Kellogg's own mystical vision of eugenics reached new heights: "The germ plasm clings tenaciously to those noble and mysterious capacities which make man the image of his Creator and stubbornly refuse to be deformed and destroyed by the abuses to which its human host subjects it. Here is the creating force, the transforming power that can rescue poor depreciated, degenerated humanity and bring it back to its Edenic excellence, which even when viewed through the eyes of infinite wisdom and judgment was pronounced 'Very good.'" Even at this late date, Kellogg believed, in the germ plasm there was still "enough left in man of the qualities planted in him by his Maker to make his salvation possible."[162]

THE END OF THE RACE BETTERMENT FOUNDATION

Although the Third Race Betterment Conference was successful enough that a fourth conference was projected, the crisis of the Wall Street crash and the onset of the Depression forced its postponement.[163] Finally, according to a newspaper article from September 1941, the Fourth Race Betterment Conference was planned to meet in Battle Creek in June 1942, timed to celebrate Dr. Kellogg's ninetieth birthday. Slated to attend were some 150 scientists and thinkers from the United States and Canada, including Charles B. Davenport, Paul Popenoe, Albert E. Wiggam, and the popular philosopher Will Durant. The theme was to be "a better race for the post-war days."[164] Three months later, however, the Japanese attacked Pearl Harbor and the United States itself was at war. The conference was canceled.

Despite their limited number, as Christine Rosen has remarked, the three national conferences on race betterment were unique in the national eugenics movement, for they "provided a less rigorously scientific environment in which to discuss race improvement" and "thus offered scientific and nonscientific supporters of eugenics an opportunity to explore common ground."[165] What's more, the conferences placed Kellogg center stage as one of the foremost promoters of eugenics during his day. Harry H. Laughlin, writing to Kellogg shortly after Pearl Harbor to urge that the fourth conference not be canceled, took the opportunity to pen this encomium to the doctor: "If Race Betterment develops into a science and a practical art, it must progress along the lines laid down by its founder, Sir Francis Galton and the few Americans who belong to his group. Among these Americans I would name Charles B. Davenport, Alexander Graham Bell, David Starr Jordan, and John Harvey Kellogg."[166]

Dr. Kellogg's zeal for the unbounded potential of eugenics never waned, even at the very end of his life. For example, in a letter written on November 1, 1943—a little more than a month before his death—Kellogg harangued Dr. Reginald M. Atwater of the American Public Health Association about race betterment: "If the American Public Health Association is indifferent to this matter or lacks the moral courage to give it consideration, it will miss a great opportunity for undertaking a work which may help to solve the world's greatest problem, how to save the human race, or at least the white portion of it."[167] In the end Kellogg felt that along with biologic living, his promotion of eugenics was one of his most important contributions to the betterment of mankind. Eugenics, he wrote just days before he died, "offers the only hope there is for civilization. [For] if the laws of biology were applied to human life as vigorously as they are applied to animals there would be no question of not only saving the human race but it might be lifted so far above the level of present types of homo sapiens and would be almost regarded as a new species of the genus homo."[168] Having pledged to sink his last penny into race betterment, the doctor was as good as his word, for when his will was filed in probate, it was found that Kellogg had left his entire estate to the Race Betterment Foundation, a fact noted with approval by Charles B. Davenport in his glowing obituary of the doctor in the journal *Eugenics*.[169]

Kellogg's eugenics dream, of course, never did come to pass, but the Race Betterment Foundation lingered on until 1967. That year the state attorney general, Frank J. Kelly, accused the four trustees of the foundation of misuse of funds; the foundation, which had $687,000 in 1947, was left with only $492.87, much of the money said to have been paid out as gifts and loans to friends and family members of the foundation's trustees. Presumably, the courts placed the Race Betterment Foundation in receivership, after which it was apparently dissolved without further ado.[170] By this time eugenics was no longer a burning issue in the popular imagination, and, ironically, people who came into contact with the Race Betterment Foundation in its last decade simply assumed it was some kind of maladroitly named civil rights organization.[171]

# Conclusion

## The Fall of the Temple of Health

As the Race Betterment Foundation faded from view in the 1960s, the Battle Creek Sanitarium was also heading toward a similar fate. Kellogg's sanitarium had remained in a thriving condition throughout most of the 1920s, but by then the doctor was spending much of his time in Florida and the active management of the Battle Creek Sanitarium had passed to a board of directors under the leadership of Dr. Charles Stewart.[1] In view of the continued popularity of the Battle Creek Sanitarium and its potential for growth, Dr. Stewart and the board embarked on a major expansion of the sanitarium's main building, adding the massive twin Italianate towers that still form a distinctive landmark on the Battle Creek skyline. Significantly, however, Dr. Kellogg opposed the expansion, concerned that it signaled the shift of the sanitarium toward pure commercialism and away from the spiritual and humanitarian mission of the institution upon which he had always insisted. Although in many ways a business success, Kellogg consistently denounced the corrupting influence of commercialism throughout his career, both because he felt it compromised his credentials as a physician and because he refused to compromise his principles and sense of mission simply to make a profit.[2] Dr. Kellogg, of course, was always happy to make money and lived well, but he spent the bulk of his profits on the sanitarium and other projects all in an effort to promote biologic living and, later, race betterment.[3] Even at the height of the Roaring Twenties, Dr. Kellogg was still unwilling to subordinate his sacred mission to simple money getting. In this he was completely out of step with the utilitarian spirit of the rest of the nation.

Battle Creek Sanitarium with towers addition.

As it turned out, Dr. Kellogg's instincts were right, at least as far as the expansion of the Battle Creek Sanitarium was concerned. The new twin towers were completed just in time for the stock market crash of 1929. Within a year the number of patients plummeted from thirteen hundred to just three hundred. Crippled by massive debt and a dearth of paying guests, the Battle Creek Sanitarium entered receivership in 1933, creating even more pressure to drop Kellogg's biologic living in favor of what the board hoped would be more attractive, because less strict, health programs. This included abandoning the vegetarian diet and allowing smoking on the premises, both of which thoroughly enraged Dr. Kellogg.[4]

Despite his age (the doctor was now in his eighties), Kellogg worked hard during the 1930s to regain control of the institution in defense of his health principles. Only in 1942 did the doctor finally succeed. By this time, however, the Battle Creek Sanitarium, now in bankruptcy, was a shell of its former glory. The main building had been sold to the federal government, which used it as an army hospital during and after World War II, and the sanitarium itself was forced to relocate to a much smaller building, the old Phelps Sanatorium, which was now owned by Kellogg's Race Betterment Foundation. Kellogg also fought off an attempt by the Adventist General Conference to reassert control over what had been historically a Seventh-day Adventist institution. The result was a court battle that ended in a division of assets, with the church receiving some $625,000 and Kellogg's associates retaining control of the rest of the Sanitarium Association's funds and its real estate. The victory, such as it was, was a pyrrhic one, for on December 14, 1943, the ninety-one-year-old Dr. John Harvey Kellogg had died suddenly in Battle Creek after a brief bout of pneumonia, ending all hopes that Kellogg by simple force of will could bring the sanitarium back to its past glory.[5] Without its charismatic prophet, the Battle Creek Sanitarium, much like a sectarian religious movement bereft of its leader, began its final decline.

The Battle Creek Sanitarium limped along until 1957, when, in an irony that would not have been lost on Dr. Kellogg, the Sanitarium Association came again under the control of members of the Seventh-day Adventist Church, in this case a consortium of Seventh-day Adventist physicians, who renamed it the Battle Creek Health Center in 1959.[6] Eventually, in response to changing needs, the new association shifted the emphasis of the facility away from general health and wellness to mental health, drug and alcohol rehabilitation, and acute care. A new building, the first in many years, was completed in 1971. It was named for James R. Jeffrey, who began his career at the sanitarium as a janitor, but was inspired to complete medical school and ended up as the sanitarium's medical director when Kellogg passed away in 1943. Long-term sanitarium care was discontinued on March 1, 1972, although the name remained the Battle Creek Sanitarium Hospital. Two years later the hospital returned to the ownership of the Seventh-day Adventist Church, which incorporated it into its ever-expanding network of health care facilities. At this point acute care was phased out due to state efficiency mandates, and mental health and drug and alcohol rehabilitation became the facility's primary focus.[7] Finally, in 1993 the hospital was sold and absorbed into the secular Battle Creek System, officially putting an end to the 126-year-old Battle Creek Sanitarium.[8] By this time Dr. Kellogg's biologic living—the so-called Battle Creek Idea—had long been forgotten in Battle Creek itself.

Despite Kellogg's ultimate failure to institutionalize biologic living, the doctor's long evolution from the Christian physiology of Seventh-day Ad-

ventism to the eugenic religion of the "germ plasm" is one of the more remarkable episodes in both American religious and medical history. Born
and bred a religious sectarian yet a physician by vocation, Kellogg spent a
lifetime trying to reconcile religious and scientific understandings of the
body. Indeed, the body was the great fact for Kellogg, the ineluctable nexus
of the material and the spiritual. When that nexus came under attack by materialist science or was in danger of being underappreciated as he believed it
was by his coreligionists, or, as in his last years, suppressed in the interests
of commercialized medicine, Kellogg fought tenaciously to keep this nexus
alive in the Battle Creek Idea. Kellogg's choice of eugenics as the capstone
of his system of sacralized medicine, perhaps inevitable given his continuing apocalyptic preoccupations, undoubtedly led to his system's perceived
irrelevance after World War II. Yet biologic living's core idea—the body as
sacred—has never completely disappeared from the American consciousness ever since it was first articulated by the Christian physiologists and other
early health reformers, a fact amply attested to by its reemergence in the 1970s
in the holistic and alternative medicine movement.[9] As an important historical exemplar of this enduring American concern, and as an important bridge
from the nineteenth century to the contemporary era of holistic medicine,
the legacy of Dr. John Harvey Kellogg's biologic living presents an invaluable
narrative. Moreover, it must be recognized, too, that, despite biologic living's failure as a mass movement, Dr. Kellogg died believing that his lifelong
theological project of reconciling science and religion was a success: "True
science is but a revelation of the Creative Intelligence and is clothed with
the sanctity of infinity," Kellogg wrote in 1942, "and rightly viewed holds
the key to spiritual harmony and peace." With this revelation Kellogg could
then dispense with "subtle theories and hypotheses" and regard "all truth as
one great whole and the infinite source of all." Doing so, Kellogg believed,
"brought one a satisfying sense of security which connotes peace of mind
and dissipates uncertainty and apprehension and so promotes optimism and
good health."[10] Such in essence was Kellogg's religion of biologic living, the
Battle Creek Idea.

*Facing.* Dr. Kellogg at the Miami–Battle Creek Sanitarium, ca. 1935.

# NOTES

### PREFACE

1. Richard Schwarz, "John Harvey Kellogg: American Health Reformer," 180.

2. Patsy Gerstner, "The Temple of Health: A Pictorial History of the Battle Creek Sanitarium."

3. D. E. Robinson, *The Story of Our Health Message*; Gerstner, "Temple of Health"; Ronald L. Numbers, *Prophetess of Health: Ellen G. White and the Origins of Seventh-day Adventist Health Reform*; Malcolm Bull and Keith Lockhart, *Seeking a Sanctuary: Seventh-day Adventism and the American Dream*. In this book I rely not on Schwarz's 1970 book, *John Harvey Kellogg, MD*, but on his 1964 dissertation, "John Harvey Kellogg," because it contains full documentation.

4. Mary Farrell Bednarowski, *New Religions and the Theological Imagination in America*.

5. John S. Haller Jr., *American Medicine in Transition, 1840–1910*, 280–84.

6. Emmett K. Vandevere, "Years of Expansion, 1865–1885," 74–75.

7. See, for example, Norman Young, "The Alpha Heresy: Kellogg and the Cross"; Bert Haloviak, "Pioneers, Pantheists, and Progressives: A. F. Ballenger and Divergent Paths to the Sanctuary" (1980), unpublished paper, Office of Archives and Statistics, General Conference of Seventh-day Adventists, Washington, DC, 1–66; C. Mervyn Maxwell, "Sanctuary and Atonement in SDA Theology: An Historical Survey"; Richard W. Schwarz, "The Perils of Growth, 1886–1905," 86–88; and George R. Knight, *A Search for Identity: The Development of Seventh-day Adventist Beliefs*, 113–14, 126. There are also a number of unpublished studies of the "Pantheism Crisis" in the archives of the Center for Adventist Research, Andrews University: Leclare Reed, "The Concept of God Expressed in the Writings of J. H. Kellogg" (1942); Stanley August Aufdemberg, "John Harvey Kellogg and Pantheism" (1970); James W. Zackrison, "The Development of Dr. John Harvey Kellogg's Theological Ideas Up to 1903" (1973); and Jim McKinley, "John Harvey Kellogg: A Controversy, 1897–1907" (1978). See also David Duffie, "Ellen White and the Theological Dimensions of the Kellogg Crisis" (1981), unpublished paper, Loma Linda Library, Loma Linda University, Loma Linda, California.

8. Schwarz, "Perils of Growth," 104–11; Knight, *Search for Identity*, 90–127.

9. See Paul A. Carter, *The Spiritual Crisis of the Gilded Age*.

10. For the connection between Progressivism and eugenics, see Donald K. Pickens, *Eugenics and the Progressives.*

## 1. BATTLE CREEK BEGINNINGS

1. John Harvey Kellogg, "Biographical Facts," June 13, 1940, JHKUM, Box 1; Schwarz, "John Harvey Kellogg," 12, 16; Lewis E. Weeks, ed., "August F. Bloese: Former Secretary to Dr. John Harvey Kellogg, An Oral History," 6, 21.

2. Kellogg, "Biographical Facts," June 13, 1940, JHKUM, Box 1; Schwarz, "John Harvey Kellogg," 12.

3. A. D. P. Van Buren, "The City of Battle Creek: Its Early History, Growth, and Present Condition"; Gerald G. Herdman, "Glimpses of Early Battle Creek"; Berenice B. Lowe, *Tales of Battle Creek,* 11–20; Mary G. Butler, "The Village of Battle Creek: 'Distinguished for Its Love of Liberty and Progress.'"

4. Dixon Ryan Fox, *Yankees and Yorkers;* David M. Ellis, "The Yankee Invasion of New York, 1783–1850"; John C. Hudson, "Yankeeland in the Middle West."

5. E. G. Rust, ed., *Calhoun County Business Directory,* 103–107; E. H. Pilcher, *Protestantism in Michigan,* 376–83; Van Buren, "City of Battle Creek," 349, 356–57; A. D. P. Van Buren, "Pioneer Annals: Containing the History of the Early Settlement of Battle Creek and Township," 310–24; Washington Gardner, ed., *History of Calhoun County,* 394–414; Lowe, *Tales of Battle Creek,* 13. Later arrivals in Battle Creek were the Reformed Church of America (1850), the African Methodist Episcopal Church (1850), the Second Baptist Church (Colored) (1859), the Roman Catholic Church (1860), and the Reform Temple (1880). Van Buren, "City of Battle Creek," 356–57; Lowe, *Tales of Battle Creek,* 40; Rust, *Calhoun County Business Directory,* 106–107.

6. Quoted in Marilyn P. Watkins, "Civilizers of the West: Clergy and Laity in Michigan Frontier Churches, 1820–1840," 166.

7. For an overview of the Quaker branches in Michigan during the nineteenth century, see John Cox Jr., "The Quakers in Michigan." For Battle Creek's Quakers, see Van Buren, "Pioneer Annals," 270–72; Gardner, *History of Calhoun County,* 897; Lowe, *Tales of Battle Creek,* 16–17; Martin L. Ashley, "The Early Quakers of Battle Creek: Followers of the Inner Light"; and Martin L. Ashley and Frances Thornton, "A Quaker Anti-slavery Family: The Merritts of Battle Creek." For Hicksite and Progressive Quakers, see Allen C. Thomas, "Congregational or Progressive Friends"; A. Day Bradley, "Progressive Friends in Michigan and New York"; Robert W. Doherty, *The Hicksite Separation: A Sociological Analysis of Religious Schism in Early Nineteenth Century America;* Carlisle G. Davidson, "A Profile of Hicksite Quakerism in Michigan, 1830–1860"; and Thomas D. Hamm, *The Transformation of American Quakerism: Orthodox Friends, 1800–1907.* For Battle Creek Progressionists, see *Battle Creek Journal,* April 25, 1856; *Liberator,* September 19, 1856, 155; *Anti-slavery Bugle,* November 8, 1856; *Proceedings of the Pennsylvania Meeting of Progressive Friends, 1857,* 39; *Liberator,* August 28, 1857, 139; *Proceedings of the Pennsylvania Meeting of Progressive Friends, 1858,* 104–105; and "A Declaration of Principles Believed and Advocated by the Progressionists of Battle Creek" (1858) (American Broadsides and Ephemera Collection, Call Number BDSDS, American Antiquarian Society). For Universalists, see Rust, *Calhoun County Business Directory,* 105–106; Van Buren, "Pioneer Annals," 323; and Edward Whipple, *Biography of James M. Peebles,* 62. For Swedenborgians, see "Notice," *Michigan Tribune,* June 19, 1847; Van Buren, "Pioneer Annals," 323; George Field, *Memoirs, Incidents, and Reminiscences of the Early History of the New Church in Michigan, Indiana, Illinois, and Adjacent States; and Canada,* 11, 32, 134; Marguerite Block, *The*

*New Church in the New World: A Study of Swedenborgianism in America,* 123–29; and Kit Lane, *Lucius Lyon: An Eminently Useful Citizen,* 152.

8. Pillsbury quoted in the *Liberator,* November 20, 1857. For notice of Andrew Jackson Davis's participation, see *Proceedings of the Pennsylvania Meeting, 1858,* 105. For Progressionists' conversion to Spiritualism, see Hugh Barbour et al., *Quaker Crosscurrents: Three Hundred Years of Friends in New York Yearly Meetings,* 135–36. Subsequent histories of Quakers in Battle Creek would all attribute the denomination's decline in the town to the inroads of Spiritualism. See, for example, Van Buren, "City of Battle Creek," 356–57; and Ashley, "Early Quakers of Battle Creek," 33.

9. The *Battle Creek Journal,* June 26, 1857; *History of Calhoun County, Michigan,* 84–85; Whipple, *Biography of Peebles,* 63–71.

10. *Kalamazoo (MI) Gazette,* September 19, 1851. For the details of Harmonia that follow, see Ashley, "Early Quakers of Battle Creek," 32–33; Carleton Mabee, *Sojourner Truth: Slave, Prophet, Legend,* 93–102; and Frances Thornton, "Harmonia: Memories of the Lost Village."

11. Ronald D. Graybill, "The Whites Come to Battle Creek: A Turning Point in Adventist History." Membership statistic from http://www.Adherents.com.

12. For the religious situation during this period in upstate New York, see Whitney R. Cross, *The Burned-Over District: The Social and Intellectual History of Enthusiastic Religion in Western New York, 1800–1850;* and Michael Barkun, *Crucible of the Millennium: The Burned-Over District of New York in the 1840s.* For the role of Vermont in the development of burned-over district spirituality, see P. Jeffrey Potash, *Vermont's Burned-Over District: Patterns of Community Development and Religious Activity, 1761–1850.*

13. Everett M. Dick, "The Millerite Movement, 1830–1845," 1–2; David L. Rowe, *God's Strange Work: William Miller and the End of the World,* 1–101.

14. Dick, "Millerite Movement," 5–13; Rowe, *God's Strange Work,* 102–57.

15. Dick, "Millerite Movement," 16–17, 20–23; Rowe, *God's Strange Work,* 158–91.

16. Ellen G. White, *Life Sketches of James White and Ellen G. White* (1888), LS88 184.1–192.1, EGWW; Dick, "Millerite Movement," 23–28; Rowe, *God's Strange Work,* 192–35.

17. E. White, *Life Sketches,* LS88 136.3–245.1, EGWW; Godfrey T. Anderson, "Sectarianism and Growth, 1846–1864." For good descriptions of Ellen White's visionary process, see Ronald D. Graybill, "The Power of Prophecy: Ellen G. White and the Women Religious Founders of the Nineteenth Century," 84–112; and Numbers, *Prophetess of Health,* 61–64. Ellen White's visions ceased in 1879, and thereafter she received her revelations through dreams. Numbers, *Prophetess of Health,* 242.

18. E. White, *Life Sketches,* LS88 192.2–192.4, 204.1, 245.2–248.1, EGWW; Dick, "Millerite Movement," 31–32; George R. Knight, "Adventist Faith Healing in the 1890s," 61–66.

19. In *Desire of the Ages* (1898), Ellen White wrote, "Christ has given signs of His coming. He declares that we may know when He is near, even at the doors. He says of those who see these signs, 'This generation shall not pass, till all these things be fulfilled.' These signs have appeared. Now we know of a surety that the Lord's coming is at hand." DA 632.2, EGWW.

20. E. White, *Life Sketches,* LS88 220.2–221.1, 259.1–260.1, 265.1, 272.2, 278.1–282.3, 287.1, EGWW; Anderson, "Sectarianism and Growth," 32, 36.

21. Schwarz, "John Harvey Kellogg," 8–9; Milton Raymond Hook, *Flames over Battle Creek,* 21–23.

22. Merritt G. Kellogg, "A Bit of Family History" (n.d.), 1–29, JHKUM, Box 1; Schwarz, "John Harvey Kellogg," 3–10.

23. E. White, *Life Sketches*, LS88 312.3–313.1, 317.2, EGWW; Schwarz, "John Harvey Kellogg," 9; Hook, *Flames over Battle Creek*, 23; Anderson, "Sectarianism and Growth," 43.

24. Hook, *Flames over Battle Creek*, 23–24, 44–46; Graybill, "Whites Come to Battle Creek," 25–29.

25. Hook, *Flames over Battle Creek*, 25–26.

26. Ibid., 37–38, 45–47; Anderson, "Sectarianism and Growth," 36–44, 46–52.

27. Schwarz, "John Harvey Kellogg," 3–10; Weeks, "August F. Bloese," 69, 83.

28. Albert E. Wiggam, "The Most Remarkable Man I Have Ever Known."

29. "Conversation Club Banquet: A Complimentary Evening to Dr. Kellogg at the Sanitarium," April 22, 1908, JHKUM, Box 5.

30. All by J. H. Waggoner: "God Is," *Review and Herald*, April 24, 1856, 13; "Dr. Randolph and Spiritualism," *Review and Herald*, January 6, 1859, 52–53; "Modern Spiritualism, No. 2," *Review and Herald*, July 28, 1874, 55; "Spiritualism, No. 9," *Review and Herald*, September 29, 1874, 119.

31. Schwarz, "John Harvey Kellogg," 10–19. John Preston Kellogg apparently had low expectations for his son, reportedly telling him, "John, if I had supposed you were going to amount to so much, I certainly would have taken more pains with you." Schwarz, "John Harvey Kellogg," 12. See also John Harvey Kellogg, "My Search for Health," January 16, 1942, JHKUM, Box 7, 1–2.

32. John Harvey Kellogg, "Biographical Facts," June 13, 1940, JHKUM, Box 1.

33. John B. Blake, "Health Reform"; Robinson, *Story of Our Health Message*, 13–17. For the metaphor of "heroic medicine," see James C. Whorton, *Nature Cures: The History of Alternative Medicine in America*, 5–6.

34. Whorton, *Nature Cures*, 34–36.

35. For an overview of these systems, see Robert C. Fuller, *Alternative Medicine and American Religious Life*, 26–37; Whorton, *Nature Cures*, 77–101. See also Catherine L. Albanese, *Nature Religion in America from the Algonkian Indians to the New Age*, 123–28, for a discussion of nineteenth-century health reform as representative of a spiritual subcurrent Albanese identifies as "American nature religion."

36. Richard H. Shyrock, "Sylvester Graham and the Popular Health Movement, 1830–1870"; William B. Walker, "The Health Reform Movement in the United States, 1830–1870," 31–62; Schwarz, "John Harvey Kellogg," 100, 103–104; Robinson, *Story of Our Health Message*, 38–49; Blake, "Health Reform," 36–41; James C. Whorton, *Crusaders for Fitness: The History of American Health Reformers*, 38–50; Numbers, *Prophetess of Health*, 97–103.

37. Charles E. Rosenberg and Carroll Smith-Rosenberg, "Piety and Social Action: Some Origins of the American Public Health Movement," in *No Other Gods: On Science and American Social Thought*, by Charles E. Rosenberg, 109–22; Whorton, *Crusaders for Fitness*, 34–35. Finney himself became a proponent of Grahamite health reforms. Whorton, *Crusaders for Fitness*, 126.

38. Whorton, *Crusaders for Fitness*, 5, 15, 29–31. See also P. Gerard Damsteegt, "Health Reform and the Bible in Early Sabbatarian Adventism."

39. Larkin B. Coles, MD, *Philosophy of Health: Natural Principles of Health and Cure; or, Health and Cure without Drugs; also, The Moral Bearings of Erroneous Appetites*, 216, quoted in Numbers, *Prophetess of Health*, 110.

40. James C. Whorton, "'Christian Physiology': William Alcott's Prescription for the Millennium," 467–68.

41. Quoted in Damsteegt, "Health Reform," 14, 16.

42. Quoted in Blake, "Health Reform," 43.

43. Whorton, "'Christian Physiology,'" 466–81; Whorton, *Crusaders for Fitness*, 49–61. See also Damsteegt, "Health Reform," 17. Graham also shared Alcott's millennial perfectionism. See, for example, Sylvester Graham, *The Philosophy of Sacred History Considered in Relation to Human Aliment and the Wines of Scripture*, 62, 314.

44. Walker, "Health Reform Movement," 161–79.

45. Ibid., 148–60, 217–21; Schwarz, "John Harvey Kellogg," 104–107; Robinson, *Story of Our Health Message*, 28–37; Blake, "Health Reform," 44–45; Whorton, *Crusaders for Fitness*, 107–108, 135–38.

46. Walker, "Health Reform Movement," 179–92, 221–35, 246–68; Schwarz, "John Harvey Kellogg," 24; Blake, "Health Reform," 45–46; Whorton, *Crusaders for Fitness*, 138–40; Numbers, *Prophetess of Health*, 177–78.

47. R. T. Trall, "July Matters," 16.

48. Walker, "Health Reform Movement," 197–203, 270; Robinson, *Story of Our Health Message*, 33–35; Numbers, *Prophetess of Health*, 95, 124–26, 127.

49. John Harvey Kellogg, "Battle Creek Ideals," October 6, 1931, JHKUM, Box 7, 1; Walker, "Health Reform Movement," 134–41.

50. Robinson, *Story of Our Health Message*, 34–36, 44; Harry B. Wiess and Howard R. Kemble, *The Great American Water-Cure Craze: A History of Hydropathy in the United States*, 135–36.

51. See the *Proceedings of the Pennsylvania Meeting of Progressive Friends, 1853* and *Proceedings of the Pennsylvania Meeting of Progressive Friends, 1859*.

52. "Declaration of Principles Believed and Advocated by the Progressionists of Battle Creek."

53. Quoted in Ashley and Thornton, "Quaker Anti-slavery Family," 41.

54. Thornton, "Harmonia," 18–19.

55. James M. Peebles, *Outlines of Dr. J. M. Peebles' Medical Standing and Medical Practice*; "A Statement of Facts: The Medical Standing of Dr. Peebles & Company Health Institution," *Battle Creek Moon*, January 23, 1900, 3; Whipple, *Biography of Peebles*, 449, 453–61, 588. Peebles would go on to manufacture patent medicines in Battle Creek in 1902, operating under the business name "Peebles Institute of Health." Arthur J. Cramp, ed., *Nostrums and Quackery*, 148–50.

56. Gerald Carson, *Cornflake Crusade*, 54–55; Mabee, *Sojourner Truth*, 193–99; Margaret Washington, *Sojourner Truth's America*, 132–33, 158, 177–78, 345–46.

57. Washington, *Sojourner Truth's America*, 175–79.

58. Whipple, *Biography of Peebles*, 46, 579; Walker, "Health Reform Movement," 197, 269.

59. "Letter of Henry C. Wright," *Liberator*, September 27, 1861, 31–39; Henry Willis and C. Euphemia Cochran, "Meeting at St. Mary's Lake," *Liberator*, October 4, 1861, 31, 40; Gardner, *History of Calhoun County*, 206. For Peterman's religious affiliation, see *The Universalist Register*. Willis put his entire holdings at St. Mary's Lake up for sale in 1864. *Liberator*, December 2, 1864, 15.

60. E. White, *Life Sketches*, LS88 131.1–134.3, 189.1, 192.5, 194.1, 196.1, 197.1, 198.4–201.1, 223.3, 257.1, 261.1, 304.2–305.2, 306.1–307.1, 317.1, 322.2, EGWW; Numbers, *Prophetess of Health*, 45–47, 76–80.

61. Ellen G. White, "Publishing and Traveling," *Spiritual Gifts*, 2SG 134.1, 135.1, EGWW; Numbers, *Prophetess of Health*, 80–81.

62. Robinson, *Story of Our Health Message*, 60–74; Numbers, *Prophetess of Health*, 43–47, 68, 76–90.

63. The following paragraphs follow closely Bull and Lockhart, *Seeking a Sanctuary*, 69–76.

64. Ellen White abhorred those who sought to "mangle the visions" and "spiritualize away their literal meaning," for she "had often been shown the lovely Jesus" and could attest to the fact that "he is a *person.*" E. White, *Life Sketches*, LS88 230.1–230.3, EGWW (emphasis in the original). See also Bull and Lockhart, *Seeking a Sanctuary*, 75–78.

65. Bull and Lockhart, *Seeking a Sanctuary*, 86.

66. Ibid., 90–91.

67. Ibid., 89–90.

68. Uriah Smith, in his *The State of the Dead and the Resurrection of the Wicked*, argued for the former position; John Harvey Kellogg, in his *Harmony of Science and the Bible on the Nature of the Soul and the Doctrine of the Resurrection*, argued for the latter.

69. Robinson, *Story of Our Health Message*, 118; Numbers, *Prophetess of Health*, 128.

70. Robinson, *Story of Our Health Message*, 50–59.

71. M. Kellogg, "Bit of Family History" (n.d.), JHKUM, Box 1, 4, 5–7, 25.

72. John Harvey Kellogg, "My Search for Health," January 16, 1942, JHKUM, Box 7, 1–2; M. Kellogg, "Bit of Family History" (n.d.), JHKUM, Box 1, 25.

73. John Harvey Kellogg, untitled, October 21, 1938, JHKUM, Box 7, 3.

74. John Harvey Kellogg, "An Address to Heads of Departments of the Battle Creek Sanitarium, Nov. 1, 1938," JHKUM, Box 7, 9–10; Schwarz, "John Harvey Kellogg," 7–8; Numbers, *Prophetess of Health*, 84–85, 128–29. Recipes for Graham Gems would continue to be featured in Kellogg's journal *Good Health* well into the twentieth century. See Lenna F. Cooper, "August Breakfasts," *Good Health*, August 1917, 390.

75. Numbers, *Prophetess of Health*, 132.

76. Robinson, *Story of Our Health Message*, 75–85; Numbers, *Prophetess of Health*, 132.

77. Robinson, *Story of Our Health Message*, 86–93, 97–98.

78. Ellen G. White, "Health (1864)," *Spiritual Gifts*, 4aSG 125.2, 4a SG 128.1, 4aSG 131.1, 4aSG 134.1, 4aSG 139.1, EGWW.

79. Ibid., 4aSG 120.1–4aSG 122.1, EGWW. Already in her 1858 edition of *The Great Controversy*, White had remarked on this process of degeneration. Ellen G. White, *The Great Controversy between Christ and His Angels and Satan and His Angels*, 69–70.

80. E. White, "Health (1864)," 4aSG 121.3–4aSG 124.2, EGWW.

81. Ibid., 4aSG 150.1, EGWW.

82. Ibid., 4aSG 148.1–4aSG 149.1, EGWW.

83. An advertisement for the pamphlet series appeared under the heading "Important Work" in the *Review and Herald*, January 24, 1865, 72. See also Robinson, *Story of Our Health Message*, 104–11, 112; and Numbers, *Prophetess of Health*, 146–49.

84. Ellen G. White, "Questions and Answers," *Review and Herald*, October 8, 1867, 260.

85. Despite the disclaimer written into the preface of this book, accusations of plagiarism would continue to dog Ellen White's health reform pronouncements; for a discussion of the controversy over the influence of other health reformers on Ellen White's health testimonies, see Robinson, *Story of Our Health Message*, 80–85; and Numbers, *Prophetess of Health*.

86. Robinson, *Story of Our Health Message*, 144–47.

87. Ibid., 80.

## 2. THE RISE OF THE TEMPLE OF HEALTH

1. Robinson, *Story of Our Health Message*, 73–74; Numbers, *Prophetess of Health*, 94. Kellogg, however, acknowledged that the Western Health Reform Institute was preceded by the

St. Mary's water cure. See "Address by John Harvey Kellogg in the Sanitarium Gymnasium, Field Day, Oct. 10, 1923," JHKUM, Box 7, 5.

2. Robinson, *Story of Our Health Message,* 97–102; Numbers, *Prophetess of Health,* 141–45.

3. For example, "When we who are now the advocates of this Hygienic philosophy shall have impressed upon our fellow-citizens the correctness of our views, to the degree that they shall consent in the main—in all essential points—to cooperate with us; to the degree that our principles shall no more be considered as the outgrowth of fanaticism, but on the other hand will be recognized as the outgrowth of an honest faith in the Gospel of Christ; then shall we have seen such results as will more than compensate us for whatever loss of reputation or character or fame or worldly consideration or wealth we shall have undergone. We shall be rich, then, in the reward of our labors, and in the consciousness that, in God's providence, we have inaugurated a revolution which shall not cease its whirl until the 'kingdoms of this world become the kingdoms of our Lord and of his Christ, and He shall reign forever and ever!'" James Caleb Jackson, *The Sexual Organism and Its Healthful Management,* 279.

4. James Caleb Jackson, *The Training of Children,* 98–99.

5. Ellen G. White, "Our Late Experience," *Review and Herald,* February 20, 1866, 89–91; "The Health Institute" (1875), 3T 172.2, EGWW; Robinson, *Story of Our Health Message,* 134–37; Numbers, *Prophetess of Health,* 150–54.

6. Ellen G. White, "Our Late Experience," *Review and Herald,* February 27, 1866, 97–99; "The Health Reform," *Testimony* 11 (1868), 1T 485.2–1T 494.3, EGWW; Robinson, *Story of Our Health Message,* 139–42; Numbers, *Prophetess of Health,* 154–55.

7. Schwarz, "John Harvey Kellogg," 170–76; Robinson, *Story of Our Health Message,* 144–54; Numbers, *Prophetess of Health,* 156–59.

8. Ellen G. White, *The Health Reform and the Health Institute,* 2, 9, 12, 10, 11–12, 15.

9. "The Health Reform," *Review and Herald,* June 12, 1866.

10. "The Western Health-Reform Institute," *Review and Herald,* June 19, 1866.

11. J. N. Loughborough, "Report from Bro. Loughborough," *Review and Herald,* August 14, 1866, 85.

12. Edwin S. Gaustad, *Historical Atlas of American Religion,* 115.

13. Jonathan Butler, "Adventism and the American Experience," 194.

14. "The Western Health Reform Institute," *Review and Herald,* August 7, 1866; Numbers, *Prophetess of Health,* 158–59.

15. "Prospectus of the Health Reformer," *Review and Herald,* June 5, 1866; Robinson, *Story of Our Health Message,* 146–49, 194–97; Numbers, *Prophetess of Health,* 162, 164–65, 173–76.

16. *Review and Herald,* September 11, 1866.

17. Ellen G. White, "The Health Institute" (1868), *Testimonies I,* 1T 553.1–563.1, EGWW; White, *Health Reform and the Health Institute,* 31–53; Robinson, *Story of Our Health Message,* 82–84, 98–100, 153–54, 172–90; Numbers, *Prophetess of Health,* 159–72.

18. Robinson, *Story of Our Health Message,* 151–52, 174; "Battle Creek Sanitarium," in *Seventh-day Adventist Encyclopedia,* 174.

19. Schwarz, "John Harvey Kellogg," 29; Robinson, *Story of Our Health Message,* 36, 143–55, 172–90, 203–205, 237–39; Numbers, *Prophetess of Health,* 172–73, 177–78.

20. Schwarz, "John Harvey Kellogg," 22; Robinson, *Story of Our Health Message,* 203–205; Numbers, *Prophetess of Health,* 177.

21. John Harvey Kellogg, "An Address to the Heads of Departments of the Battle Creek Sanitarium, Nov. 1, 1938," JHKUM, Box 7, 8.

22. Schwarz, "John Harvey Kellogg," 17–23.

23. There are snapshots taken in 1925 showing Kellogg inspecting the now empty site of the old Hygeio-Therapeutic College, now completely gone; although Kellogg did not record his impressions of the trip, it is clear by his return after all those years that his time there did have an impact. JHKUM, Box 19.

24. For an engaging account of Kellogg's time at Trall's Hygeio-Therapeutic College, see Merritt G. Kellogg's reminiscences dictated to Clara K. Butler, October 12, 1916, JHKUM, Box 1. See also John Harvey Kellogg, "My Search for Health," January 16, 1942, JHKUM, Box 7, 7–10; Schwarz, "John Harvey Kellogg," 23–36; Robinson, *Story of Our Health Message*, 205, 207–208; and Numbers, *Prophetess of Health*, 176–79.

25. Quoted in Wiggam, "Most Remarkable Man," 120.

26. Kellogg spent much of 1883, 1889, 1900, 1902, 1907, and 1911 on such study tours. See "Biographical Facts," June 13, 1940, JHKUM, Box 1, 3; and Schwarz, "John Harvey Kellogg," 183n37, 266–76.

27. Schwarz, "John Harvey Kellogg," 22–36, 174–76; Robinson, *Story of Our Health Message*, 204–12.

28. "Outline of History of the Battle Creek Sanitarium for Use of Mrs. Fannie Sprague Talbot, in Preparing an Article for the Sunday Free Press, of Detroit" (n.d.), JHKUM, Box 7, 3.

29. Schwarz, "John Harvey Kellogg," 44–52.

30. John Harvey Kellogg, "The Return to Nature," October 11, 1900, JHKUM, Box 3, 6; Wiggam, "Most Remarkable Man," 118; Schwarz, "John Harvey Kellogg," 176.

31. Schwarz, "John Harvey Kellogg," 178–79.

32. John Harvey Kellogg, "Address to the Medical Missionary College," October 15, 1896, JHKUM, Box 3, 5. See also John Harvey Kellogg, "Rational Medicine," June 15, 1897, JHKUM, Box 3. Dr. Bigelow's famous 1858 essay, "The Paradise of Doctors," which ends with a call for "RATIONAL MEDICINE," was republished in the *Health Reformer* in April 1879 (97–100) and again in September 1897 (537–41).

33. Gerstner, "Temple of Health," 7–12.

34. John Harvey Kellogg, *Ladies Guide in Health and Disease*, 119, 225, 227, 228, 237.

35. Gerstner, "Temple of Health," 8.

36. Schwarz, "John Harvey Kellogg," 181–82; Gerstner, "Temple of Health," 8–13; "Battle Creek Sanitarium," in *Seventh-day Adventist Encyclopedia*, 175.

37. For Kellogg's aesthetic concerns, see John Harvey Kellogg, "The Study of the Beautiful," *Good Health*, February 1897, 65–69.

38. John Harvey Kellogg, untitled, October 21, 1938, JHKUM, Box 7, 7.

39. E. H. W., "The Dedication of the Sanitarium Chapel," *Medical Missionary* 6, no. 10 (1896): 307–308.

40. Schwarz, "John Harvey Kellogg," 183–85; Gerstner, "Temple of Health," 13–15, 23; "Battle Creek Sanitarium," in *Seventh-day Adventist Encyclopedia*, 175.

41. See, for example, Ellen G. White, *Testimony for the Physicians and Helpers of the Sanitarium* (1879), PH100 1.1–94.1, EGWW; and "Testimony to the Battle Creek Sanitarium" (1882) (Manuscript Release no. 951), 12MR 129.1–135.1, EGWW. See also Robinson, *Story of Our Health Message*, 154–55, 177–78, 189.

42. Robinson, *Story of Our Health Message*, 220–21.

43. "The Adventist Cult: A Sojourner at a Battle Creek Sanitarium Writes of the Unique Atmosphere of That Food Center," *Cereal and Feed* 3, no. 8 (1902): 1–6 (typescript in Battle Creek Sanitarium Materials, II. Writings, Charles MacIvor Collection).

44. Marion B. Baxter, *Seen through the Eyes of a Visitor* (n.p., 1897), JHKUM, Box 13, 7, reprinted in *Good Health,* August 1897, 463–66; and *Bible Echo,* March 28, 1898, 97–98.

45. Baxter, *Seen through the Eyes of a Visitor,* JHKUM, Box 13, 11, 13.

46. Ibid., 13.

47. Ibid., 10, 18.

48. Ibid., 11. See also John Harvey Kellogg to G. I. Butler, July 24, 1905, JHKMSU, Collection 13, Box 2, File 10; Schwarz, "John Harvey Kellogg," 274–75; "An Authentic Interview between Elder G. W. Amadon, Elder A. C. Bourdeau, and Dr. John Harvey Kellogg in Battle Creek, Michigan, on Oct. 7th, 1907," 26–27. White's comment that Dr. Kellogg was aided by angels is found in *General Conference Bulletin,* April 12, 1901, 203, GCA.

49. The following two paragraphs draw from Ella Eaton Kellogg, "Recollection of My Babyhood," "My Childhood Home," "Early School Days," "Reminiscences of University Days," "Beginning the Days of Work," JHKUM, Box 1; "Mrs. Ella Eaton Kellogg," *Good Health,* July 1920, 428–31; *In Memoriam: Ella Eaton Kellogg;* and Schwarz, "John Harvey Kellogg," 88–95.

50. Schwarz, "John Harvey Kellogg," 89–92.

51. Ella Eaton's diary, which runs from 1908 to 1919, contains numerous expressions of her affection for Dr. Kellogg and his attentions to her, especially on their wedding anniversary; the quotation is from April 16, 1910 (93). A copy of the diary can be found at Heritage Battle Creek, while the original is held by Garth "Duff" Stoltz of Historic Adventist Village, Battle Creek, Michigan.

52. *In Memoriam: Ella Eaton Kellogg,* 42.

53. Kellogg adopted the phrase "biologic living" in the 1910s; however, following Schwarz ("John Harvey Kellogg," 114n48, 115n115), for convenience I will use the label for Kellogg's set of health ideas after they were first enunciated in "The Hygienic Platform," *Health Reformer* 10, no. 1 (1875).

54. For example, see "Vincent Priessnitz, the Founder of Water Cures," *Good Health,* February 1881, 33–36; Larkin B. Coles, MD, "Bearing of Erroneous Appetites on Intellectual Character," *Good Health,* January 1884, 7–10; and Elizabeth Blackwell, "Dr. Blackwell on Impure Literature," *Good Health,* August 1888, 303–304. A series of articles on William A. Alcott by his son appeared in *Good Health* in 1899: William P. Alcott, "William Andrus Alcott, M.D.," *Good Health,* January 1899, 6–8; "Dr. Alcott as an Educational Reformer," *Good Health,* March 1899, 130–33; and "Dr. Alcott as Author and Humanitarian," *Good Health,* July 1899, 385–87. In addition, William P. Alcott wrote an appreciation of Sylvester Graham: "Sylvester Graham," *Good Health,* February 1902, 67–72. Kellogg cites Graham's *Ten Lectures on the Science of Human Life,* Cole's *Philosophy of Health,* and the works of William A. Alcott in "Battle Creek Ideals," a lecture in Los Angeles, March 12, 1921, JHKUM, Box 7, 4.

55. Schwarz, "John Harvey Kellogg," 113–48. As late as 1928, Kellogg was still condemning the use of aspirin, maintaining that "all drugs are baneful, some causing mental and moral as well as physical injury." John Harvey Kellogg, "Habits in Relation to Longevity," in *Proceedings of the Third Race Betterment Conference,* 344.

56. Robinson, *Story of Our Health Message,* 88–90; Ronald L. Numbers, "Sex, Science, and Salvation: The Sexual Advice of Ellen G. White and John Harvey Kellogg."

57. John Harvey Kellogg, *Plain Facts for Old and Young* (1881), 22 (Kellogg was quoting from John Ware, *Hints to Young Men on the True Relation of the Sexes,* 13). For a discussion of Kellogg's *Plain Facts,* see M. E. Melody and Linda M. Peterson, *Teaching America about Sex: Marriage Guides and Sex Manuals from the Late Victorians to Dr. Ruth,* 215–22.

58. Later, Kellogg would equate vital energy to electrical energy, which, because it can be measured, might be used to quantify a person's vital force and therefore their likely life span. Kellogg, "Habits in Relation to Longevity," in *Proceedings of the Third Race Betterment Conference*, 344–45.

59. Kellogg, *Plain Facts for Old and Young* (1881), 127, 225–39, 333, 347–76.

60. Ibid., 102–13, 126–35, 239–47, 376–77.

61. Numbers, *Prophetess of Health*, 207–12.

62. Kellogg, *Plain Facts for Old and Young* (1881), 436.

63. Ibid., 344–46, 383–84. The application of carbolic acid is recommended in the 1888 edition of *Plain Facts for Old and Young* (296).

64. Kellogg, *Plain Facts for Old and Young* (1881), 429–30.

65. John Harvey Kellogg, *Shall We Slay to Eat?*, 108–15.

66. Ibid., 148–65. For a succinct summation of Kellogg's antimeat teachings on sanitary grounds, see Wilson J. Warren, *Tied to the Great Packing Machine: The Midwest and Meatpacking*, 120–24.

67. Schwarz, "John Harvey Kellogg," 117–20. Kellogg would later write, "The writer has been a strict vegetarian for thirty-four years, and for some years back has abstained from the use of milk and eggs as well as from flesh-meats" (*Shall We Slay to Eat?*, 108). Today we would label such a strict vegetarian diet "vegan." Kellogg was following Ellen White's earlier recommendations about these animal products. Numbers, *Prophetess of Health*, 223–24.

68. John Harvey Kellogg to Irving Fisher, September 8, 1940, JHKUM, Box 2; "[Kellogg] Predicts No Cattle or Fowl, Only Nuts and Beans on Farms," *New York Times*, February 18, 1927, 1.

69. Kellogg, *Shall We Slay to Eat?*, 126–28.

70. John Harvey Kellogg, "Lecture to the Patients of the Miami–Battle Creek Sanitarium Lobby by Dr. John Harvey Kellogg," January 31, 1938, JHKUM, Box 7, 3.

71. Many of Kellogg's moral arguments were the standard vegetarian arguments dating back to the late eighteenth and early nineteenth centuries. See Whorton, *Crusaders for Fitness*, 62–91. One of the more famous pleas for animal rights—Mrs. C. M. Fairchild's *Pleadings for Mercy for the Animal World* (1883)—could be found in Kellogg's library. "Catalog of Kellogg Library," JHKUM, Box 7.

72. John Harvey Kellogg, *Plain Facts for Old and Young* (1881), 25–26.

73. Kellogg, *Shall We Slay to Eat?*, 133, 135, 136–37, 162.

74. John Harvey Kellogg, "Getting Well," November 1, 1900, JHKUM, Box 3, 16.

75. Schwarz, "John Harvey Kellogg," 418–21.

76. John Harvey Kellogg, "Memo," June 28, 1935, JHKUM, Box 1; Schwarz, "John Harvey Kellogg," 282; Weeks, "August F. Bloese," 27.

77. Schwarz, "John Harvey Kellogg," 421; Numbers, *Prophetess of Health*, 251.

78. John Harvey Kellogg to Henry S. Clubb, January 24, 1877, Box 1, Henry S. Clubb Papers.

79. Schwarz, "John Harvey Kellogg," 149–52.

80. Ibid., 257, 412, 487; John Harvey Kellogg, "Fruits—Diet and Disease," May 5, 1898, JHKUM, Box 3, 14–15.

81. John Harvey Kellogg, "The Significance of Our Work," *Medical Missionary* 14, no. 2 (1905): 46–49.

82. Whorton, *Crusaders for Fitness*, 8–9.

83. John Harvey Kellogg, *The Living Temple*, 431; see also 436–39. Kellogg was never reluctant to admit his intellectual debts to Sylvester Graham and his "gospel of biologic

living." See, for example, "A Half Century of Progress," *Good Health,* October 1916, 521. Near the end of his life, Kellogg wrote, "His teachings were adopted wholly or in part by numerous groups of religious cultists and communal experimentalists, and were the chief sources of information and inspiration to the early beginnings of the Battle Creek health movement which began in the sixties of the last century and is now widely known throughout the world." John Harvey Kellogg, *How to Have Good Health through Biologic Living,* plate after 70. See also John Harvey Kellogg to Irving Fisher, September 11, 1938, JHKUM, Box 2, 1–2.

84. See also "An Unchristian Diet," *Good Health,* May 1910, 363–64.

85. John Harvey Kellogg, "The Greater Gospel," *Good Health,* June 1898, 377–80. See also John Harvey Kellogg, "Moses as Sanitarian," *Medical Missionary* 15, no. 15 (1906): 130–31.

86. John Harvey Kellogg, *Neurasthenia or Nervous Exhaustion,* 259.

87. John Harvey Kellogg, "The 'Why' of the Religious Phase of the Sanitarium," *Medical Missionary* 16, no. 33 (1907): 259–61. "Beloved, I wish above all things that thou mayest prosper and be in health, even as thy soul prospereth" (3 John 1:2, King James Version). See also John Harvey Kellogg, "The Medical Profession," April 29, 1894, JHKUM, Box 3.

88. Kellogg, "'Why' of the Religious Phase of the Sanitarium," 259–61.

89. Schwarz, "John Harvey Kellogg," 37–38, 40–41, 61, 199–201; Gerstner, "Temple of Health," 7–12.

90. Schwarz, "John Harvey Kellogg," 215–21; Gerstner, "Temple of Health," 19; Numbers, *Prophetess of Health,* 251–53. See also Maxine Atteberry, "Seventh-day Adventist Nurses: A Century of Service."

91. "The American Missionary College," JHKUM, Box 3. See also John Harvey Kellogg, "Medical Missionary College Opening," October 1, 1895, October 15, 1896, JHKUM, Box 3.

92. John Harvey Kellogg, "The Medical Profession," April 29, 1894, JHKUM, Box 3, 35; "Address by Dr. Dowkontt," *Medical Missionary* 17, no. 11 (1909): 195–97; "Death of Dr. Dowkontt," *Medical Missionary* 18, no. 25 (1909): 498–500; John Harvey Kellogg, "Doctor Dowkontt," *Medical Missionary* 18, no. 26 (1909): 531; C. C. Creegan, "George D. Dowkontt, M.D.," *Medical Missionary* 18, no. 26 (1909): 532–35; Schwarz, "John Harvey Kellogg," 17; and Robinson, *Story of Our Health Message,* 249–75, 278, 331.

93. John Harvey Kellogg, "The American Medical Missionary College," 14; Richard W. Schwarz, "Dr. John Harvey Kellogg as a Social Gospel Practitioner"; Robinson, *Story of Our Health Message,* 275–83, 296–97.

94. Robinson, *Story of Our Health Message,* 223–35, 246–48; Numbers, *Prophetess of Health,* 229–30. Seventh-day Adventists initially had qualms about working with the WCTU because of its involvement in Sunday Sabbath legislation (Schwarz, "Perils of Growth," 78).

95. John Harvey Kellogg, *Social Purity,* 35.

96. For an overview of the WCTU, see Jack S. Blocker Jr., *American Temperance Movements: Cycles of Reform,* 79–85.

97. Schwarz, "John Harvey Kellogg," 204, 249–50; David J. Pivar, *Purity Crusade: Sexual Morality and Social Control, 1868–1900,* 116.

98. "Program of the Normal Institute on Hygiene and Heredity Held under the Auspices of the Women Christian Temperance Union of the District of Columbia, May 5th, 6th, 7th, 1884," JHKUM, Box 13; Frances Willard, "The Workshop, No. 1," *Union Signal,* February 21, 1884, 5; Schwarz, "John Harvey Kellogg," 94, 204; Pivar, *Purity Crusade,* 117, 150–51, 174; Lorine Swainston Goodwin, *The Pure Food, Drink, and Drug Crusaders, 1879–1914,* 27–31, 92–95.

99. For example, see Mary Wood Allen, "Influence of Heredity on Children," *Good Health,* October 1893, 304–305; Mary Wood Allen, "A Sermon on Heredity," *Good Health,* July 1895, 200–201; "Alcoholic Heredity," *Good Health,* July 1895, 233–34 (reprinted from the *Union Signal*).

100. Pivar, *Purity Crusade,* 37–40.

101. Kellogg, *Social Purity,* 8–9. See also John Harvey Kellogg, "Chastity and Health," in *The National Purity Congress,* edited by Aaron M. Powell, 250–68.

102. Knight, "Adventist Faith Healing in the 1890s." Beilhart quite possibly participated in the Holy Flesh movement, to be mentioned below. See H. Roger Grant, *Spirit Fruit: A Gentle Utopia,* 18–19. For Beilhart's own description of his faith healing at the sanitarium, see Grant, *Spirit Fruit,* 21–22; and James L. Murphy, *Reluctant Radicals: Jacob L. Beilhart and the Spirit Fruit Society,* 27–29.

103. See, for example, John Harvey Kellogg, "Heath Principles," *General Conference Bulletin* (March 1, 1897): 185–89, GCA; G. I. Butler to John Harvey Kellogg, March 17, 1905, JHKMSU, Collection 13, Box 2, File 8; Kellogg to S. N. Haskell, June 8, 1908, JHKMSU, Collection 13, Box 4, File 13; Schwarz, "John Harvey Kellogg," 348–53; Robinson, *Story of Our Health Message,* 286–90; Richard W. Schwarz, "The Kellogg Schism: The Hidden Issues," 24–25; and Numbers, *Prophetess of Health,* 230–32.

104. John Harvey Kellogg to S. N. Haskell, June 8, 1908, JHKMSU, Collection 13, Box 4, File 13.

105. John Harvey Kellogg, "True Christianity a Medical Missionary Movement," *Medical Missionary* 15, no. 5 (1906): 129–33.

106. G. I. Butler to Kellogg, March 7, 1906, JHKMSU, Collection 13, Box 3, File 8.

107. *Daily Bulletin of the General Conference,* March 2, 1899, 128, GCA.

108. John Harvey Kellogg, "Fruits—Fruit-Cure in Obesity, &c," May 9, 1898, JHKUM, Box 3, 38.

109. In 1907 Kellogg said, "A brother asked me the question awhile ago, 'Do you believe the Lord is coming in this generation?' 'Now,' I said, 'The text says that those that see these things, this generation shall not pass until all things be fulfilled. The Bible says it. I believe the Bible and I believe that.' If anybody should ask me to explain it, to limit and to tell exactly what it means, I do not know whether I could; but I believe that whatever it means is true.... When I was a boy 'this Generation' meant thirty years. When I got older, got to be about eighteen or twenty years old, then it meant sixty years. A little later it meant the persons who saw the sun darkened (1780), that there would still be some of them alive when the Lord came. Time has kept going on and these people have died off, and I told them I did not know what to believe about it exactly, but I believed it nevertheless." "Authentic Interview," 17.

110. John Harvey Kellogg, "The Medical Profession," April 29, 1894, JHKUM, Box 3, 35.

111. *Battle Creek Daily Journal,* January 8, 1903, quoted in Schwarz, "John Harvey Kellogg," 378. Kellogg's sentiments in regards to the religious role of doctors were not peculiar to him. We tend to forget that in the nineteenth century, as medical historian John S. Haller reminds us, "doctors, along with clergy . . . served as moral philosophers for Victorian society." A widely held maxim was that no "physician was thoroughly educated until his intellectual and moral faculties had been submitted to the purifying influences of Christianity." Medicine, after all, was not just a body of knowledge and a set of techniques, but foremost a sacred vocation. Many medical educators of the era would have agreed with Dr. Clarence J. Blake, who, in the commencement address to the 1898 graduating class of the Harvard Medical School, spoke quite seriously of a "medical priesthood" and a "medical ministry." Haller, *American*

*Medicine in Transition*, 280–84. See also Jonathan B. Imber, *Trusting Doctors: The Decline of Moral Authority in American Medicine*, 1–103.

112. Schwarz, "John Harvey Kellogg," 65.

113. *Daily Bulletin of the General Conference*, March 2, 1899, 129, GCA.

114. Schwarz, "Perils of Growth," 100, 110.

115. "First Annual Session of the Michigan Sanitarium and Benevolent Association (March 9, 1899)," *Medical Missionary Conference Bulletin*, March 9–14, 1899, 1–8, GCA; Schwarz, "John Harvey Kellogg," 353–60; Schwarz, "Kellogg Schism," 27–28; "Battle Creek Sanitarium," in *Seventh-day Adventist Encyclopedia*, 176.

116. "Statement of M. G. Kellogg" (1908), JHKMSU, Collection 13, Box 4, File 13.

117. Schwarz, "John Harvey Kellogg," 357, 359.

118. Ellen G. White, "Not for Pleasure Seekers," *Testimonies for the Church* 7 (1902), 7T 97.2, EGWW; Robinson, *Story of Our Health Message*, 297–99.

119. Quoted in Robinson, *Story of Our Health Message*, 298.

120. *Daily Bulletin of the General Conference*, March 2, 1899, 129, GCA; Robinson, *Story of Our Health Message*, 295–96.

121. Schwarz, "John Harvey Kellogg," 378–81; Richard W. Schwarz, "Reorganization and Reform: The 1901 General Conference Session, Battle Creek, Michigan."

122. Numbers, *Prophetess of Health*, 230.

123. John Harvey Kellogg, "Prospective and Retrospective," *Medical Missionary* 8, no. 1 (1898): 1; Schwarz, "Perils of Growth," 102.

124. *Medical Missionary Conference Bulletin*, May 1899, quoted in Robinson, *Story of Our Health Message*, 293.

125. Editorial in *Review and Herald*, October 22, 1903, quoted in Robinson, *Story of Our Health Message*, 299.

126. See William R. Hutchinson, *The Modernist Impulse in American Protestantism*, 132–44.

127. Kellogg ridiculed the idea that there should be a set Seventh-day Adventist creed. John Harvey Kellogg to G. I. Butler, June 1, 1904, JHKMSU, Collection 13, Box 2, File 2.

128. Schwarz, "Perils of Growth," 110.

129. Robinson, *Story of Our Health Message*, 301–309; Schwarz, "Reorganization and Reform," 11–18; Schwarz, "Perils of Growth," 103–104.

130. Quoted in Robinson, *Story of Our Health Message*, 304.

131. Ibid., 309–11.

132. Alonzo L. Baker, "My Years with John Harvey Kellogg," 44.

133. John Harvey Kellogg to Ellen G. White, March 8, 1899, JHKMSU, Collection 13, Box 1, File 1. See also "Authentic Interview," 65.

### 3. THE THEOLOGY OF BIOLOGIC LIVING

1. Schwarz, "John Harvey Kellogg," 155–57.

2. John Harvey Kellogg, "Address to Medical Students," March 30, 1901, JHKUM, Box 3, 6–7; untitled, October 13, 1917, JHKUM, Box 1, 2–3; Schwarz, "John Harvey Kellogg," 62–63.

3. Schwarz, "John Harvey Kellogg," 388n115.

4. M. G. Kellogg, "A Confession," *Review and Herald* 64, no. 25 (1887): 397–98.

5. Schwarz, "John Harvey Kellogg," 26–27.

6. John Harvey Kellogg, "Lectures of Dr. Palmer," Student Notebooks, JHKUM, Box 16.

7. John Harvey Kellogg, "Thesis Bellevue," February 14, 1875, JHKUM, Box 3, 2–3.

8. Schwarz, "John Harvey Kellogg," 363. In a letter to Ellen White, Kellogg wrote, "I have loved and respected you as a mother, especially since my mother's death" (March 8, 1899, JHKMSU, Box 1, File 1). Later he wrote, "Aside from my parents she was the best friend I ever had. She treated me as a son" (John Harvey Kellogg, untitled, October 21, 1938, JHKUM, Box 7, 15).

9. Quoted in Schwarz, "John Harvey Kellogg," 62–63.

10. Schwarz, "John Harvey Kellogg," 63–64; Schwarz, "Perils of Growth," 108.

11. Minutes of the Seventeenth Annual General Conference of Seventh-day Adventists, October 4, 1878, 127, GCA.

12. Kellogg, *Harmony of Science*, 27.

13. Ibid., 9–31. The theme of religious superstition versus medical progress is most forcefully advanced in the talk "Materialism in the Medical Profession," October 20, 1894, JHKUM, Box 3.

14. Kellogg, *Harmony of Science*, 27–28. True to his Adventist education, Kellogg rejected both the Trinitarian formulations of the Athanasian Creed and the doctrine of eternal punishment (32–33).

15. Kellogg, *Harmony of Science*, 21–22. Uniformitarian geology argues that the state of the earth is due to uniform natural forces acting over extremely long periods of time. Biblical catastrophism, on the other hand, argues that the state of the earth is due primarily to the catastrophe of the flood (for more on these debates within Seventh-day Adventism, see Ronald L. Numbers, *The Creationists*).

16. E. White, *Life Sketches*, LS88 1701–171.4, EGWW; Knight, *Search for Identity*, 72–74. In Battle Creek Adventists encountered and debated Spiritualists, whose tradition was based precisely on the doctrine that souls did not sleep, but were active and available for communication with the living after death. Kellogg was careful to discount the testimony of Spiritualists in *Harmony of Science* (51, 120). It should be noted that Kellogg did not specifically use the term *soul sleep* in *Harmony of Science and the Bible,* but in an undated lecture he cites the book as providing arguments for those "who were unwilling to accept the opprobrious title of 'soul-sleeper.'" John Harvey Kellogg, "Is the Soul Immortal, or Does It Survive the Death of the Body?," JHKUM, Box 12, 3. Apparently, Kellogg circulated this lecture to a group of Adventist administrators (who found it "a little hard to understand") and to a commercial publisher (who found it "too suggestive of materialism to please a large majority of our clergymen"). See N. P. Nelson to John Harvey Kellogg, January 14, 1898, and J. K. Frank (?), Funk and Wagnalls Company, to Kellogg, February 21, 1898, JHKUM, Box 1.

17. A remarkably similar theory had already been put forth several years before in Edward Hitchcock, *The Religion of Geology and Its Connected Sciences,* 8–9.

18. Kellogg, *Harmony of Science*, 104.

19. John Harvey Kellogg, "What Is the Soul? Gymnasium Talks," April 29, 1893, JHKUM, Box 3, 1–39.

20. Ibid., 2–10. See also "Relation of Muscles to Religion," June 15, 1893, JHKUM, Box 3.

21. Kellogg, "What Is the Soul?," JHKUM, Box 3, 33–34.

22. Ibid., 36–37.

23. E. White, *Life Sketches,* LS88 151.2–153.2, EGWW; Knight, *Search for Identity,* 72–74.

24. John Harvey Kellogg, "Creed" (n.d.), JHKUM, Box 12, 2.

25. Kellogg, *Social Purity,* 30–33. See also John Harvey Kellogg, "The Medical Profession," April 29, 1894, JHKUM, Box 3, 29–30, 35.

26. John Harvey Kellogg, *General Conference Daily Bulletin*, February 18, 1897, 72, GCA. See also "Physical Basis of Faith," January 8, 1897, JHKUM, Box 3, 23–24. For an exceptionally clear account of Kellogg's quandary, see John Harvey Kellogg, "'New Thought,'" *Medical Missionary* 8, no. 7 (1904): 201–203.

27. John Harvey Kellogg, October 21, 1938, JHKUM, Box 7, 13–14.

28. For a good overview of Haeckel's religion of Monism, see Niles R. Holt, "Ernst Haeckel's Monistic Religion."

29. John Harvey Kellogg, *General Conference Daily Bulletin*, February 18, 1897, 73–74, GCA.

30. Schwarz, "John Harvey Kellogg," 360–63.

31. John Harvey Kellogg, untitled talk, October 21, 1938, JHKUM, Box 7, 13–14.

32. God's control of the cosmos through secondary causes seems to have been the common understanding in the denomination. G. I. Butler to John Harvey Kellogg, July 15, 1904, JHKMSU, Collection 13, Box 2, File 3.

33. Maxwell, "Sanctuary and Atonement." It is true, though, that Kellogg did occasionally stray into statements that could be characterized as pantheism. For example, "What is Nature?—Nature is simply the philosophical name of God, who is the active force in Nature—the 'All in All'" (Kellogg, *The Living Temple*, 483). See also Kellogg, *Neurasthenia or Nervous Exhaustion*, 37.

34. John Harvey Kellogg, "Address to Medical Students," March 30, 1901, JHKUM, Box 3, 7.

35. Kellogg, "What Is the Soul?," April 29, 1893, JHKUM, Box 3, 32. See also John Harvey Kellogg, "Rational Medicine," June 15, 1897, JHKUM, Box 3: "Of course, when we say 'Nature,' we mean God, for nature is simply an expression of God. It is the habit of the world to speak of nature as a power, whereas nature is simply a picture,—it is simply an external or material representation of the power which is behind nature and in nature—and this is the power that cures disease" (2).

36. Kellogg, "What Is the Soul?," April 29, 1893, JHKUM, Box 3, 33. It is interesting to note that this is a complete reversal from the position Kellogg outlined in *Harmony of Science and the Bible* (1879), in which he asserted the hypermaterialist view that "no new force is required to account for all the phenomenon of life. The mystery of life all lies in organization, not in any occult force." Kellogg, *Harmony of Science*, 125.

37. Kellogg, *Shall We Slay to Eat?*, 133–35.

38. Kellogg's arguments parallel and are possibly derived from William Paley's *Natural Theology*, which relies primarily on arguments from anatomy and astronomy to prove the reality of the divine design of the universe. See Paley, *Natural Theology; or, Evidences of the Existence and Attributes of the Deity*.

39. John Harvey Kellogg, "Physical Basis of Faith," January 8, 1897, JHKUM, Box 3, 5–7, 16–23.

40. John Harvey Kellogg, "Materialism in the Medical Profession," October 20, 1894, JHKUM, Box 3, 9; "The Medical Profession," April 29, 1894, JHKUM, Box 3, 31–34; "Religion of the Body," January 2, 1896, JHKUM, Box 3, 14–16; "Physical Basis of Faith," January 8, 1897, JHKUM, Box 3, 10–15, 25–29.

41. John Harvey Kellogg, "The Medical Profession," April 29, 1894, JHKUM, Box 3, 30–31.

42. John Harvey Kellogg, "The Man Wonderful in the House Beautiful," January 27, 1895, JHKUM, Box 3, 20–23.

43. John Harvey Kellogg, "Religion of the Body," January 2, 1896, JHKUM, Box 3, 14.

44. John Harvey Kellogg, "Physical Basis of Faith," January 8, 1897, JHKUM, Box 3, 6–8, 23–24.

45. Ibid., 18, 22.

46. John Harvey Kellogg, "God in Man.—No. 1," *General Conference Daily Bulletin,* February 18, 1897, 76–80, GCA; "God in Man.—No. 1," *General Conference Daily Bulletin,* February 19, 1897, 81–84, GCA; "God in Man.—No. 3," *General Conference Daily Bulletin,* February 19, 1897, 90–96, GCA; "God in Man.—No. 3," *General Conference Daily Bulletin,* February 22, 1897, 98–99, GCA.

47. John Harvey Kellogg, "God in Man.—No. 1," *General Conference Daily Bulletin,* February 19, 1897, 83, GCA.

48. John Harvey Kellogg, "God in Man.—No. 3," *General Conference Daily Bulletin,* February 19, 1897, 96, GCA.

49. John Harvey Kellogg, "God in Man.—No. 1," *General Conference Daily Bulletin,* February 18, 1897, 78, GCA.

50. John Harvey Kellogg to Ellen G. White (June 28, 1898), quoted in Schwarz, "Kellogg Schism," 24. The idea of physical infirmity as the mark of Cain appeared in Horace Mann, "Words from Horace Mann," in *Health: or, How to Live,* edited by James White and Ellen White, 46.

51. In terms of the importance of physical beauty as a mark of holiness, see John Harvey Kellogg, "Relation of the Muscles to Religion," June 15, 1893, JHKUM, Box 3; and John Harvey Kellogg, "The Body a Temple," *Good Health,* December 1897, 772–73. For Kellogg's aesthetic, see John Harvey Kellogg, "The Study of the Beautiful," *Good Health,* February 1897, 65–69.

52. John Harvey Kellogg to Ellen G. White, June 28, 1898, quoted in Schwarz, "Kellogg Schism," 24.

53. This idea was echoed a year later by W. W. Prescott: "The message of health reform now centers just as much on that simple statement, 'This is my body,' as it centers in that simple statement, 'The seventh day is the Sabbath of the Lord thy God'" (*Daily Bulletin of the General Conference,* February 23, 1899, 59, GCA).

54. John Harvey Kellogg, "God in Nature.—No. 2," *General Conference Daily Bulletin,* February 18, 1897, 72–76, GCA.

55. A. O. Tait to Ellen G. White, March 22, 1898, quoted in Schwarz, "Perils of Growth," 86.

56. Ellen G. White, "The True Relation of God and Nature," *General Conference Bulletin,* March 6, 1899, 187, GCA.

57. Ibid.

58. Norval F. Pease, "'The Truth as It Is in Jesus': The 1888 General Conference Session, Minneapolis, Minnesota"; Vandevere, "Years of Expansion," 75; Knight, *Search for Identity,* 100–110.

59. Schwarz, "John Harvey Kellogg," 63–64; "Ellen G. White Letters to J. H. Kellogg," 11MR 299.1–320.3, EGWW.

60. John Harvey Kellogg, "The Physical Basis of Faith," October 3, 1899, JHKUM, Box 3, 1–2.

61. Ibid., 5.

62. Ibid., 6, 28. This position was first adumbrated in John Harvey Kellogg, "God in Man.—No. 1," *General Conference Daily Bulletin,* February 18, 1897, 78, GCA.

63. John Harvey Kellogg, "Some Popular Fallacies in Relation to Things Medical," February 3, 1898, JHKUM, Box 3, 26.

64. Kellogg, " Physical Basis of Faith," October 3, 1899, JHKUM, Box 3, 22. This is repeated again in "Address to Medical Students," March 30, 1901, with a slight caveat: "God does not

sin, but he permits man to use his divine energy, power and life in committing sin, and so he is serving with him in his sin" (JHKUM, Box 3, 7).

65. Again, Kellogg would attempt to qualify this later: "As regards life, there are three kinds of life, three lives;—the tissue life or animal life . . . ; the conscious or somatic life, which wicked men have in common with Christian men; then there is spiritual life which Christian men only have. . . . I was talking only of the physiological life, which all men have in common." John Harvey Kellogg to S. N. Haskell, July 3, 1904, JHKMSU, Collection 13, Box 2, File 3.

66. Kellogg, "Physical Basis of Faith," October 3, 1899, JHKUM, Box 3, 25.

67. Kellogg, "Address to Medical Students," March 30, 1901, JHKUM, Box 3, 17–20. See also "General Missionary Committee Meeting," March 16, 1901, JHKUM, Box 12, 12–14.

68. "General Missionary Committee Meeting," March 16, 1901, JHKUM, Box 12, 19.

69. E. White, *Great Controversy*, 187–88.

70. Kellogg, "Divine Healing," April 16, 1901, JHKUM, Box 6, 19–20.

71. John Harvey Kellogg, "General Missionary Committee Meeting," May 11, 1901, JHKUM, Box 12, 11.

72. Schwarz, "John Harvey Kellogg," 365–68; Gary Land, "Shaping the Modern Church," 124–30.

73. Kellogg, "Divine Healing," April 16, 1901, JHKUM, Box 6, 19–20.

74. Quoted in Schwarz, "Perils of Growth," 87; see also 104–11.

### 4. THE LIVING TEMPLE

1. Ellen G. White, "Testimony for the Physicians and Helpers of the Sanitarium" (1879), PH100 53.2, EGWW; Robinson, *Story of Our Health Message*, 292–300; Schwarz, "Kellogg Schism."

2. Ellen G. White, "Centering Too Much in Battle Creek," *Testimonies for the Church* 8 (1904), 8T 133.3, EGWW; Schwarz, "Dr. John Harvey Kellogg as a Social Gospel Practitioner," 382–83; Ellen G. White to Judge Jesse Arthur, January 14, 1903, 13MR 120.1–128.3, EGWW.

3. Schwarz, "John Harvey Kellogg," 185–88; Gerstner, "Temple of Health," 25–29.

4. *A Brief Account of the Dedicatory Services of the New Main Building of the Battle Creek Sanitarium*, 115–20.

5. "For the Afternoon Papers" (n.d. but probably 1903), JHKUM, Box 7. See also Kellogg's speech at the laying of the sanitarium's cornerstone in ibid., 119.

6. W. W. Prescott, "The Forward Movement," *Medical Missionary* 14, no. 1 (1902): 7–8. The Forward Movement was to be under the supervision of W. W. Prescott as chairman, W. A. Spicer and G. W. Thomason as secretaries, and J. H. Kellogg, A. J. Read, and E. R. Palmer as members. Kellogg mentions it in "Authentic Interview," 8.

7. This story is related in Mary Foote Henderson, *The Aristocracy of Health: A Study of Physical Culture, Our Favorite Poisons, and a National and International League for the Advancement of Physical Culture*, 673. Perhaps this was the case, because much of *The Living Temple* consisted of ideas that Kellogg had been developing in his lectures during the previous decade, and some of it consisted of republication of material that had already appeared elsewhere. For example, Kellogg, *Shall We Slay to Eat?* and "The Mystery of Life," *Good Health*, January 1902, 1–4.

8. John Harvey Kellogg to W. C. White, January 8, 1904, and to G. I. Butler, January 12, 1904, JHKMSU, Collection 13, Box 1, File 7; Kellogg to S. N. Haskell, February 24, 1904, JHKMSU, Collection 13, Box 1, File 8; Butler to Kellogg, January 23, 1905, JHKMSU, Collection 13, Box 2, File 7; Kellogg to Sarah MacEnterfer, January 28, 1906, JHKMSU, Collec-

tion 13, Box 3, File 6; Kellogg to Butler, January 31, 1906, JHKMSU, Collection 13, Box 3, File 6; "Authentic Interview," 8–14, 92–94; John Harvey Kellogg, untitled, October 21, 1938, JHKUM, Box 7, 14; Schwarz, "John Harvey Kellogg," 189–90; Schwarz, "Perils of Growth," 86–88. Ads for *The Living Temple* appeared in the *Medical Missionary* (for example, 12, no. 2 [1903], 47), and excerpts were published in the same journal (John Harvey Kellogg, "God: The Explanation of Nature," *Medical Missionary* 12, no. 2 [1903]: 32–33) and in the *Life Boat* ("In Tune for the Infinite," *Life Boat,* March 1902, 49–50).

9. Kellogg, *The Living Temple,* 5.

10. Ibid., 28; see also 451–55, 486.

11. Ibid., 483.

12. Ibid., 29, 30, 38, 39, 63, 451, 452, 483.

13. Ibid., 29. Although the book never reached the hands of very many Adventists, these specific ideas were published as excerpts in the *Medical Missionary,* thus giving them fairly wide distribution. Kellogg, "God: The Explanation of Nature," *Medical Missionary* 12, no. 2 (1903): 32–33.

14. Kellogg, *The Living Temple,* 36.

15. Ibid., 64–67, 84, 86, 87–89, 98, 100, 101–106, 111, 194–95, 250–52, 256, 260–61, 277–78, 336–37, 388, 396–98, 412, 435–39, 440–47, 491.

16. Kellogg, *The Living Temple,* 191, 440–42. This was republished several times: for example, "The Ministry of Pain," *Life Boat,* August 1903, 207–209; and "The Ministry of Pain" in Kellogg, *Ideas,* 17–18. Kellogg's notion of "The Ministry of Pain" (although not the phrase) can be found as far back as his editorial "A 'Regular' Kill," *Health Reformer* 8, no. 9 (1873): 275–76.

17. For one's personal responsibility in contracting infectious disease, see "The Power of Nature," May 2, 1901, JHKUM, Box 3, 10. See also "Nature in Disease," *Good Health,* April 1902, 183–84.

18. Kellogg, *The Living Temple,* 423–24, 455–60; Young, "Alpha Heresy," 37–38; James W. Zackrison, "The Development of Dr. John Harvey Kellogg's Theological Ideas Up to 1903" (1973), unpublished paper, Center for Adventist Research, Andrews University, 23–24.

19. Kellogg, *The Living Temple,* 427. This joke appeared at least a decade earlier: "A thorough reformation in cooks and cookery would do more toward ushering in the wished for millennium than would be accomplished by half the preachers in Christendom in trying to evangelize men and women who subsist upon a worse than heathen diet and whose bad hearts are largely born of bad food and bad blood. Total depravity is in at least a large proportion of cases synonymous with total indigestion. In their efforts to reform men and women philanthropists seldom reach the root of the difficulty. Nothing is more needed at the present time than a vigorous crusade against bad food and bad cookery" ("A Powerful Personage," *Good Health,* March 1893, 88–89). See also his 1894 talk "The Medical Profession," April 29, 1894, JHKUM, Box 3, 22; and "Is Depravity Acquired or Inherited?," *Life Boat,* May 1902, 97–98.

20. Kellogg, *The Living Temple,* 29–30. It is interesting to note that some of Kellogg's earliest attempts at defining religion make faith in Jesus secondary. See *Harmony of Science,* 27–28; and *Social Purity,* 30.

21. Kellogg, *The Living Temple,* 484–85.

22. Ibid., 453.

23. Schwarz, "Perils of Growth," 87. The letter was subsequently printed in the *Review and Herald* on October 22, 1903.

24. Ellen G. White, "Teach the Word," *Review and Herald,* October 22, 1903, 8–9.

25. "Some Friction Apparently Exists in the Adventist Denomination," *Battle Creek Daily Journal*, October 26, 1903. See also "Dove of Peace," *Battle Creek Daily Journal*, October 27, 1903. Kellogg was not happy that this controversy made its way into the papers. John Harvey Kellogg to W. C. White, October 28, 1903, JHKMSU, Collection 13, Box 1, File 6.

26. Ellen White, "Pantheism and the Alpha of Heresies," November 26, 1903, 11MR 247.1, 249.1, EGWW.

27. Kellogg, *The Living Temple*, 30–31.

28. Ibid., 32–33. See also John Harvey Kellogg to G. I. Butler, December 21, 1902, JHKMSU, Collection 13, Box 1, File 2; and Kellogg to Butler, May ?, 1904, JHKMSU, Collection 13, Box 1, File 11.

29. Kellogg, *The Living Temple*, 30–31.

30. Ibid., 29, 31.

31. Ibid., 486–88; John Harvey Kellogg, "A Lecture in the Old Sanitarium Lobby," July 6, 1936, JHKUM, Box 7, 14–15, 17–22.

32. Ellen G. White, *The Ministry of Healing*, 428; originally published in a slightly different form in Ellen G. White, "Pantheistic Theories" (1904), 8T 291.1–292.3, EGWW.

33. Knight, *Search for Identity*, 90–127.

34. G. I. Butler to John Harvey Kellogg, July 12, 1904, JHKMSU, Collection 13, Box 2, File 3.

35. E. J. Waggoner, "Studies in the Book of Hebrews, No. 6," *General Conference Daily Bulletin*, February 18, 1897, 71–72, GCA; "Remarks on the Gospel of Health," *General Conference Daily Bulletin*, February 23, 1899, 57–58, GCA.

36. "W. W. Prescott, Part 2, 1901–1944."

37. Schwarz, "John Harvey Kellogg," 387; Schwarz, "Perils of Growth," 86–87. Kellogg later said in 1904 that this was because he had prevented Prescott's appointment at Emmanuel Missionary College in 1901 and that "Prof. Prescott's objection to the book [*The Living Temple*] was an afterthought" (Schwarz, "Kellogg Schism," 29). However, this does not account for why Prescott would have been participating in the Forward Movement in 1902.

38. Schwarz, "Perils of Growth," 87. See also the remarks of "Elder Hibbard" and "Bro. Hinkel" appended to John Harvey Kellogg, "Address to Medical Students," March 30, 1901, JHKUM, Box 3. Dr. William Sadler wrote a long defense of Dr. Kellogg and an attack on the testimonies in a letter to Ellen G. White, April 26, 1906, JHKMSU, Collection 13, Box 3, File 9.

39. See, for example, John Harvey Kellogg to G. I. Butler, October 13, 1904, JHKMSU, Collection 13, Box 2, File 4; and Butler to Kellogg, March 10, 1905, JHKMSU, Collection 13, Box 2, File 8.

40. John Harvey Kellogg, "Untitled Autobiographical Statement," October 21, 1938, JHKUM, Box 7, 14. See also John Harvey Kellogg to Ellen G. White, February 6, 1906, JHKMSU, Collection 13, Box 3, File 7.

41. Schwarz, "John Harvey Kellogg," 387–88. A copy of *Education* was listed as part of Kellogg's library in 1904. "Catalog of Kellogg Library," JHKUM, Box 7. Kellogg commented on "God in Nature" in Ellen White's *Education* in letters to S. N. Haskell (November 3, 1903) and G. I. Butler (November 6, 1903), JHKMSU, Collection 13, Box 1, File 6.

42. White, *Education*, 99–100.

43. Ibid., 101.

44. See, for example, Kellogg, *The Living Temple*, 477–78. Commenting on criticisms of *The Living Temple* in a talk to nurses entitled "General Diseases," Kellogg made the lengthy argu-

ment that, while man may be perverted, he could never pervert the laws of nature because they are God's laws, and at one point Kellogg asserts that "we might cut someone's throat. This light would help us do it. The sunlight shining upon a murder, which enables a man to murder, is just as pure light as ever shown. So the life of God that is on our bodies is all right. It does the very best it can for us under the circumstances" (January 12, 1904, JHKUM, Box 4, 4–6).

45. John Harvey Kellogg, "General Diseases—Nurses' Post-Graduate," January 12, 1904, JHKUM, Box 4, 4–5. Another example: "There is something far more than Battle Creek in the Battle Creek Idea and that is the importance of following nature. Formerly, nature was thought to be depraved. I was brought up to believe that man was naturally, totally depraved. I was taught the doctrine of total depravity and I think the general impression of my father was that I had it pretty bad. The idea was that nature was necessarily wicked, that God when he made the world turned it over to the devil to do with as he had a mind to and he had not interfered with it since except by special request. There are still some people who entertain that antiquated notion I think. The fundamental idea of this institution is, that there is a great beneficent power in the institution that is working for the good of everybody, waiting for every man and helping everybody." John Harvey Kellogg, "The Battle Creek Idea at the Sanitarium Parlor, Battle Creek, Michigan, Monday, July 29, 1918 at 8:00 P.M.," JHKUM, Box 7, 1.

46. John Harvey Kellogg to S. N. Haskell, March 15, 1904, quoted in Schwarz, "John Harvey Kellogg," 66.

47. Uriah Smith, *Review and Herald*, October 28, 1890, quoted in Knight, *Search for Identity*, 112.

48. Schwarz, "Reorganization and Reform," 16–18; Knight, "Adventist Faith Healing in the 1890s"; Bull and Lockhart, *Seeking a Sanctuary*, 79–80, 92.

49. For example, Alan Stump, *The Foundation of Our Faith: 160 Years of Christology in Adventism*, 193; Knight, *Search for Identity*, 114.

50. Quoted in Stump, *Foundation of Our Faith*, 195, 197. The Holy Spirit is actually mentioned only three times in *The Living Temple*, each time in reference to 1 Corinthians 6:19 ("Know ye not that your body is the temple of the Holy Ghost?"). In an earlier Sanitarium lecture, "How We Can Aid Nature in the Struggle against Disease" (October 4, 1900), Kellogg characterizes the Holy Spirit thus: "Now this Spirit of God, that is in man, is doing the best it can to keep man alive and well; this divine Spirit,—this Holy Ghost in man—is all the while laboring to keep man alive and well" (JHKUM, Box 3, 4). Later, Kellogg said that "I thought I had cut out entirely the theological side of questions of the trinity and all that sort of things" from *The Living Temple*. ("Authentic Interview," 96).

51. Kellogg admits as much in a letter to G. I. Butler: "I never undertook to differentiate between God the Father, God the Son, and God the Holy Ghost. I did not know that it was necessary for me to do so" (August 5, 1905, JHKMSU, Collection 13, Box 2, File 11, 6); and in "Extracts from letter from Dr. Kellogg to Dr. Hayward": "These theologians [e.g. Prescott] have sought to darken the minds of people and to make this sweet and beautiful truth [divine immanence] appear loathsome to them, by dragging into it the old controversy about the Trinity" (August 15, 1905, JHKMSU, Collection 13, Box 2, File 11, 2).

52. John Harvey Kellogg, "The Religion of the Body," January 2, 1896, JHKUM, Box 3, 14.

53. For more on Spencer's American influence, see James R. Moore, *The Post-Darwinian Controversies: A Study of the Protestant Struggle to Come to Terms with Darwin in Great Britain and America, 1870–1900*, 153–73.

54. Herbert Spencer, *First Principles*, 101.

55. See, for example, John Harvey Kellogg, "The Religion of the Body," January 2, 1896, JHKUM, Box 3, 14; "Rational Mind-Cure," *Good Health,* April 1898, 200.

56. For example, John Harvey Kellogg, "Physical Basis of Faith," January 8, 1897, JHKUM, Box 3, 12–16.

57. Spencer, *First Principles,* 108–13.

58. Kellogg, "Physical Basis of Faith," January 8, 1897, JHKUM, Box 3, 2–3. See also "God in Nature," *General Conference Daily Bulletin,* February 18, 1897, 80, GCA; and *General Conference Daily Bulletin,* February 19, 1897, 83, GCA.

59. Moore, *Post-Darwinian Controversies,* 168, 220, 237.

60. Ellen White, "A Warning against Deceptive Teaching," June 23, 1904, SpTB06 41.1–64.1; Land, "Shaping the Modern Church," 127.

61. Arthur Cushman McGiffert, *The Rise of Modern Religious Ideas,* 187–99; Ira V. Brown, *Lyman Abbott, Christian Evolutionist: A Study in Religious Liberalism,* 128–29. See also Bruce Kuklick, *Churchmen and Philosophers: From Jonathan Edwards to John Dewey,* 216–25; and for the importance of the doctrine of immanent theism in Protestant modernism in general, see Hutchinson, *Modernist Impulse.*

62. McGiffert, *Rise of Modern Religious Ideas,* 180–82; Brown, *Lyman Abbott,* 140–41. See also Jon H. Roberts, *Darwinism and the Divine in America: Protestant Intellectuals and Organic Evolution, 1859–1900,* 136–44; and D. H. Meyers, "American Intellectuals and the Victorian Crisis of Faith."

63. John Harvey Kellogg to Dr. Hamilton Holt, June 5, 1940, JHKUM, Box 2; John Harvey Kellogg, "A Lecture in the Old Sanitarium Lobby," July 6, 1936, JHKUM, Box 7, 1.

64. *Good Health,* July 1884, 223.

65. Rev. George G. Lyon, "New Theology."

66. For the life and thought of Abbott, see Brown, *Lyman Abbott.*

67. While a student in New York during the early 1870s, Kellogg joined the Eucleian Society at New York University, of which Lyman Abbott was a past member, and Kellogg attended services at Plymouth Church to hear Henry Ward Beecher, whom Abbott would succeed as pastor in 1887. The doctor is also known to have visited the offices of Abbott's *Outlook* (*Good Health* 31, no. 10 [1896]: 323), and articles by Lyman Abbott's wife were occasionally excerpted in *Good Health* (32, no. 6 [1897]: 378–79; 32, no. 7 [1897]: 448).

68. Lyman Abbott, *A Study in Human Nature,* 64.

69. Lyman Abbott, *The Evolution of Christianity,* v.

70. Lyman Abbott, "The Supernatural," *Outlook,* July 2, 1898, 580–84.

71. "Nature, that is, God, implants in man himself the help-giving powers that remove disease; and, in addition, stores the world full of remedies also, so that specifics may be found for almost every disease to which flesh is heir. The laws of healing are wrought into the physical realm; they are a part of the divine economy; and shall we think that He who helps the man to a new skin and to a new bone cares nothing for his moral nature, and will not help him when he has fallen into sin?" (*Good Health,* September 1898, 572).

72. Lyman Abbott, *The Temple,* 8.

73. Ibid., 81–92.

74. Brainard S. Sabin, "The Progress of Our Faith: An Outline of the Theological History of the First Congregational Church of Battle Creek," 32. See also Edward Z. Boies and Doris E. Ware, *The First Congregational Church of Battle Creek: Its First One-Hundred and Fifty Years,* 1–18. Reed Stuart was born in Moundsville, Virginia, in 1842 and brought by his family to Warren County, Illinois, before the Civil War. He graduated from Monmouth College in 1865

and took a theological degree six years later and was called to his first pastorate in Oneida, Illinois, from whence he was called to Battle Creek. Reed Stuart died in 1910. Coller File 72–601, Helen Warner Branch Local History.

75. Back when Stuart was called to Battle Creek in 1877, the church was still "Presbyga-tional," having been organized forty years before during the operation of the Plan of Union. The more conservative Presbyterians in Reed's congregation eventually charged him with heterodoxy to the Lansing Presbytery in 1881, and while Stuart was ultimately exonerated, the Congregationalists and Presbyterians dissolved their union and formed separate churches in 1883. Stuart stayed with the Congregationalists, who adopted in 1885 the adjective *Indepen-dent* to signal their liberalism and freedom from any constraining orthodoxies. Stuart was then called to the First Unitarian Church of Detroit in 1886, where he served for twenty years until his death. See Sabin, "Progress of Our Faith," 32–34; and Boies and Ware, *First Congre-gational Church of Battle Creek,* 15–18.

76. *Battle Creek Weekly Moon,* October 11, 1884, 1, 8.

77. A glance at the catalog of Kellogg's personal library prepared sometime after 1903 also reveals a distant but possible influence by an Anglican of modernist leanings. Under the catalog heading of "God in Man," under which Kellogg listed his own *Living Temple,* there appears J. R. Illingworth's *Divine Immanence* (1898). "Catalog of Kellogg Library," JHKUM, Box 7. Illingworth, who was a contributor to the famous modernist volume *Lux Mundi,* ar-gued in *Divine Immanence* for the spiritual importance of matter, especially as it is organized into the body by which human consciousness is expressed. Moreover, somewhat like Kel-logg's notion of the exemplary theory of the atonement, Illingworth also contended that Christ's incarnation was to demonstrate to humanity that a sinless soul in a sinless body would never die, although, unlike Kellogg, the English divine was careful to point out that such complete sinlessness and consequent immortality were impossible for people here on earth; for that, they would have to wait to receive their resurrection bodies in heaven. Perhaps most important, throughout his work Illingworth promoted an understanding of divine im-manence that he was careful to differentiate from pantheism; it is likely that when Kellogg was later forced to defend himself against charges of pantheism, it was to Illingworth's char-acterization of God as being both immanent in but transcending matter that Kellogg turned, albeit without acknowledgment. J. R. Illingworth, *Divine Immanence: An Essay on the Spiri-tual Significance of Matter,* 69–73, 99–100.

78. Mimeograph headed "The 'pantheism' of J. H. K. originated with M. G. Kellogg, who makes the following statement," JHKAM, MS 2007–12, Box 1, Folder 12.

79. Bull and Lockhart, *Seeking a Sanctuary,* 40, 45–47.

80. For a history of the Seventh-Day Baptists, see Dan A. Sanford, *A Choosing People: The History of Seventh-Day Baptists.*

81. Ella Eaton Kellogg, "Reminiscences of University Days," JHKUM, Box 1.

82. Sanford, *Choosing People,* 346–48.

83. Abigail Ann Maxson Allen, ed., *Life and Sermons of Jonathan Allen,* 229, 294. It is no-table that the Pacific Press Publishing Company was the Seventh-day Adventist press on the West Coast. See also E. H. Lewis, ed., *Allen of Alfred: Some of His Words to His Students.*

84. Pivar, *Purity Crusade,* 116.

85. Arthur L. White, *Ellen G. White: The Early Elmshaven Years,* vol. 5 (1900–1905), 5BIO 281.5, EGWW.

86. Ella Eaton Kellogg's will specified bequests to Alfred University of one thousand dol-lars to establish a scholarship in her name, a donation of one thousand dollars to the Seventh-

Day Baptist Missionary Society for Medical Missionary work, and a donation of five hundred dollars to the Seventh-Day Baptist Memorial Fund. August 20, 1923, Minutes of the Transactions of the Board of Trustees of the American Medical Missionary Board, bk. 2, JHKMSU, Collection 13, 117:178.

87. John Harvey Kellogg to S. N. Haskell, September 21, 1903, JHKMSU, Collection 13, Box 1, File 6; Kellogg to G. I. Butler, February 21, 1904, JHKMSU, Collection 13, Box 1, File 8. Butler in a letter to Kellogg wrote, "You have drifted, and have not perhaps been conscious of it. The drifting process is a peculiar one. We may think we are standing just the same as we did before, or sitting on the old hen's nest, but our positions have changed imperceptibly to ourselves" (March 27, 1906, JHKMSU, Collection 13, Box 3, File 8).

88. John Harvey Kellogg to S. N. Haskell, April 4, 1904, JHKMSU, Collection 13, Box 1, File 10.

89. John Harvey Kellogg, *The Miracle of Life*, 5–6. *The Miracle of Life* was republished in 1910 under the title *Life, Its Mysteries and Miracles: A Manual of Health Principles*. Much of the wisdom of *The Living Temple* was also repackaged—sometimes verbatim—into what can only be called a self-help book targeted at a popular audience; it was called simply *Ideas* (1916). Kellogg after this time routinely excoriated pantheism and reiterated his commitment to Christianity. See, for example, "Pantheism," *Medical Missionary* 8, no. 5 (1904): 131–32; "'Neither Is There Salvation in Any Other,'" *Life Boat*, July 1904, 193; and "Vain Philosophy," *Medical Missionary* 8, no. 8 (1904): 234–35.

90. S. N. Haskell to John Harvey Kellogg, October 25, 1904, JHKMSU, Collection 13, Box 2, File 4; John Harvey Kellogg, untitled, October 21, 1938, JHKUM, Box 7, 15.

91. Henderson, *Aristocracy of Health*; Wu Tingfang, *America, through the Spectacles of an Oriental Diplomat*, 217. Wu made frequent trips to the sanitarium while in the United States. See, for example, "Wu Ting Fang Upheld the Battle Greek Idea," *Battle Creek Idea*, December 12, 1907, 3.

92. John Harvey Kellogg, *The Living Temple*, translated by Rev. M. C. Wilcox and Mr. Wong Cang-Hwo (Shanghai: Methodist Publishing House in China, 1912), JHKUM, Publications, Box 3. See also "Memorandum in Reference to Pantheism in the Living Temple," in which Wilcox is quoted as writing, "I have now gone over this entire book with great care preliminary to translating it into Chinese classical language, and I find nothing to justify the charge which I understand has been made against it—that it contains pantheism" (May 19, 1908, JHKMSU, Collection 13, Box 4, File 13). Notice of the translation duly appeared in the *Medical Missionary*: "The book entitled 'The Living Temple,' by J. H. Kellogg, M.D., has been translated into the Chinese language by Rev. M. C. Wilcox, D.D., who has attained eminence in the study of the Chinese language and literature. A copy of this book has been sent to the Sanitarium medical library, and is a very pleasing sample of Chinese printing. In a review of this work the *Chinese Recorder*, a prominent periodical, says, "'The Living Temple,' by Dr. J. H. Kellogg, of Battle Creek, Mich., called in the Chinese, *Yong Seu Tung Laung*, is an exposition of hygienic principles reinforced by religious considerations, and is designed to be of real help to the Chinese, especially to Christians, who are better prepared to appreciate the religious standpoint. We can heartily commend it to the Christian Church in China" (*Medical Missionary* 23, no. 8 [1914]: 225).

93. Ellen White frequently criticized Kellogg's character. According to Schwarz, "John Preston Kellogg had observed that his doctor son tended to be headstrong and self-willed, and shortly before his death the elder Kellogg requested Ellen White to do all in her power to help John Harvey develop pleasing traits of character. This Mrs. White promised to do."

Through the years she counseled the doctor against the dangers of being driven by too much ambition and the tendency to take too much personal credit for the success of the work in which he was engaged. She repeatedly referred him to the Biblical example of the humiliation of Nebuchadnezzar, which, according to Daniel 4, had come about because of excessive pride." Schwarz, "John Harvey Kellogg," 69. "There is a love for supremacy whether you see it or not," wrote Ellen White to Kellogg in 1886 (71; see also 368–76). "You are in no case to consider that you're the man with the power to set up and to cast down. You are not to feel that in the exercise of your power you may exalt whom you will and tear down as you see fit. God's servants are not given this power. . . . The Lord is not to be hindered in His workings by any monopolies" (372–73).

94. Ellen White to Brethren Faulkhead and Salisbury, January 17, 1904, 2MR 243.2, EGWW.

95. Ellen White to Dr. Paulsen, October 14, 1903, 5MR 375.2, EGWW.

96. Ellen G. White, "A Warning against Deceptive Teaching," *Testimonies to the Church Regarding Our Youth Going to Battle Creek* (1905), SpTB06 41.1–SpTB06 44.1, EGWW; "The Remarks of Mrs. E. G. White to the Delegates of the 36th Session of the General Conference at Takoma Park, Washington D.C., May 30th, 1905," JHKMSU, Collection 13, Box 2, File 9; John Harvey Kellogg to G. I. Butler, July 24, 1905, JHKMSU, Collection 13, Box 2, File 10; Ellen G. White, "To Ministers and Physicians," May 1, 1906, JHKMSU, Collection 13, Box 3, File 10; Ellen G. White, "To Drs. Paulson, Reed, Edwards, Morse, Riley, and Judge Arthur," May 8, 1906, JHKMSU, Collection 13, Box 3, File 10.

97. Knight, *Search for Identity,* 128–59.

### 5. DR. KELLOGG'S BREAK WITH THE SEVENTH-DAY ADVENTIST CHURCH

1. "A Grand Temple of Health," *Battle Creek Morning Inquirer,* June 1, 1903, 1–4; *Brief Account of the Dedicatory Services,* 3–6.

2. "A Grand Temple of Health," *Battle Creek Morning Inquirer,* June 1, 1903, 1–4; *Brief Account of the Dedicatory Services,* 9–10.

3. *Brief Account of the Dedicatory Services,* 12, 21, 33, 39, 40–43.

4. Ibid., 58.

5. John Harvey Kellogg, *The Battle Creek Sanitarium: History, Organization, Methods,* 203. See also "Religious Life as It Is in the Sanitarium," *Battle Creek Idea,* August 6, 1909, 1, 7; and "Christianity at the Sanitarium," *Battle Creek Idea,* September 16, 1910, 1–2.

6. *Principles of the Battle Creek Sanitarium* (Battle Creek, MI: n.p.), JHKUM, Box 13, 3–7. The board membership listed in the manual indicates that it was published sometime after 1904.

7. John Harvey Kellogg, "There Is Only One Kind of Healing," *Medical Missionary* 22, no. 1 (1913): 9. The window can still be seen today at what is now the Hart-Dole-Inouye Federal Building.

8. John Harvey Kellogg to G. I. Butler, July 10, 1903, and August 4, 1903, JHKMSU, Collection 13, Box 1, File 6.

9. In a letter to W. C. White, August 7, 1895, Kellogg complained that "the only real obstacle to the work in this country is the numerous 'little Popes' in the shape of conference presidents" (JHKMSU, Collection 13, Box 1, File 1). For a good example of Kellogg's relationship with Daniells, see John Harvey Kellogg to G. I. Butler, May ?, 1904, and May 2, 1904, JHKMSU, Collection 13, Box 1, File 11.

10. "Report of a Portion of a Council-Meeting Held at Mrs. E. G. White's Home, 'Elmshaven,' St. Helena, Cal. 8 A.M., Oct. 19, 1902," JHKMSU, Collection 13, Box 1, File 2; John Harvey Kellogg to G. I. Butler, October 30, 1902, JHKMSU, Collection 13, Box 1, File 2.

11. For Kellogg's account of this, see John Harvey Kellogg to S. N. Haskell, June 8, 1908, JHKMSU, Collection 13, Box 4, File 13. For the formation of the American Medical Missionary Board, see Jesse Arthur to John Harvey Kellogg, November 11, 1906, JHKMSU, Collection 13, Box 4, File 4.

12. These events are reviewed in Schwarz, "Kellogg Schism," 28–31; and Schwarz, "Perils of Growth," 104–105, 107–11.

13. I. H. Evans to John Harvey Kellogg, February 22, 1906, JHKMSU, Collection 13, Box 3, File 7. Apparently, Dr. Kellogg stopped attending the General Conference Meetings in 1905. G. I. Butler to John Harvey Kellogg, March 17, 1905, JHKMSU, Collection 13, Box 2, File 8; Kellogg to Butler, May 12, 1905, and Butler to Kellogg, March 17, 1905, JHKMSU, Collection 13, Box 2, File 9; Jesse Arthur to Kellogg, March 29, 1906, JHKMSU, Collection 13, Box 3, File 8.

14. Much of the correspondence and other materials in the JHKMSU Collection 13 reflects this state of affairs from 1905 onward; among many possible examples, see John Harvey Kellogg to G. I. Butler, February 1, 1905, JHKMSU, Collection 13, Box 2, File 7; Butler to Kellogg, April 5, 1905; Kellogg to S. N. Haskell, August 27, 1905, JHKMSU, Collection 13, Box 2, File 11; M. E. Simmons to Kellogg, August 28, 1905, JHKMSU, Collection 13, Box 2, File 11; George Thomason to Kellogg, December 13, 1905, JHKMSU, Collection 13, Box 3, File 4; J. E. Froom to Dr. B. F. Rand, December 31, 1905, JHKMSU, Collection 13, Box 3, File 4; A. G. Daniells to L. C. Leake, February 18, 1906, JHKMSU, Collection 13, Box 3, File 7; "Address of A. T. Jones," March 4, 1906, JHKMSU, Collection 13, Box 3, File 8; A. E. Place to G. C. Tenney, March 18, 1906, JHKMSU, Collection 13, Box 3, File 8; C. P. Farnsworth to Kellogg, March 26, 1906, JHKMSU, Collection 13, Box 3, File 8; M. G. Kellogg to Kellogg, March 21, 1906, JHKMSU, Collection 13, Box 3, File 8; M. G. Kellogg to Kellogg, May 3, 1906, JHKMSU, Collection 13, Box 3, File 10; Jesse Arthur to Kellogg, May 15, 1906, JHKMSU, Collection 13, Box 3, File 10; Daniells to Morris Lukons, October 9, 1905, JHKMSU, Collection 13, Box 4, File 3; W. C. White to Daniells, December 20, 1906, JHKMSU, Collection 13, Box 4, File 4; "Statement of Herbert Ossig," June 27, 1907, JHKMSU, Collection 13, Box 4, File 7; Herbert Ossig to Kellogg, June 27, 1907, JHKMSU, Collection 13, Box 4, File 7. Rumors reached such a pitch that it was alleged that Dr. Kellogg was "using his position to lead from the paths of virtue both his lady nurses and patients" and that he was running a "bawdy house downtown" with W. K. Kellogg. "Statement of Irving Keck," January 21, 1907, JHKMSU, Collection 13, Box 4, File 6.

15. John Harvey Kellogg to G. I. Butler, January 8, 1906, JHKMSU, Collection 13, Box 3, File 5. There were also rumors that the sanitarium was contemplating a takeover of the Battle Creek Tabernacle: W. C. White to A. G. Daniells, December 20, 1906, and Kellogg to Irving Keck, February 9, 1907, JHKMSU, Collection 13, Box 4, File 4; "Resolution Passed by the Board of Trustees of the Battle Creek Sanitarium," February 8, 1907, JHKMSU, Collection 13, Box 4, File 6; Kellogg to Keck, February 9, 1907, JHKMSU, Collection 13, Box 4, File 6; White to R. A. Hart, February 12, 1907, JHKMSU, Collection 13, Box 4, File 6.

16. John Harvey Kellogg, "Untitled Autobiographical Statement," October 21, 1938, JHKUM, Box 7, 16; Schwarz, "John Harvey Kellogg," 408–409.

17. "Authentic Interview," 1–100.

18. Ibid., 14.

19. Ibid., 79. Kellogg had long claimed that the charges against *The Living Temple* were brought for purely political reasons: John Harvey Kellogg to G. I. Butler, March 14, 1904, JHKMSU, Collection 13, Box 1, File 9; Kellogg to Butler, April 22, 1904, JHKMSU, Collection 13, Box 1, File 10.

20. Apparently, a copy of the transcript of the interview was circulated, at least on a limited basis, after Kellogg felt he had been maligned in the press by Elders Amadon and Bourdeau. See G. W. Amadon to John Harvey Kellogg, November 26, 1907, JHKMSU, Collection 13, Box 4, File 9; Kellogg to Amadon, November 26, 1907, JHKMSU, Collection 13, Box 4, File 9; Amadon to Kellogg, December 2, 1907, JHKMSU, Collection 13, Box 4, File 10; Kellogg to Amadon, December 3, 1907, JHKMSU, Collection 13, Box 4, File 10; Amadon to Kellogg, December 22, 1907, JHKMSU, Collection 13, Box 4, File 10; M. G. Kellogg to Kellogg, February 11, 1908, JHKMSU, Collection 13, Box 4, File 11.

21. "Authentic Interview," 64.

22. In Kellogg's words, "In theological matters I have never been in very good standing with the denomination. Nearly thirty years ago I was accused of heresy, and doubtless would have been expelled but for the fact that James White took sides with me against all the other theologians of the denomination. My medical and scientific training made it impossible for me to believe some of the doctrines of the church, and I frankly said so." John Harvey Kellogg, "My First and Last Word," December 16, 1907, JHKMSU, Collection 13, Box 4, File 10.

23. See, for example, G. I. Butler to John Harvey Kellogg, March 7, 1906, JHKMSU, Collection 13, Box 2, File 9; Butler to Kellogg, March 27, 1906, JHKMSU, Collection 13, Box 3, File 8.

24. John Harvey Kellogg to T. H. Robinson, November 18, 1907, JHKMSU, Collection 13, Box 4, File 9; Schwarz, "Kellogg Schism," 35.

25. John Harvey Kellogg to G. I. Butler, April 2, 1906, JHKMSU, Collection 13, Box 3, File 5.

26. John Harvey Kellogg to G. I Butler, July 30, 1904, JHKMSU, Collection 13, Box 2, File 2.

27. John Harvey Kellogg, "Talk at Banquet for Christian Endeavor," June 30, 1910, JHKUM, Box 5, 3.

28. "Authentic Interview," 9, 91.

29. "Funeral Is Held for Dr. Kellogg," *Battle Creek Enquirer and News,* December 19, 1943, 10.

30. Schwarz, "John Harvey Kellogg," 353–60, 413–14; Robinson, *Story of Our Health Message,* 325–28. For Kellogg's version of the rechartering, see Kellogg, "My First and Last Word," December 16, 1907, JHKMSU, Collection 13, Box 4, File 10.

31. Schwarz, "John Harvey Kellogg," 374, 382–83; Kit Watts, "Seventh-day Adventist Headquarters: From Battle Creek to Takoma Park"; Numbers, *Prophetess of Health,* 247–48.

32. *Review and Herald,* February 5, 1901, 96.

33. Schwarz, "John Harvey Kellogg," 382–86.

34. Watts, "Seventh-day Adventist Headquarters," 45; Schwarz, "Perils of Growth," 105–107.

35. G. I. Butler to John Harvey Kellogg, January 2, 1905, JHKMSU, Collection 13, Box 2, File 6; George Thomason to Kellogg, October 11, 1905, JHKMSU, Collection 13, Box 3, File 2.

36. Robinson, *Story of Our Health Message,* 285–86, 335–425; Numbers, *Prophetess of Health,* 247.

37. Schwarz, "John Harvey Kellogg," 415–17; Numbers, *Prophetess of Health,* 248–50, 562–64, 566.

38. Kellogg, "My First and Last Word," December 16, 1907, JHKMSU, Collection 13, Box 4, File 10.

39. On Shakers, see "The Shakers Exempt from Cancer," *Good Health,* May 1911, 393–94; and "The Shakers an Example of Simple Life," *Good Health,* March 1919, 150–51. On Transcendentalists, see "Address by Dr. J. H. Kellogg, at the Dedication of the Tri-City Sanitarium, Moline, Ill.," *Medical Missionary* 8, no. 3 (1904): 65–69; "A Sketch of Brook Farm," *Battle Creek Idea,* April 28, 1901, 4; and "Notable Modern Examples of the Simple Life," *Good Health,* May 1919, 269–72. On Salvation Army, see "Booth a Vegetarian," *Good Health,* November 1907, 632. On Tolstoy, see T. C. O'Donnell, "Tolstoy and the Simple Life," *Good Health,* January 1911, 70–77; and Leo Tolstoy, "The Imp and the Crust," *Good Health,* May 1911, 460–61.

40. John Harvey Kellogg, untitled, *Good Health,* April 1898, 255–57; John Harvey Kellogg, "How Can a Sick Man Get Well?," April 20, 1905, JHKUM, Box 4, 11–12. Kellogg's various books and *Good Health* enjoyed popularity among both the Latter-day Saints (LDS) of Utah and the Reorganized Latter-day Saints of Missouri (RLDS). In 1928 Frederick M. Smith, grandson of Joseph Smith Jr. and the leader of the RLDS, after reading Kellogg's *Tobaccoism* (1922), made a point of sending Kellogg a copy of the *Doctrine and Covenants,* highlighting Section 86, "Word of Wisdom," the canonical purity teachings of the Mormons. Frederick M. Smith to John Harvey Kellogg, October 21, 1928, JHKUM, Box 1. Several years later Kellogg's interest in the "Word of Wisdom" was rekindled through conversations with an RLDS student at the Battle Creek College (Edna Haynie to Kellogg, April 1, 1937, JHKUM, Box 2) and through an article by John A. Widstoe, noted LDS author and member of the Council of Twelve. This resulted in a *Good Health* article that noted that Joseph Smith's teaching "was practically identical with that of the late Sylvester Graham, who was the real founder of the health reform movement which began in this country in the early part of the last century" ("The Word of Wisdom," *Good Health,* May 1936, 140–42). Kellogg quoted Widstoe with approval: "In the true gospel of Jesus Christ, the sanctity of the body is second only to that of the spirit." Commenting on the health statistics in Widstoe's article, Kellogg proclaimed that the "Word of Wisdom" had made the "Mormon settlement in Utah" "really a great biologic experiment as well as a unique religious and social venture." Kellogg to M. Hinhede, April 19, 1937, JHKUM, Box 2. Two years later, perhaps in response to the article, Widstoe sent Kellogg a copy of his book *The Word of Wisdom: A Modern Interpretation* (1937), noting in his cover letter that "since we have followed your teachings for so long and made use of your printed matter, at least by absorption, we should like you to have a copy of this book." Widstoe and his family would remain faithful subscribers to *Good Health* for years. John A. Widstoe to Kellogg, October 17, 1938, April 11, 1940, JHKUM, Box 2.

41. Rev. Henry S. Clubb, "The Status of Vegetarianism in the United States," *Good Health,* November 1907, 609–11; "A Century of Vegetarianism, an Interesting Visitor," *Battle Creek Idea,* October 1, 1909, 6; John Harvey Kellogg, "Talk to Conference of Institutions Giving Professional Training in Physical Education Held at Washington, DC, May 7–8, 1925," JHKUM, Box 7, 8–9.

42. John Harvey Kellogg to C. W. Barron, November 7, 1922; Barron to Kellogg, November 14, 1922; Kellogg to Barron, November 29, 1922, February 1, 4, May 28, 1924, June 17, 1927, JHKUM, Box 1. See also "A Philosopher Who Condemned the Use of Flesh," *Good Health,* June 1938, 175.

43. John Harvey Kellogg, "In Tune with the Infinite," *Good Health,* October 1902, 475–77; John Harvey Kellogg, "In Tune with the Infinite," *Life Boat,* March 1902, 49–50; Kellogg, *The Living Temple,* 457–60.

44. A long quotation from Trine's 1896 *What All the World's a-Seeking* appeared in *Good Health* in 1897 (Ralph Waldo Trine, "Growth in Service to Others," *Good Health,* May 1897,

277); a publisher's squib for *In Tune with the Infinite* appeared in the same journal two years later ("In Tune with the Infinite," *Good Health,* June 1899, 372–73); and an excerpt from *In Tune with the Infinite* with an attribution to Trine, but not his book, appeared in *Good Health* in 1900 ("The Effect of Thought on the Body," *Good Health,* March 1900, 145–47). Moreover, Kellogg also later had a copy of it in his personal library ("Catalog of Kellogg Library," JHKUM, Box 7). For a very late use of the phrase "in tune with the Infinite," see John Harvey Kellogg to R. D. Walker, May 11, 1943, JHKUM, Box 3.

45. Ellen G. White, "Shall We Consult Spiritualist Physicians?," *Review and Herald,* June 27, 1882, 401–403; "The Dangers of Mind-Cure—Letter to Dr. Sanderson," October 6, 1901, 18MR 263.1–273.3, EGWW. For an overview of the rise of the New Thought movement, see Catherine L. Albanese, *A Republic of Mind and Spirit: A Cultural History of American Metaphysical Religion,* 300–329.

46. John Harvey Kellogg, "The Mind-Cure," *Good Health,* July 1885, 210–11.

47. John Harvey Kellogg, "Pseudo Mind-Cure," *Good Health,* March 1898, 135–40. According to Kellogg, in a brief review of Beard's *Practical Treatise on Nervous Exhaustion (Neurasthenia),* "The writer had the pleasure of intimately knowing that able physician, scientist, and neurologist, having served as his assistant in his work at the DeMilt Dispensary in 1875, at which time he was collecting the data which was later utilized in the production of this interesting volume" (*Modern Medicine* 15, no. 2 [1906]: 45). See also John Harvey Kellogg, "Lecture to Patients of the Miami–Battle Creek in the Sanitarium Lounge by Dr. John Harvey Kellogg," April 17, 1938, JHKUM, Box 7, 1–25. Here Kellogg describes the success of Dr. Beard's placebo experiments in which Beard posed as a "magnetic doctor" administering "magnetic cures" to his patients using a galvanic battery (15–18). For more on Beard, see Charles E. Rosenberg, "George M. Beard and American Nervousness," in *No Other Gods,* 98–108; and F. G. Gosling, *Before Freud: Neurasthenia and the American Medical Community.*

48. John Harvey Kellogg, untitled, *Good Health,* March 1887, 82; John Harvey Kellogg, "Quarreling Like Brothers," *Good Health,* January 1888, 30.

49. John Harvey Kellogg, "The Mind Cure Delusion," *Good Health,* October 1889, 309–10. On the Transcendentalist connection, see John S. Haller Jr., *The History of New Thought: From Mind Cure to Positive Thinking and the Prosperity Gospel,* 21–24.

50. John Harvey Kellogg, untitled, *Good Health,* March 1887, 82.

51. Kellogg, "Quarreling Like Brothers," 30. New Thought also incorporated elements of Theosophy, which may have added to Kellogg's hostility toward the movement. See Albanese, *Republic of Mind and Spirit,* 328–29.

52. Ralph Waldo Trine, *In Tune with the Infinite; or, Fullness of Peace, Power, and Plenty,* 11–13, 25, 37, 38, 178, 199.

53. Ibid., 121–22.

54. Ibid., 82, 84.

55. "The Effect of Thought on the Body," *Good Health,* March 1900, 145–47.

56. See, for example, John Harvey Kellogg, "Simple Therapeutic Measures," *Good Health,* October 1881, 293–95; John Harvey Kellogg, "How to Live a Century," February 15, 1884, JHKUM, Box 3, 21–26; John Harvey Kellogg, "Psychosomatic Diseases, Sanitarium Lecture," July 10, 1889, JHKUM, Box 3; John Harvey Kellogg, "Health and Good Cheer," *Good Health,* May 1903, 220–21. The Battle Creek Sanitarium School of Hygiene offered courses in "mental philosophy" beginning in 1878 (Robinson, *Story of Our Health Message,* 244). Kellogg shared this conviction with Ellen White and the Christian physiologists (Robinson, *Story of Our Health Message,* 133).

57. Trine, *In Tune with the Infinite,* 119–34. For a good exposition of Kellogg's theory of the connection between ideas, dreams, the unconscious mind, and the Infinite Power behind them all, see John Harvey Kellogg, "A Lecture in the Old Sanitarium Lobby," July 6, 1936, JHKUM, Box 7, 1–32. For Kellogg's dream of the flaking process, see "The Early Beginnings," January 13, 1927, JHKUM, Box 7, 4–5. Kellogg also claimed to have overcome the fear of death after seeing himself murdered in a dream. John Harvey Kellogg, "An Address to Members of the Miami Three Score and Ten Club, 3:00 PM, March 17, 1931," JHKUM, Box 7.

58. John Harvey Kellogg, "Does This Happen by Chance?," *Life Boat,* April 1902, 73–75.

59. Trine, *In Tune with the Infinite,* 51. A brief review of Trine's *Land of Living Men* appeared in *Good Health,* January 1911, 95; and of Trine's *New Alinement* [*sic*] *of Life* in *Good Health,* December 1913, 17–18. Reviews of New Thought books continued to be featured periodically in *Good Health:* "*The Message of New Thought* by Abel Leighton Allen," *Good Health,* May 1914, 280; "*The Renewal of the Body* by Annie Rix Militz," *Good Health,* October 1914, 560; "*New Thought Christianized* by James M. Campbell," *Good Health,* July 1917, 358; "New Thought by Horatio W. Dresser," *Good Health,* September 1917, 464; and "*A History of the New Thought Movement* by Horatio W. Dresser," *Good Health,* November 1919, advertising section, 18.

60. William James, *The Varieties of Religious Experience,* 96, 178–80. In 1904, in the wake of "Pantheism Crisis," Kellogg claimed never to have read a New Thought book in his life, which was clearly not the case (John Harvey Kellogg to G. I. Butler, February 21, 1904, JHKMSU, Collection 13, Box 1, File 8); he also defended himself against teaching New Thought ideas in *The Living Temple* (Kellogg to Butler, June 27, 1904, JHKMSU, Collection 13, Box 2, File 2).

61. Horace Fletcher, *Menticulture; or, The A-B-C of True Living,* v, 9, 19–20, 21, 32, 36, 43.

62. Horace Fletcher, *Happiness as Found in Forethought Minus Fearthought,* 52, 53, 58, 89–99, 109–14, 151 (emphasis in the original).

63. Schwarz, "John Harvey Kellogg," 129–30; James C. Whorton, "'Physiologic Optimism': Horace Fletcher and Hygienic Ideology in Progressive America"; Whorton, *Crusaders for Fitness,* 205–206.

64. Horace Fletcher, *The A. B. –Z. of Our Own Nutrition,* 5; Horace Fletcher, *Fletcherism; or, How I Became Young at Sixty,* 79.

65. On "Physiologic Optimism," see Horace Fletcher, *Optimism: A Real Remedy,* 14. On "Fletcherize," John Harvey Kellogg, "Horace Fletcher" (obituary), *Good Health,* March 1919, 132–34. On "Chewing Song," see Horace Fletcher, *The New Glutton or Epicure,* 60–61; copies of the "Chewing Song" can be found in JHKAM, MS 2007-12, Box 2, File 4; and JHKUM, Box 12.

66. Fletcher, *Fletcherism,* 173.

67. See, for example, "Chewing Reform," *Medical Missionary* 13, no. 11 (1904): 342–43; "Five Remarkable Books by Horace Fletcher" (advertisement for Good Health Publishing), *Good Health,* September 1905, 498; "Horace Fletcher," *Battle Creek Idea,* March 12, 1908, 1; "Mr. Fletcher's New Book," *Battle Creek Idea,* March 19, 1908, 3; "Tells Adventurous Life of Horace Fletcher," *Battle Creek Idea,* August 6, 1908, 1–2; "Two Distinguished Men Visit Sanitarium," *Battle Creek Idea,* August 13, 1908, 1–2; "Mr. Horace Fletcher Pays Another Visit," *Battle Creek Idea,* November 19, 1908, 1–3; "Forethought the Key to Felicity," *Battle Creek Idea,* September 24, 1909, 1; Horace Fletcher, "Fletcherizing the W.C.T.U.," *Good Health,* May 1911, 409–12;

and John Harvey Kellogg, "Horace Fletcher" (obituary), *Good Health*, March 1919, 132–34. Rather uncharitably, Dr. Kellogg was not above criticizing certain aspects of Fletcherism after Fletcher's death. John Harvey Kellogg, "Horace Fletcher's Fatal Mistake," *Good Health*, April 1919, 194–96.

68. Horace Fletcher to John Harvey Kellogg, October 31, 1909, Horace Fletcher Papers, 1898–1915, Letters to John Harvey Kellogg, 1903–1915 and undated, MS Am 791 (20), Houghton Library; Fletcher, *New Glutton or Epicure*, 46–72, 309–11.

69. John Harvey Kellogg, "Optimism: Look Upward and Outward and Cheer Up!," *Good Health*, March 1915, cover. See also, for example, John Harvey Kellogg, "The Simple Life in a Nutshell," *Good Health*, November 1907, 593–98; this article was reprinted greatly expanded in Kellogg, *Neurasthenia or Nervous Exhaustion*, 233–58.

70. Kellogg, *The Living Temple*, 486.

71. Kellogg, *Neurasthenia or Nervous Exhaustion*, 16–24, 180–82, 183–205, 261, 319–21, 333.

72. Ibid., 169, 180–82.

73. Ibid., 151–82.

74. For information on the Emmanuel Movement, see John Gardner Greene, "The Emmanuel Movement, 1906–1929"; and Raymond J. Cunningham, "The Emmanuel Movement: A Variety of American Religious Experience."

75. John Harvey Kellogg, "Treatment by Suggestion," *Battle Creek Idea*, July 8, 1910, 1–2; John Harvey Kellogg, "Psychotherapeutics or Mind-Cure," *Battle Creek Idea*, December 2, 1910, 1–3.

76. Kellogg, *Neurasthenia or Nervous Exhaustion*, 172.

77. For background on Christian Science, see Stephen Gottschalk, *The Emergence of Christian Science in American Religious Life*; and Albanese, *Republic of Mind and Spirit*, 283–300.

78. William F. Hutchinson, "The 'Christian Science' Delusion," *Good Health*, September 1888, 346–47; John Harvey Kellogg, "What the Mind-Cure Doctors Profess to Do," *Good Health*, August 1889, 246–28; John Harvey Kellogg, "The Mind-Cure Delusion," *Good Health*, September 1889, 277–79.

79. For the history of the conflict between "medical freedom" and the enforcement of licensing laws, see Whorton, *Nature Cures*, 133–39; and Rennie B. Schoepflin, *Christian Science on Trial: Religious Healing in America*.

80. "Killed by Christian Science," *Good Health*, February 1892, 56; "Another Victim of Christian Science," *Good Health*, August 1892, 245.

81. John Harvey Kellogg, "The Menti-cure," *Good Health*, August 1906, 423–26.

82. John Harvey Kellogg, "Question Box Lecture," November 22, 1906, JHKUM, Box 4, 1–5.

83. John Harvey Kellogg, "The Errors of Christian Science," *Medical Missionary* 16, no. 6 (1907): 42–43; "The Errors of Christian Science, Continued," *Medical Missionary* 16, no. 7 (1907): 50–51; "The Errors of Christian Science, Continued," *Medical Missionary* 16, no. 8 (1907): 58–59; "The Errors of Christian Science, Concluded," *Medical Missionary* 16, no. 8 (1907): 66–67; "Loopholes for Error," *Medical Missionary* 22, no. 11 (1913): 323–25; "Fallacies of Christian Science Pointed Out," *Battle Creek Idea*, December 12, 1907, 1–2; "The True Christian Science," *Battle Creek Idea*, December 12, 1907, 5–6; "The Real Test," *Battle Creek Idea*, January 14, 1909, 4; "The Influence of the Mind on the Body," *Battle Creek Idea*, January 21, 1909, 1–3; "What about Psychotherapy?," *Battle Creek Idea*, January 28, 1910, 1–3; "Christian Science Only So in Name," *Battle Creek Idea*, April 8, 1910; "The Strongholds of Christian Sci-

ence," *Battle Creek Idea,* April 8, 1910, 4; "Christian Science Only So in Name, Continued," *Battle Creek Idea,* April 15, 1910, 1–3.

84. John Harvey Kellogg, "Is Christian Science Dead," *Good Health,* January 1911, 1–2.

85. For example, "The Tragedy of Christian Science," *Good Health,* February 1910, 107–108; "Christian Science and the Grippe," *Good Health,* December 1918, 694; "The Christian Science Umbrella," *Good Health,* January 1919, 6; "The Slaughter of the Innocents by Christian Science," *Good Health,* July 1920, 388–89.

86. Kellogg claimed that Daniells and Prescott accused him of teaching Christian Science during the Pantheism Crisis. John Harvey Kellogg to G. I. Butler, April 27, 1904, JHKMSU, Collection 13, Box 1, File 10.

87. *Kalamazoo (MI) Gazette,* October 17, 1895, 1; February 14, 1896, 1; May 1, 1896, 1. Mrs. Chester was back in court in October to answer a coroner's inquest about one of her patients, but this resulted in no charges. *Kalamazoo (MI) Gazette,* October, 2, 1896, 1.

88. See, for example, Schoepflin, *Christian Science on Trial,* 213–19.

89. The best overviews of the life and thought of C. W. Post are Peyton Paxson, "Charles William Post: The Mass Marketing of Health and Welfare," 147–75; and Nettie Leitch Major, *C. W. Post: The Hour and the Man,* 28–37.

90. Paxson, "Charles William Post," 36–56.

91. Post maintained membership throughout his life in Battle Creek's Independent Congregational Church, a church that was liberal enough to be comfortable with his New Thought beliefs. Ibid., 65.

92. C. W. Post, *I Am Well! The Modern Practice of Natural Suggestion as Distinct from Hypnotic or Unnatural Influence,* 4, 8, 10, 11, 22, 56, 91, 103, 106, 116, 119–23, 128–29, 131.

93. A second edition, titled *I Am Well!* and from which the following quotations are taken, was published the following year.

94. Ibid., 8, 77–88, 95, 96, 105, 109, 118, 133–37.

95. Grant, *Spirit Fruit;* James L. Murphy, *Reluctant Radicals.*

96. C. W. Post, *The Road to Wellville* (Battle Creek, MI: Postum Cereal, n.d.), 9, 10, 14, Atwater Ephemera Box 4/77, Edward G. Miner Library; Paxson, "Charles William Post," 36, 52–56, 69–96.

97. Horace B. Powell, *Original Has This Signature—W. K. Kellogg,* 100; Carson, *Cornflake Crusade,* 5; Garth "Duff" Stoltz, "A Taste of Cereal" and "101 Cereal Manufacturing Companies in Battle Creek, Michigan."

98. "Memo," June 28, 1935, JHKUM, Box 1.

99. Kellogg, *Battle Creek Sanitarium System,* 205, 207.

100. The following paragraphs rely on Powell, *Original Has This Signature.* See also Carson *Cornflake Crusade,* 124–25, 145–46, 198, 200ff; and Schwarz, "John Harvey Kellogg," 418–24.

101. Powell, *Original Has This Signature,* 51–52.

102. Ibid., 96–97. On the bicycle fad in full bloom in the 1890s, see Whorton, *Crusaders for Fitness,* 304–30.

103. W. K. Kellogg to John Harvey Kellogg, two letters, both dated September 4, 1907, JHKMSU, Collection 13, Box 4, File 8.

104. Powell, *Original Has This Signature,* 145–56; Schwarz, "John Harvey Kellogg," 425–38.

105. Powell, *Original Has This Signature,* 67–156, 268–336.

106. Ibid., iii, 28, 69, 259, 265–67, 269, 296, 344.

### 6. DR. KELLOGG AND RACE BETTERMENT

1. Kellogg could not help gloating over the fact that not only did Phelps go out of business, but he committed suicide, his wife went insane, and his investors lost all their money. John Harvey Kellogg to S. N. Haskell, October 31, 1904, JHKMSU, Collection 13, Box 2, File 4. Other attempted sanitariums in turn-of-the-century Battle Creek included that of Mrs. M. E. Pendill (known as the "Indian Doctress"), that of A. Dana Batram, and the "Health Home" of Dr. Theodore Sands (Lowe, *Tales of Battle Creek*, 74–75).

2. "The Sanitarium Annex," *Good Health*, June 1911, 9–12; Lowe, *Tales of Battle Creek*, 267–69; Whorton, *Crusaders for Fitness*, 297–303; Paxson, "Charles William Post," 124–25. Kellogg learned about Macfadden's trouble with the obscenity laws from none other than Anthony Comstock ("Statement," November 4, 1907, JHKMSU, Collection 13, Box 4, File 9), and on a couple of occasions the doctor helped keep tabs on Macfadden for him (Anthony Comstock to John Harvey Kellogg, January 2, 8, 1908, both in JHKMSU, Collection 13, Box 4, File 11). Kellogg was convinced that Macfadden was stealing his customers. See "Statement of Mrs. Greenblatt," June 28, 1908, and handbill for Macfadden Sanatorium, both in JHKMSU, Collection 13, Box 4, File 13. Near the end of his life, Macfadden attempted to create a new religion of health —"Cosmotarianism"—based on his book *Science of Divine Healing with a Key to Health and Happiness: The Cosmotarian Gospel*, whose dependence on Kellogg's *The Living Temple* is obvious.

3. John Harvey Kellogg, *Light Therapeutics*, 26.

4. Tatiana Tolstoy Souheline to John Harvey Kellogg, November, 16, 1907, JHKUM, Box 1, published as "A Word from Tolstoy," *Good Health*, January 1908, 7; T. Pawlow to Kellogg, August 8, 1907, JHKMSU, Collection 13, Box 4, File 7; R. S. Owen to Kellogg, June 16, 1907, JHKMSU, Collection 13, Box 4, File 8; T. Joe Willey, "Kellogg and Pavlov: Portrait of a Friendship."

5. John Harvey Kellogg to Sarah McEnterfer, March 5, 1908, JHKMSU, Collection 13, Box 4, File 12.

6. John Harvey Kellogg to W. C. White, January 24, 1904, JHKMSU, Collection 13, Box 1, File 7; John Harvey Kellogg to G. I. Butler (February 8, 1904), JHKMSU, Collection 13, Box 1, File 8; "Authentic Interview," 50; Schwarz, "John Harvey Kellogg," 383, 415–17; Robinson, *Story of Our Health Message*, 330–32. For the Flexner report's evaluation of the American Medical Missionary College, see Abraham Flexner, *Medical Education in the United States and Canada*, 119, 244–45. In addition to citing the fact that Christians only are admitted, the report also observes with disapproval that the "school and the sanitarium are inextricably interwoven" and that the curriculum is limited to "the therapeutic theories approved by the sanitarium authorities; a critical and investigative spirit is not cultivated" (244–45).

7. Ella Eaton Kellogg recorded in her diary (July 23, 1915) that she and the doctor were officially invited to attend Mrs. White's funeral service at the Oak Hill Cemetery, but doubted they would attend (a copy of the diary can be found at Heritage Battle Creek, while the original is held by Garth "Duff" Stoltz of Historic Adventist Village, Battle Creek, Michigan).

8. See L. T. to A. G. Daniells, January 26, 1906, JHKMSU, Collection 13, Box 3, File 6.

9. "Authentic Interview," 9, 16–19, 29–30, 45. As he stated in *The Living Temple*, the fact that God was everywhere did not preclude him from being in the heavenly sanctuary as well. John Harvey Kellogg to G. I. Butler, September 14, 1903, JHKMSU, Collection 13, Box 1, File 6. Kellogg also claimed that his interpretation of the sanctuary doctrine referred both to the cleansing of the heavenly sanctuary *and* to the cleansing of the human body. Kellogg to S. N. Haskell, June 30, 1904, JHKMSU, Collection 13, Box 2, File 2.

10. *Principles of the Battle Creek Sanitarium,* 10–14. For a description of the Sabbath Services and the religious life generally at the sanitarium during this time, see "Statement of Irving Keck," January 21, 1907, JHKMSU, Collection 13, Box 4, File 6.

11. *The Battle Creek Sanitarium Book,* 100.

12. William M. Danner to Dr. John Harvey Kellogg, July 10, 1909, JHKMSU, Collection 13, Box 4, File 14.

13. John Harvey Kellogg, "At the Sanitarium Chapel," August. 2, 1906, JHKUM, Box 4, 1–2; Upton Sinclair, *The Profits of Religion,* 237–38. Sinclair's interpretation of why Kellogg maintained the Saturday Sabbath was cynical, to say the least: "You get the shrewd little doctor who is running this establishment alone in his office, and he will smile and admit that of course it is not necessary to take all Bible phrases literally; but you know how it is—there are different levels of intelligence, and so on. Yes, I know how it is. You have an institution founded upon a certain dogma, and run by means of that dogma, and it is hard to change without smashing things. It is especially convenient when servants and nurses have a religious upbringing, and do not steal the pocket-books of the patients" (238). For a much more positive perspective on Kellogg and the sanitarium, see Upton Sinclair and Michael Williams, *Good Health and How We Won It.*

14. John Harvey Kellogg, "At the Sanitarium Chapel," August 2, 1906, JHKUM, Box 4. The fact that Kellogg's wife was a Seventh-Day Baptist probably also had a bearing on the Sabbath issue.

15. Schwarz, "John Harvey Kellogg," 411. For evidence of Ella Eaton Kellogg's rigid Sabbatarianism and distaste at "Sabbath desecration," see her diary on September 3, 1909, 67–70 (a copy of the diary can be found at Heritage Battle Creek, while the original is held by Garth "Duff" Stoltz of Historic Adventist Village, Battle Creek, Michigan). Another indication of the growing nondenominational nature of the sanitarium at the end of the first decade was the fact that when Dr. Dowkontt came to advise the Medical Missionary College, he proposed creating an Evangelical Union Church in Battle Creek to serve the transient population of the sanitarium; the church would be characterized by "liberty of thought and action allowed in regard to baptism, observance of Sabbath, premillennial or post millennial advent of Christ, etc." "Controversial topics [were] to be avoided in public preaching," with the "aim" of the new church to be "to emphasize points of agreement and minimize points of difference." Apparently, Dowkontt died before he could put his plan into action. "Synopsis of Constitution outlined by Dr. Dowkontt: Corporation to Be Known as the Evangelical Union Church," JHKMSU, Collection 13, Box 4, File 15.

16. John Harvey Kellogg, "An Address to Heads of Departments of the Battle Creek Sanitarium, Nov. 1, 1938," JHKUM, Box 7; Schwarz, "John Harvey Kellogg," 51, 55, 191–94, 464. Another indication of the eclipse of Seventh-day Adventist practices at the sanitarium is that by 1929, Easter Sunday, traditionally ignored by Adventists, was now being celebrated at the Sanitarium. "Easter Songs," *Sanitarium News Bulletin,* March 29, 1929, 1.

17. For Kellogg's statements on premillennialism, see John Harvey Kellogg, "The Significance of Our Work," *Medical Missionary* 14, no. 2 (1905): 46–49; John Harvey Kellogg, "True Christianity a Medical Missionary Movement," *Medical Missionary* 15, no. 5 (1906): 130–33; and unsigned editorials "San Francisco Earthquake," *Medical Missionary* 15, no. 5 (1906): 136; "Signs of a Storm," *Medical Missionary* 21, no. 1 (1912): 7; "Now Is the Crisis of This World: Now Shall the Prince of This World Be Cast Out," *Medical Missionary* 23, no. 8 (1914): 230–31; "The Kingdom That Can Not Be Shaken," *Medical Missionary* 23, no. 9 (1914): 260–61; "Editorial Notes," *Medical Missionary* 23, no. 10 (1914): 289; and "Can We Still Be Christians?," *Medi-*

*cal Missionary* 23, no. 11 (1914): 323–24. A robust defense of premillennialism by Billy Sunday was printed in the *Medical Missionary* in 1914 (Rev. William A. Sunday, "The Second Coming of Christ," *Medical Missionary* 23, no. 2 [1914]: 55–59), and talks on dispensationalism and the Scofield Reference Bible were held at the sanitarium in 1912 ("News and Personals," *Battle Creek Idea*, January 26, 1912, 7; "News and Personals," *Battle Creek Idea*, February 9, 1912, 6, 7).

18. John Harvey Kellogg, "True Christianity a Medical Missionary Movement," *Medical Missionary* 15, no. 5 (1906): 129–33.

19. By the 1930s Kellogg had completely abandoned literal apocalypticism. In 1934 an Adventist named Harry Rigg wrote to Kellogg, hoping to enlist his aid circulating a letter in which he excoriated the General Conference of the Seventh-day Adventists for not condemning Roosevelt's National Recovery Act (NRA), which, Rigg contended, was actually the work of the Beast in the Last Times. Kellogg wrote back, stating, "I have your letter of Jan. 1 with circular enclosed. I doubt if the distribution of your circular will do any good. Character is the only thing that counts. Piety induced by fear is only skin deep. I do not think we ought to be worried about the end of probation or about judgment or anything of that sort. The thing that should concern us is whether we are making the best of our opportunities for rendering service to our fellows. The things we love to do are the things that indicate what we really are." Harry Rigg to A. R. Forbush, National Recovery Administration, December 11, 1933; Rigg to the General Conference of Seventh-day Adventists, December 11, 1933, JHKUM, Box 1; Rigg to John Harvey Kellogg, January 1, 1934; Kellogg to Rigg, January 18, 1954.

20. Kellogg was still convinced of the special creation of human beings at least at late as 1906 (John Harvey Kellogg, "Question Box Lecture," October 18, 1906, 19–20, JHKUM, Box 4), and was still expressing doubts about human evolution from lower life forms in the 1920s (John Harvey Kellogg, "Fundamentalism," *Good Health*, July 1925, 32; John Harvey Kellogg, "Fundamentals," *Good Health*, August 1925, 33–34). Even at the end of his life, it appears the issue was still unsettled for the doctor. In a lecture to his patients at the Miami–Battle Creek Sanitarium in 1938, Kellogg wrote, "I do not imagine we are descended from apes, but we may have a common ancestor. If there is a common ancestor he has not been discovered yet." Perhaps unsure of his audience, Kellogg seems to have lost his nerve with this bold declaration of the descent of man, crossing out in the typescript everything beginning with "may" and writing in pencil that we merely "resemble them in our bodily structures." "Lecture to Patients of the Miami–Battle Creek in the Sanitarium Lobby by Dr. John Harvey Kellogg, Jan. 31, 1938," 2, JHKUM, Box 7, 2.

21. Kellogg, *Shall We Slay to Eat?*, 113–14, 132, 140, 141–42. Later in life Kellogg adopted a secular version of this myth: "All paleontologists agree that man did not become a flesh eater until after the arrival of the Glacial Period, when the great forests of nut trees and wild fruits, which had previously constituted his chief food resources, were destroyed by the ice cap that crept down over the Northern Hemisphere and compelled those who did not migrate to the South to seek shelter in caves." John Harvey Kellogg, "Habits in Relation to Longevity," in *Proceedings of the Third Race Betterment Conference*, 331.

22. "A word further in reference to old age: A famous Italian bacteriologist says that he has discovered the germ of old age. I don't think that old age is due to germs, in a great majority of cases,—in fact I am not sure but that it is always due to germs, because old age began about the time when germs began. I think there is pretty good reason to believe that germs were introduced into the world about the time Adam fell. . . . Adam and his successors, up to the time of the flood, lived nearly a thousand years. The tissues of the human race were then so resistant that it took a thousand years of the infection of germs before they could destroy the body. It

used to be a great mystery to me why a man could not live forever, if he lived properly,—I believe he could, if he would live hygienically, if it were not for germs. These germs are constantly present in the alimentary canal, in the intestines and in the colon,—you can't find a mammal but what has germs in the colon. And these germs are all the time producing toxins in the body,—they are all the time being produced in the body. And there is a condition which reaches beyond germs in shortening man's life. It does not seem reasonable that God constructed the body in such a manner that the poisons produced by the body should kill it. The poisons produced in a tree do not kill the tree, and why should the poisons produced in the body or an animal kill the animal? But what does kill it? It is not the poisons which are physiologically produced in the body, but the poisons which are the results of man's sinning which kill the body." John Harvey Kellogg, "Fruits—Diet and Disease," May 5 1898, JHKUM, Box 3, 14–16.

23. Ruth C. Engs, *Clean Living Movements: American Cycles of Health Reform*, 69, 74. See also Charles E. Rosenberg, "The Bitter Fruit: Heredity, Disease, and Social Thought," in *No Other Gods*, 37–38.

24. Elizabeth Blackwell, *The Laws of Life with Special Reference to the Education of Girls*, 8.

25. Sylvester Graham, *Lectures on the Science of Human Life*, 161. The idea of biblical degeneration after Eden was not simply an American idea, but could be found, for example, in the writings of the French psychiatrist Benedict Morel (Rosenberg, *No Other Gods*, 43), an author whose works were known to Kellogg (see "Drunkenness and Heredity," *Good Health*, December 1881, 362–63). See also S. C. Gilman, "Degeneracy and Race in the Nineteenth Century: The Impact of Clinical Medicine."

26. Engs, *Clean Living Movements*, 68–69; Rosenberg, *No Other Gods*, 29, 31.

27. For the importance of Lamarckian thinking among the antebellum Christian physiologists, see Engs, *Clean Living Movements*, 68–69, 72–74.

28. Quoted in ibid., 68.

29. Ibid., 68–69.

30. Quoted in Rosenberg, *No Other Gods*, 36–37.

31. Quoted in Engs, *Clean Living Movements*, 67, 74.

32. "Words from Horace Mann," in *Health: or, How to Live*, edited by J. White and E. White, 181–92.

33. Kellogg, *Plain Facts for Old and Young* (1881), 109.

34. "The Medical Profession," April 29, 1894, JHKUM, Box 3, 21. See also "Literary Notices," *Good Health*, February 1892, 64–65: "We do not believe in total depravity, nevertheless, there is a certain amount of inherited depravity, which, while mixed with certain elements of good in the character of the individual, is amply sufficient to sink him in perdition" (64).

35. John Harvey Kellogg, "Drunkenness and Heredity," *Good Health*, December 1881, 362–63; "An Evil Heritage," *Good Health*, May 1884, 135–38; "A Bad Inheritance," *Good Health*, September 1884, 279; "A New Race of Human Beings," *Good Health*, July 1888, 271; "The Propensity to Kill," *Good Health*, January 1889, 25; "The Heredity of Mutilations," *Good Health*, November 1892, 345; "Heredity," *Good Health*, December 1892, 378; "Heredity (a Poem)," *Good Health*, February 1893, 41; "Child Training," *Good Health*, March 1893, 80–82; "Is Cancer Hereditary?," *Good Health*, May 1893, 150–52; "The Disinherited," *Good Health*, July 1894, 216–17; "The Awful Heredity of Drunkenness," *Good Health*, November 1895, 330–31; "Tea-Smoking," *Good Health*, April 1996, 120.

36. Kellogg, *Plain Facts for Old and Young* (1881), 102–13, 116–40, 347–418; John Harvey Kellogg, "Race Poisons," *Good Health*, November 1910, 929; "Heredity and Crime," *Good Health*, December 1896, 377; "Offspring of Drunkards," *Good Health*, April 1897, 212.

37. Kellogg, *The Living Temple*, 445–46. See also John Harvey Kellogg, "Hereditary Diseases," *Good Health*, March 1888, 110; "How to Exchange a Poor Constitution for a Good One," *Good Health*, September 1891, 263–64; and "Is There Hope for the Transgressor?," *Life Boat*, September 1903, 240–41.

38. Kellogg, *The Living Temple*, 446.

39. Ibid., 444. See also John Harvey Kellogg, "The Greater Gospel," *Good Health*, June 1898, 377–80.

40. "Heredity Not Fate," *Good Health*, January 1897, 51–52. See also Kate Lindsay, "How to Modify Inherited Tendencies," *Good Health*, November 1896, 350–51.

41. John Harvey Kellogg, "The Disinherited," *Good Health*, July 1894, 216–17.

42. For Weismann, see Daniel J. Kevles, *In the Name of Eugenics: Genetics and the Uses of Human Heredity*, 18–19, 70–71.

43. Kellogg was not alone in his stubborn refusal to abandon Lamarckianism; this was also generally the case among many health reformers of the era and for precisely the same reasons. See Whorton, *Crusaders for Fitness*, 154–61.

44. John Harvey Kellogg, "Mendel's Law of Heredity and Race Degeneration," *Good Health*, 1910, 135–37.

45. "A New Book on Eugenics," *Good Health*, April 1917, 166.

46. "Is Eugenics 'Scientific Calvinism'?," *Eugenics* 3, no. 1 (1930): 18–19; Kathy Jane Cooke, "A Gospel of Social Evolution: Religion, Biology, and Education in the Thought of Edwin Grant Conklin," 5, 135, 156.

47. Kellogg, *The Living Temple*, 450.

48. Kellogg, *Plain Facts for Old and Young* (1881), 110.

49. Spencer famously observed, "An unquestionable injury is done by agencies which undertake in a wholesale way to foster good-for-nothings: putting a stop to that natural process of elimination by which society continually purifies itself." Herbert Spencer, *The Study of Sociology*, 346. Fear of the dire effects of "indiscriminate benevolence" became widespread in the United States during this period. See Christine Rosen, *Preaching Eugenics: Religious Leaders and the American Eugenics Movement*, 26–29.

50. "A Sanitary Convention," *Good Health*, February 1881, 61. See also John Harvey Kellogg, "Race Degeneracy: Its Cause and Cure," *Good Health*, December 1909, 929–31.

51. John Harvey Kellogg, "A Startling Truth," *Good Health*, December 1897, 771–72; "Health and Sanitation," *New York Times*, October 14, 1897.

52. John Harvey Kellogg, "Are We a Dying Race?," *Good Health*, December 1897, 723–26; *Good Health*, January 1898, 1–4; *Good Health*, February 1898, 69–72. See also John Harvey Kellogg, "The Race Is Going Down," *Good Health*, February 1898, 118–19.

53. Kellogg, "Are We a Dying Race?," 723, 726.

54. John Harvey Kellogg, "Tendencies toward Race Degeneracy," JHKUM, Box 5, 27; John Harvey Kellogg, "Race Suicide," *Good Health*, August 1911, 730–31; "The Declining Birth Rate Threatens Race Suicide," *Good Health*, August 1935, 243–44; John Harvey Kellogg, "The Melancholy Outlook for White Nations," *Good Health*, May 1938, 140. Kellogg had met Ross while a member of the American Eugenics Society; he was later a presenter at the Third Race Betterment Conference ("Who Outbreeds Whom?," in *Proceedings of the Third Race Betterment Conference*, 72–81) and wrote a eulogy of Kellogg at his death (Schwarz, "John Harvey Kellogg," 487). Kellogg had met Roosevelt while both were speaking at a Chautauqua in Austin, Texas, in 1910 (Schwarz, "John Harvey Kellogg," 206).

55. Kellogg, *Ladies Guide in Health and Disease*, 353

56. In the genealogical fragments in the JHKUM, Box 1, Kellogg claimed descent from William the Conqueror through his father's side and the pilgrim fathers through his mother's side.

57. "Our Country," *Good Health*, November 1886, 351.

58. John Harvey Kellogg, "Where Are All the Healthy Young Men?," *Good Health*, August 1898, 513–14.

59. "Degeneration of the Anglo Saxon Race," *Modern Medicine* 10, no. 2 (1901): 44.

60. John Harvey Kellogg, "Deterioration in Great Britain," *Good Health*, April 1904, 332.

61. M. V. O'Shea and John Harvey Kellogg, *Making the Most of Life*, 45.

62. Kellogg, *Plain Facts for Old and Young* (1881), 164.

63. For the history of scientific racism, see John S. Haller Jr., *Outcasts from Evolution: Scientific Attitudes of Racial Inferiority, 1859–1900*; and Jonathan Peter Spiro, *Defending the Master Race: Conservation, Eugenics, and the Legacy of Madison Grant*.

64. John Harvey Kellogg, "Physical Influence of the Weather," October 31, 1891, JHKUM, Box 3, 3.

65. John Harvey Kellogg, "A Foolish Experiment," *Good Health*, May 1914, 251–53.

66. Spiro, *Defending the Master Race*, 100–101, 138–40, 155, 242.

67. "Norway to the Fore," *Good Health*, May 1917, 221. Articles decrying race mixing often appeared in *Good Health* in the 1920s. See Reynold Spaeth, "Eugenic Aspects of the Negro," *Good Health*, October 1919, 590–93; Roswell H. Johnson, "The Eugenic Program," *Good Health*, June 1920, 350–55; "Eugenics and Migration," *Good Health*, July 1923, 297–99; Wilhelmine E. Key, "Race and Nationality," *Good Health*, July 1924, 303–304; Wilhelmine E. Key, "Eugenics in South America," *Good Health*, August 1922, 344–46; and Luther S. West, "Eugenics and American Government," *Good Health*, December 1928, 36–38.

68. Schwarz, "John Harvey Kellogg," 339; Ashley, "Francis Titus," 41; Margaret Washington, *Sojourner Truth's America*, 377.

69. Schwarz, "John Harvey Kellogg," 340; Ronald D. Graybill, *Ellen G. White and Church Race Relations*, 61–64.

70. "News and Personals," *Battle Creek Idea*, March 10, 1911, 8; "News and Personals," *Battle Creek Idea*, March 17, 1911, 8; "News and Personals," *Battle Creek Idea*, March 24, 1911, 8; "The Progress of a Race," *Battle Creek Idea*, March 24, 1911, 1–5.

71. Kellogg, *Ladies Guide in Health and Disease*, 193.

72. John Harvey Kellogg, "The Degeneration of the Negro," *Good Health*, October 1908, 588. See also Reynold Spaeth, "Eugenic Aspects of the Negro," *Good Health*, October 1919, 590–93.

73. "Chinese Statesman Rebukes American Drinking Customs," *Good Health*, April 1914, 178–81; "America through the Spectacles of an Oriental Diplomat," *Good Health*, May 1914, 277–78; "Race Betterment in the Far East," *Good Health*, October 1918, 583–86.

74. "Lecture to Patients of the Miami–Battle Creek in the Sanitarium Lobby by Dr. John Harvey Kellogg, Jan. 31, 1938," JHKUM, Box 7, 23–24.

75. John Harvey Kellogg to Albert Wiggam, April 6, 1930, JHKUM, Box 1. See also John Harvey Kellogg, "Chaos Coming—Prepare," *Good Health*, February 1938, 44–45; "Will the Yellow Races Dominate the Future World?," *Good Health*, October 1938, 301; and "The White Race Is Dying Fast but There's 'No Cause for Gloom'!!," *Good Health*, December 1938, 366.

76. Kellogg, "Are We a Dying Race?," 726; "'Are We a Dying Race?,' Continued," *Good Health*, January 1898, 3–4.

77. Kellogg, "Are We a Dying Race?," 726; "'Are We a Dying Race?,' Continued," 3–4.

78. *Good Health,* February 1898, 71–72.

79. According to Rosenberg, *No Other Gods,* "The environmentalism and optimism which had characterized mid-century discussions of heredity were gradually replaced in the 1880s by a growing biological reductionism and emphasis on authoritarian solutions" (46).

80. Kellogg, *Plain Facts for Old and Young* (1881), 108.

81. John Harvey Kellogg, "The Medical Profession," April 29, 1894, JHKUM, Box 3, 13.

82. *Good Health,* February 1898, 70–72.

83. John Harvey Kellogg, "Are We a Dying Race?," *Modern Medicine* 7, no. 7 (1898): 168–69.

84. For an overview of Dr. Kellogg's involvement in eugenics, see Schwarz, "John Harvey Kellogg," 441–63.

85. For overviews of eugenics in the United States, see Engs, *Clean Living Movements,* 137–42; Mark H. Haller, *Eugenics: Hereditarian Attitudes in the American Thought;* and Kevles, *In the Name of Eugenics.*

86. Quoted in Schwarz, "John Harvey Kellogg," 446. Upton Sinclair was appalled to find that evolution was not being taught at the American Medical Missionary College: "I went to the Battle Creek Sanitarium to investigate hydrotherapy, and found myself in a nest of Seventh day Adventists. . . . They are decent and kindly people, and you learn to put up with their eccentricities; it is really convenient in some ways, because, as not all the city shares their delusions, there are some stores open every day of the week. But then you discover that the Sanitarium is training 'medical missionaries' to send to Africa, and is teaching these supposed-to-be-scientists that evolution is a doctrine of the devil, and not proven anyhow! . . . People will come from all over the country, and pay high prices to stay in such a sanitarium; you can make vegetarians of them, which you think more important than teaching abstract notions about their being descended from monkeys." Sinclair, *The Profits of Religion,* 237–38.

87. See Kevles, *In the Name of Eugenics,* 21. Kellogg was well aware of the Oneida perfectionists, excoriating them in *Plain Facts for Old and Young* (1881), 258–59, although he eventually used Noyes's term for eugenics, "stirpiculture," in an approving article ("Stirpiculture," *Good Health,* April 1899, 234). As for Victoria Woodhull, she lectured on more than one occasion to Battle Creek's spiritualists. "A Spiritualist" wrote to the *Michigan Tribune* on October 2, 1873, to denounce "Woodhullism" in anticipation of her Battle Creek lecture, which was announced for Thanksgiving Day. Spiritualism file, Heritage Battle Creek. According to the Coller file, Helen Warner Branch Local History, Woodhull lectured again in Battle Creek on or around February 25, 1875.

88. Goodwin, *Pure Food, Drink, and Drug Crusaders,* 95.

89. "Adopts 22 Children to Make 'Gentlemen' in One Generation," *North American* (Philadelphia), April 13, 1902; "Educating Slum Children: Dr. Kellogg's Experiments in Proving That Environment Is Greater than Heredity," *New York Tribune,* August 3, 1901; "Unique Experiments in the Training of Slum Children by Dr. J. H. Kellogg," *New York Sunday Recorder,* August 4, 1901, JHKUM, Box 13; Schwarz, "John Harvey Kellogg," 88, 92, 303–309. For Kellogg's description of the rescue of Huldah's kid, see John Harvey Kellogg, "What Must Be Done for the Street Waif," *Life Boat,* February 1902, 26–28.

90. See, for example, John Harvey Kellogg, "The Social Purity Question from a Medical Standpoint," *Good Health,* April 1908, 194–96; and "Race Degeneracy: Its Cause and Cure," *Good Health,* December 1909, 929–31.

91. Kellogg, "Are We a Dying Race?"; *Good Health,* January 1898, 1–4; *Good Health,* February 1898, 69–72. See also Kellogg, "Race Is Going Down," 118–19.

92. John Harvey Kellogg, "The Race Is Growing Old," *Good Health*, November 1906, 668–69.

93. "New Comers Given 'Freshman' Banquet," *Battle Creek Idea*, November 1, 1913, 1–5; Irving Fisher, "The Vitality Record Office," *Good Health*, June 1937, 174–75, 188; Irving Norton Fisher, *My Father, Irving Fisher,* 105–22.

94. Annie L. Cot, "'Breed Out the Unfit and Breed In the Fit': Irving Fisher, Economics, and the Science of Heredity," 799, 812.

95. Irving Fisher, *Report on National Vitality: Its Wastes and Conservation,* 49–54.

96. Ruth Clifford Engs, *The Eugenics Movement: An Encyclopedia,* 7–8.

97. Irving Fisher, "A Modern Crusade against Consumption," *Good Health*, May 1905, 213–18; Irving Fisher, "Health as a National Asset," *Battle Creek Idea*, August 15, 1913, 1–4, 8, 10.

98. William Jay Schieffelin, "Work of the Committee of One Hundred on National Health"; George E. Rosen, "The Committee of One Hundred on National Health and the Campaign for a National Health Department, 1906–1912." See also "Professor Irving Fisher Coming to Speak to Sanitarium on Work of National Health Committee," *Battle Creek Idea*, December 26, 1907, 1, 5; "$700 Subscribed for Health League," *Battle Creek Idea*, January 9, 1908, 1–2; "Health Perils in the United States," *Battle Creek Idea*, March 11, 1910, 1, 3–5; "Christian Science vs. the Proposed Federal Department of Health," *Good Health*, September 1911, 810–12; "The Animus behind the Opposition to the National Department of Health," *Good Health*, August 1910, 637–39; "Regarding John D. Works," *Good Health*, January 1914, 11–12. Later in 1914, when Fisher created the Life Extension Institute, a for-profit company designed to supply insurance companies with health maintenance programs, Kellogg was appointed to its Hygiene Reference Board and provided much written material for LEI publications, including the best-selling *Health: or, How to Live.* See Laura Davidow Hirshbein, "Masculinity, Work, and the Fountain of Youth: Irving Fisher and the Life Extension Institute, 1914–31."

99. Quoted in Charles E. Rosenberg, "Charles B. Davenport and American Eugenics," in *No Other Gods,* 91. See also E. Carlton MacDowell, "Charles Benedict Davenport, 1866–1944: A Study in Conflicting Influences"; and Garland E. Allen, "The Eugenics Record Office at Cold Springs Harbor, 1910–1940: An Essay in Institutional History."

100. *Good Health*, March 1911, 272–74.

101. John Harvey Kellogg to Charles B. Davenport, February 8, 1912; Davenport to Kellogg, March 2, 1912; Kellogg to Davenport, March 7, 1912; Davenport to Kellogg, March 13, 1912; Kellogg to Davenport, March 18, 1912; and Davenport to Kellogg, March 21, 1912, all in the Davenport Papers. See also Spiro, *Defending the Master Race,* 211, 250–52, 320–21. Kellogg's close associate Dr. William Sadler wrote a book entitled *Race Decadence* (1922) that showed a marked dependence on Madison Grant's book *The Passing of the Great Race.* Spiro, *Defending the Master Race,* 169–70, 189.

102. See "The Physical Degeneracy of Man," *Good Health*, January 1920, 25; and "History in Terms of Race," *Good Health*, February 1931, 41–42, 50. Another major work of scientific racism, *The Rising Tide of Color* by Lothrop Stoddard, was also given a glowing review in *Good Health*, December 1922, 536–38. In one significant aspect, Kellogg was very different from Madison Grant, Chase Osborn, and their ilk because he was not anti-Semitic. Kellogg believed that because the Jews had been practicing biologic living since the days of Moses, they actually represented superior genetic stock on a par with Grant's so-called Nordics or Anglo-Saxons. In a 1935 article commenting on Nazi Germany's "race hygiene" program, Kellogg observed, "The ejection from their country of a people whose blood is far superior to their own (the Jews) as indicated by all racial tests would seem to be a poor start towards race improvement. Breeders improve their stock by inbreeding new and better strains." "Germany's Futile

Effort at Race Betterment," *Good Health,* October 1935, 307. For a more complimentary article on Nazi Germany's racial programs, see "Germany Fighting Race Degeneracy," *Good Health,* September 1935, 277. See also "Vitality of Jewish Race," *Good Health,* March 1912, 166–67.

103. Charles B. Davenport to John Harvey Kellogg, August 17, 1923; Kellogg to Davenport, August 27, October 29, 1923; Davenport to Kellogg, September 4, 1923; Kellogg to Davenport, September 9, 1923; and Davenport to Kellogg, September 14, October 8, 18, 1923, all in Davenport Papers. See also Spiro, *Defending the Master Race,* 211, 250–52, 320–21.

104. John Harvey Kellogg, "A New Introduction of an Old Term," *Battle Creek Idea,* August 19, 1910, 4.

105. Kellogg, *Plain Facts for Old and Young* (1881), 114–15.

106. "A Sensible Law," *Good Health,* March 1881, 86; John Harvey Kellogg, "The New Hygiene," *Battle Creek Idea,* September 30, 1910, 1–3; "Eugenics Pioneer Visits Sanitarium," *Battle Creek Idea,* November 1, 1913, 9.

107. John Harvey Kellogg, *Tendencies toward Race Degeneracy,* 32.

108. Schwarz, "John Harvey Kellogg," 263n166, 447–49; Jeffrey Alan Hodges, "Dealing with Degeneracy: Michigan Eugenics in Context," 111.

109. Hodges, "Dealing with Degeneracy," 112, 130, 134, 141–58, 172. The text of the bills can be found in Jeffrey Alan Hodges, "Euthenics, Eugenics, and Compulsory Sterilization in Michigan, 1897–1960," 141–54.

110. Numerous articles in *Good Health* reported on the implementation of new state sterilization laws when they went into effect throughout the country. For example, see "Wisconsin's Eugenics Law," *Good Health,* January 1916, 50; "The New Eugenics Law of Oregon," *Good Health,* August 1924, 346; "Sterilization of the Unfit," *Good Health,* September 1925, 32; and "Sterilization Laws," *Good Health,* September 1930, 40.

111. "Argument for the Sterilization of the Unfit," *Good Health,* February 1913, 106.

112. John Harvey Kellogg, "The Perils of Personal Liberty," *Good Health,* April 1919, 191–93.

113. Martin S. Pernick, *The Black Stork: Eugenics and the Death of "Defective" Babies in American Medicine and Motion Pictures since 1915,* 3–8.

114. John Harvey Kellogg, "Testing Eugenics," *Good Health,* January 1916, 7–8. Nevertheless, O. C. Glaser, who wrote the "Department of Eugenics" column for *Good Health,* saw fit to commend the eugenic teachings of *The Black Stork.* "The Black Stork," *Good Health,* November 1917, 571.

115. *Proceedings of the First National Conference on Race Betterment, January 8, 9, 10, 11, 12, 1914,* 1.

116. Schwarz, "John Harvey Kellogg," 454–55; C. Rosen, *Preaching Eugenics,* 85–88.

117. John Harvey Kellogg to Charles B. Davenport, September 24, 1913, Davenport Papers.

118. *Proceedings of the First National Conference,* 595, 597–98, 600–625.

119. Ibid., 599. It also apparently had an impact on popular culture. Shortly after the conference, a silent film was produced entitled *Eugenics vs. Love* (1914): in it a cereal company in a town called "Battle River" offered a prize to the man and woman judged to be the most eugenically fit if they agreed to get married; the plot revolved around the fact that the most eugenically fit man in town was appalled by the prospect of marrying the most eugenically fit woman. Ultimately, the hero did manage to marry his sweetheart, despite the fact that she did not score very high in eugenic fitness. Pernick, *Black Stork,* 131.

120. Schwarz, "John Harvey Kellogg," 62.

121. John Harvey Kellogg, "Needed: A New Human Race," in *Proceedings of the First National Conference,* 446. For the distinction between eugenics and euthenics, see M. Haller, *Eugenics,*

77. See also Kathy Jane Cooke, "The Limits of Heredity: Nature and Nurture in American Eugenics before 1915." The word *euthenics* was coined by Ellen Swallow Richards of MIT in 1906 (270); a brief review of Richards's book *Euthenics* ran in *Good Health*, September 1911, 838–40.

122. If this sounded in part like science fiction, perhaps it was: Kellogg was charmed by the description of the new humanity as described in Bulwer-Lytton's short story "The Coming Race." See John Harvey Kellogg, "Bulwer-Lytton's Vision of the Coming Race," *Good Health*, May 1916, 253.

123. Kellogg, "Needed: A New Human Race," 447–48. The development of the data form for the Eugenics Registry and the composition of the registry's board occupied several letters between Davenport and Kellogg from 1914 to 1916 (Davenport Papers), after which it apparently took several more years for the registry to begin functioning.

124. John Harvey Kellogg, "Race Degeneracy and Race Improvement," *Good Health*, June 1935, 179.

125. "The Race Betterment Foundation," *Good Health*, December 1914, 609–10. On July 22, 1914, a meeting was held to change the name from the American Medical Missionary Board to the Race Betterment Foundation, and on October 3, 1914, the foundation began meeting under its new name. At the February 21, 1916, meeting, Kellogg announced that the name change had been approved by the State of Michigan. Minutes of the Transactions of the Board of Trustees of the American Medical Missionary Board, bk. 2, JHKMSU, Collection 13, 117:25–27, 31, 60.

126. "Finis," *Medical Missionary* 23, no. 12 (1914): 354.

127. John Harvey Kellogg to Albert Wiggam, April 6, 1930, JHKUM, Box 1; "Changes in Missionary Ideals," *Good Health*, December 1933, 18–19. See also "Japanese Good Sense," *Good Health*, July 1928, 38.

128. *Official Proceedings of the Second National Conference on Race Betterment, August 4, 5, 6, 7, and 8, 1915, Held in San Francisco, California, in Connection with the Panama-Pacific International Exposition*, 144; "Race Betterment Week at San Francisco Fair," *Good Health*, August 1915, 371–72. See also Robert W. Rydell, *World of Fairs: The Century-of-Progress Expositions*, 38–58.

129. *Official Proceedings of the Second National Conference*, 5.

130. John Harvey Kellogg, "The Eugenics Registry," in *Official Proceedings of the Second National Conference*, 76. Also published as "Practical Eugenics," *Good Health*, October 1915, 423–31.

131. Kellogg, "The Eugenics Registry," 79–87.

132. *Official Proceedings of the Second National Conference*, 89–91.

133. A. E. Hamilton, "Exhibiting an Idea," *Good Health*, April 1915, 150–52.

134. *Official Proceedings of the Second National Conference*, 145–61. Many of these posters were republished in the *Battle Creek Idea*, as well as an updated edition of *Plain Facts*, which was expanded to included chapters titled "Heredity and Eugenics" and "Race Degeneracy and Improvement." Education about these areas was essential, Kellogg believed, to the development of man's "sex conscience" and in order to bring him closer to the purity of a "sexual millennium." John Harvey Kellogg, *Plain Facts* (1917), 765–810, 865–918. See also "The Sex Conscience," *Good Health*, July 1915, 298–99.

135. *Official Proceedings of the Second National Conference*, 6–7.

136. Tamen Wolff, *Mendel's Theatre: Heredity, Eugenics, and Early Twentieth-Century American Drama*, 106–10. See also Sheldon Cheney, *Conversations with Sheldon Cheney: An Interview Conducted by J. R. K. Kantor and Suzanne Riess for the Regional Oral History Office, the Bancroft Library, University of California, Berkeley*, 3–4 (Cheney was the director of the "Morality Masque").

137. *Proceedings of the Third Race Betterment Conference*, 120–21, 739–42.

138. John Harvey Kellogg, "The Responsibilities of Those Who Are Fit," in *Proceedings of the Third Race Betterment Conference*, 118–19.

139. *Proceedings of the Third Race Betterment Conference*, 741.

140. John Harvey Kellogg, "Habits in Relation to Longevity," in ibid., 346–47. For Kellogg's earliest statement of the need for a religion of eugenics, see "Cultivating the Religion of Health," *Good Health*, March 1914, 117–19.

141. Quoted in C. Rosen, *Preaching Eugenics*, 38.

142. John Harvey Kellogg to Charles B. Davenport, September 8, 1916; Davenport to Kellogg, September 13, 1916; Kellogg to Davenport, September 21, 1916; and Davenport to Kellogg, October 23, November 3, 1916, all in Davenport Papers.

143. John Harvey Kellogg to Aldred Scott Warthin, June 13, 1927, Aldred Scott Warthin Papers, Box 1.

144. Aldred Scott Warthin, "A Biologic Philosophy or Religion a Necessary Foundation for Race Betterment," in *Proceedings of the Third Race Betterment Conference*, 86–90. Two years later Warthin expanded his thoughts on the religion of the germ plasm in a short book, *The Creed of a Biologist: A Biologic Philosophy of Life*.

145. C. Rosen, *Preaching Eugenics*, 117–28; John M. Bozeman, "Eugenics and the Clergy in the Early Twentieth-Century United States." See also Leila Zenderland, "Biblical Biology: American Protestant Social Reformers and the Early Eugenics Movement."

146. Kenneth C. MacArthur, "Eugenics and the Church: Eugenics and Unity." A list of clerical supporters of eugenics given in a later article were all noted modernists. Kenneth C. MacArthur, "Eugenics and the Church: Answering Some Critics." For a classic statement of the religious importance of eugenics from a modernist perspective, see Shailer Mathews, "Science Gives Content to the Religious Life," in *Contributions of Science to Religion*, edited by Shailer Mathews, 410–13.

147. Florence Brown Sherbon, "The Preacher's Part."

148. Edwin Grant Conklin, *Heredity and Environment in the Development of Men*; Alexis Carrel, *Man, the Unknown*.

149. For a brief biography of Wiggam up to 1927, see Jay Arthur Meyers, *Fighters of Fate: A Story of Men Who Have Achieved Greatly Despite the Handicaps of the Great White Plague*, 294–305. Once the public lost interest in eugenics in the 1940s, Wiggam became a syndicated columnist on topics of psychology, dying in 1957. "Albert E. Wiggam, Columnist, Was 84," *New York Times*, April 27, 1957, 19.

150. "Chautauqua Bill at Last Arranged," *Battle Creek Evening News*, April 20, 1912, 2; ad for Battle Creek Chautauqua (June 30–July 7, 1912), *Battle Creek Daily Moon*, June 29, 1912, 4; "Chautauqua Now Near Its Finish," *Battle Creek Daily Moon*, July 5, 1912, 3.

151. Albert E. Wiggam, *The New Decalogue of Science*, 17–19, 8–82.

152. Ibid., 19, 60, 90–91, 95, 99–101, 110–11, 185, 288.

153. Ibid., 104, 105, 117, 197, 239, 244, 252, 256, 262, 263, 269.

154. John Harvey Kellogg, "A Foolish Experiment," *Good Health*, May 1914, 251–53.

155. Albert E. Wiggam, "Eugenics and the State," *Good Health*, July 1922, 299–30.

156. "The New Decalogue," *Good Health*, November 1924, 450; "A Health Code," *Good Health*, August 1927, 24–25.

157. "Funeral Is Held for Dr. Kellogg," *Battle Creek Enquirer and News*, December 19, 1943, 10; John Harvey Kellogg, "Philosophy of Life," June 5, 1940, JHKUM, Box 7.

158. Schwarz, "John Harvey Kellogg," 485–86.

159. John Harvey Kellogg, "An Aristocracy of Health: What It Is and Why," *Good Health*, February 1936, 38–39; John Harvey Kellogg, "The Aristocracy of Health: Endowed by Mrs. Mary F. Henderson," *Good Health*, June 1937, 166–67.

160. Carrel, *Man, the Unknown*. For Carrel's life and work, see Joseph T. Durkin, SJ, *Hope for Our Time: Alexis Carrel on Man and Society*; David Le Vay, *Alexis Carrel: The Perfectability of Man*; and Andrés Horacio Reggiani, *God Eugenicist: Alexis Carrel and the Sociobiology of Decline*. Although best known for his "immortal chicken heart," a piece of tissue supposedly kept alive for years in his laboratory at the Carnegie Institute, Carrel was also interested in eugenics. "Doctor Carrel Studies Race Betterment," *Good Health*, March 1939, 108. Learning of this interest, Kellogg invited Carrel to Battle Creek for the Third Race Betterment Conference, where he gave a paper titled "The Immortality of Animal Tissues and Its Significance" (in *Proceedings of the Third Race Betterment Conference*, 309–14). It was here that Kellogg and Carrel apparently got to know each other's work, with Carrel later writing Kellogg that he was "extremely interested in your ideas and in the way you have realized them" and inviting him to the Rockefeller Institute to observe techniques of tissue culture for possible replication at the sanitarium laboratories. Alexis Carrel to John Harvey Kellogg, February 2, November 24, 1928, Alexis Carrel Papers. For the next several years, Kellogg repeatedly tried to coax Carrel back to the sanitarium, but it was not until 1939, shortly before Carrel was to be forced into mandatory retirement from the Rockefeller Institute, that he finally visited Kellogg at the Miami–Battle Creek Sanitarium. Looking for a place to continue his work, Carrel spent a week with Kellogg, giving a lecture to the sanitarium patients on March 5. In it he praised Dr. Kellogg as a "pioneer" and a "prophet" for race betterment, after which Carrel extolled the virtues of tissue culture for combating the degeneration of civilization and improving the "condition of the great white races." John Harvey Kellogg to Alexis Carrel, August 4, 6, October 17, 1929, June 27, 1932, Carrel Papers. A copy of Dr. Carrel's talk, "Lecture Given by Dr. Alexis Carrel, at the Miami–Battle Creek, Sunday, March 5th, 1939," can be found in JHKUM, Box 7. Kellogg apparently was even inspired by Carrel to entertain fascism. John Harvey Kellogg, "Are Dictators Becoming Necessary?," *Good Health*, March 1939, 80.

161. John Harvey Kellogg to Alexis Carrel, March 21, 1939, JHKUM, Box 3, 3.

162. John Harvey Kellogg, "The Mission of Good Health Is to Save Civilization through Race Betterment and Biologic Living," January 23, 1940, JHKUM, Box 7, 3–4.

163. Schwarz, "John Harvey Kellogg," 459–61.

164. "Noted Scientists to Lecture Here, Will Attend Fourth Conference of Race Betterment Foundation in 1942," clipping from unidentified newspaper, September 16, 1941, JHKUM, Box 13.

165. C. Rosen, *Preaching Eugenics*, 91–92.

166. Harry H. Loughlin to John Harvey Kellogg, December 19, 1941, JHKUM, Box 2.

167. John Harvey Kellogg to Dr. Reginald M. Atwater, November 1, 1943, JHKUM, Box 3, 3–4.

168. John Harvey Kellogg to Dr. Henry F. Vaughan, November 21, 1943, JHKUM, Box 3, 4.

169. "Dr. Kellogg Wills Entire Estate to Promote Health," *Battle Creek Enquirer and News*, December 22, 1943, 1; Charles B. Davenport, "John Harvey Kellogg, 1852–1943."

170. "Kelly Files Race Betterment Suit," *Battle Creek Enquirer and News*, April 18, 1967, 1–2; "Fund Faces Charge of Wasting $687,000," *New York Times*, April 19, 1967, 42; "Race Betterment Group Denies Squander Claims," *Battle Creek Enquirer and News*, September 28, 1968, 2.

171. Schwarz, "John Harvey Kellogg," 462n131.

### CONCLUSION

1. Schwarz, "John Harvey Kellogg," 51, 55, 191–94, 464.

2. Ibid., 191, 421, 464–67; Weeks, "August F. Bloese," 13–14, 77.

3. Schwarz, "John Harvey Kellogg," 421, 439.

4. For example, "For many years back there has been a very determined attempt to change the ideals of the institution and it has been a very grievous thing for me. I have had a pretty stiff battle to keep the principles where they should be." Kellogg specifically complained that some of the doctors were now promoting a "light meat diet" to patients at the sanitarium. The principles of the Battle Creek Sanitarium were like "the Ten Commandments," according to Kellogg, and every doctor at the institution should strive to live up to them. "An Address to Heads of Departments of the Battle Creek Sanitarium, November 1, 1938," JHKUM, Box 7.

5. "Dr. Kellogg Is Dead at 91," *Battle Creek Enquirer and News,* December 15, 1943, 1; Schwarz, "John Harvey Kellogg," 467–85; "Battle Creek Sanitarium," in *Seventh-day Adventist Encyclopedia,* 177.

6. *Battle Creek Idea,* Spring 1959, 1, JHKUM, MS 2007–12, Box 1, Folder 7.

7. Gerstner, "Temple of Health," 76–77; "Battle Creek Sanitarium," in *Seventh-day Adventist Encyclopedia,* 177–78.

8. Gerstner, "Temple of Health," 77; "Battle Creek Sanitarium," in *Seventh-day Adventist Encyclopedia,* 178.

9. Whorton, *Nature Cures,* 246–56.

10. John Harvey Kellogg, "My Search for Health," January 16, 1942, JHKUM, Box 7, 5–6. See also John Harvey Kellogg, "Seeing the Invisible," *Good Health,* August 1930, 35–36.

# BIBLIOGRAPHY

## Additional Manuscript Collections

American Antiquarian Society Library. Worcester, MA.

Carrel, Alexis. Papers. Georgetown University, Washington, DC.

Center for Adventist Research. Andrews University, Berrien Springs, MI.

Clubb, Henry S. Papers. Bentley Historical Library, University of Michigan, Ann Arbor.

Davenport, Charles B. Papers. American Philosophical Society, Philadelphia.

Edward G. Miner Library. University of Rochester Medical Center, Rochester, NY.

Fletcher, Horace. Papers. Houghton Library, Harvard University, Cambridge, MA.

Helen Warner Branch Local History. Willard Library, Battle Creek, MI.

Heritage Battle Creek. Battle Creek, MI.

MacIvor, Charles. Collection. Center for Adventist Research, Andrews University, Berrien Springs, MI.

Warthin, Aldred Scott. Papers. Bentley Historical Library, University of Michigan, Ann Arbor.

## Other Sources

Abbott, Lyman. *The Evolution of Christianity*. Boston: Houghton Mifflin, 1900.

———. *A Study in Human Nature*. New York: Chautauqua Press, 1885.

———. "The Supernatural." *Outlook,* July 2, 1898, 580–84.

———. *The Temple*. New York: Macmillan, 1909.

Albanese, Catherine L. *Nature Religion in America: From the Algonkian Indians to the New Age*. Chicago: University of Chicago Press, 1991.

———. *A Republic of Mind and Spirit: A Cultural History of American Metaphysical Religion*. New Haven, CT: Yale University Press, 2007.

Allen, Abigail Ann Maxson, ed. *Life and Sermons of Jonathan Allen*. Oakland, CA: Pacific Press, 1894.

Allen, Garland E. "The Eugenics Record Office at Cold Springs Harbor, 1910–1940: An Essay in Institutional History." *Osiris,* 2nd ser., 2 (1986): 225–64.

Altherr, Thomas L. "A Convention of 'Moral Lunatics': The Rutland, Vermont, Free Convention of 1858." *Vermont History* 69 (2001): 90–104.

Anderson, Godfrey T. "Sectarianism and Growth, 1846–1864." In *Adventism in America: A History*, edited by Gary Land, 29–31. Berrien Springs, MI: Andrews University Press, 1998.

Ashley, Martin L. "The Early Quakers of Battle Creek: Followers of the Inner Light." *Heritage
Battle Creek* 9 (Winter 1999): 31–36.

———. "Frances Titus: Sojourner Truth's 'Trusted Scribe.'" *Heritage Battle Creek* 8 (Fall
1997): 35–43.

Ashley, Martin L., and Frances Thornton. "A Quaker Anti-slavery Family: The Merritts
of Battle Creek." *Heritage Battle Creek* 9 (Winter 1999): 38–45.

Atteberry, Maxine. "Seventh-day Adventist Nurses: A Century of Service." *Adventist Heritage*
8, no. 2 (1983): 3–11.

"An Authentic Interview between Elder G. W. Amadon, Elder A. C. Bourdeau, and Dr. John
Harvey Kellogg in Battle Creek, Michigan, on October 7th, 1907." Typescript, Heritage
Room, the Library, La Sierra University, Riverside, CA.

Avery, A., ed. *The Averell-Averill-Avery Family*. Vol. 1. Cleveland, OH: Press of Evangelical
Publishing House, 1914.

Baker, Alonzo L. "My Years with John Harvey Kellogg." *Spectrum* 4, no. 4 (1972): 40–45.

Barbour, Hugh, et al. *Quaker Crosscurrents: Three Hundred Years of Friends in the New York
Yearly Meetings*. Syracuse, NY: Syracuse University Press, 1995.

Barkun, Michael. *Crucible of the Millennium: The Burned-Over District of New York in the
1840s*. Syracuse, NY: Syracuse University Press, 1986.

*The Battle Creek Sanitarium Book*. Battle Creek, MI: n.p., 1912.

Baxter, Albert. *History of the City of Grand Rapids, Michigan*. New York: Munsell, 1891.

Bednarowski, Mary Farrell. *New Religions and the Theological Imagination in America*. Bloomington: Indiana University Press, 1989.

Blackwell, Elizabeth. *The Laws of Life with Special Reference to the Education of Girls*. London:
Sampson Low, Son, 1859.

Blake, John B. "Health Reform." In *The Rise of Adventism*, edited by Edwin Scott Gaustad,
30–49. New York: Harper and Row, 1974.

Block, Marguerite. *The New Church in the New World: A Study of Swedenborgianism in America*. 1932. Reprint, New York: Octagon Books, 1984.

Blocker, Jack S., Jr. *American Temperance Movements: Cycles of Reform*. Boston: Twayne, 1989.

Boies, Edward Z., and Doris E. Ware. *The First Congregational Church of Battle Creek: Its First
One-Hundred and Fifty Years*. Battle Creek, MI: B & R Letter Shop, 1986.

Bozeman, John M. "Eugenics and the Clergy in the Early Twentieth-Century United States."
*Journal of American Culture* 27, no. 4 (2004): 422–31.

Bradley, A. Day. "Progressive Friends in Michigan and New York." *Quaker History* 52, no. 2
(1963): 95–103.

Braude, Ann. "News from the Spirit World: A Checklist of American Spiritualist Periodicals,
1847–1900." *Proceedings of the American Antiquarian Society* 99 (October 1989): 399–462.

Bressler, Ann Lee. *The Universalist Movement in America, 1770–1880*. Oxford: Oxford University Press, 2001.

*A Brief Account of the Dedicatory Services of the New Main Building of the Battle Creek Sani-
tarium*. Battle Creek, MI: n.p., 1904.

Britten, Emma Hardinge. *Modern American Spiritualism*. New York: published by the author,
1870.

Brown, Ira V. *Lyman Abbott, Christian Evolutionist: A Study in Religious Liberalism*. 1953. Reprint, Westport, CT: Greenwood Press, 1970.

Bull, Malcolm, and Keith Lockhart. *Seeking a Sanctuary: Seventh-day Adventism and the American Dream*. 2nd ed. Bloomington: Indiana University Press, 2007.

Butler, Jonathan. "Adventism and the American Experience." In *The Rise of Adventism*, edited by Edwin Scott Gaustad, 173–206. New York: Harper and Row, 1974.

Butler, Mary G. "The Village of Battle Creek: 'Distinguished for Its Love of Liberty and Progress.'" *Heritage Battle Creek* 9 (Winter 1999): 23–30.

Carrel, Alexis. *Man, the Unknown*. New York: Harper and Brothers, 1935.

Carroll, Brett E. *Spiritualism in Antebellum America*. Bloomington: Indiana University Press, 1997.

Carson, Gerald. *Cornflake Crusade*. New York: Rinehart, 1957.

Carter, Paul A. *The Spiritual Crisis of the Gilded Age*. DeKalb: Northern Illinois University Press, 1971.

Cheney, Sheldon. *Conversations with Sheldon Cheney: An Interview Conducted by J. R. K. Kantor and Suzanne Riess for the Regional Oral History Office, the Bancroft Library, University of California, Berkeley*. Berkeley: Regents of the University of California, 1977.

*Cleave's Biographical Cyclopedia of Homeopathic Physicians and Surgeons*. Philadelphia: Galaxy, 1873.

Coles, Larkin B., MD. *Philosophy of Health: Natural Principles of Health and Cure; or, Health and Cure without Drugs; also, The Moral Bearings of Erroneous Appetites*. Boston: Ticknor, Fields, and Richards, 1851.

Conklin, Edwin Grant. *Heredity and Environment in the Development of Men*. Princeton, NJ: Princeton University Press, 1915.

Cooke, Kathy Jane. "A Gospel of Social Evolution: Religion, Biology, and Education in the Thought of Edwin Grant Conklin." PhD diss., University of Chicago, 1994.

———. "The Limits of Heredity: Nature and Nurture in American Eugenics before 1915." *Journal of the History of Biology* 31 (1998): 263–78.

Cot, Annie L. "'Breed Out the Unfit and Breed In the Fit': Irving Fisher, Economics, and the Science of Heredity." *American Journal of Economics and Sociology* 64, no. 3 (2005): 793–826.

Cowan, Ruth Schwartz. "Nature and Nurture: The Interplay of Biology and Politics in the Work of Francis Galton." *Studies in the History of Biology* 1 (1977): 133–208.

Cox, John, Jr. "The Quakers in Michigan." *Michigan History* 29 (1945): 512–21.

Cramp, Arthur J., ed. *Nostrums and Quackery*. Chicago: American Medical Association, 1921.

Cross, Whitney R. *The Burned-Over District: The Social and Intellectual History of Enthusiastic Religion in Western New York, 1800–1850*. New York: Harper Touchstone, 1950.

Cunningham, Raymond J. "The Emmanuel Movement: A Variety of American Religious Experience." *American Quarterly* 14, no. 1 (1962): 48–63.

Damsteegt, P. Gerard. "Health Reform and the Bible in Early Sabbatarian Adventism." *Adventist Heritage* 5, no. 2 (1978): 13–21.

Davenport, Charles B. "John Harvey Kellogg, 1852–1943." *Eugenical News* 28, no. 1 (1943): 43–44.

Davidson, Carlisle G. "A Profile of Hicksite Quakerism in Michigan, 1830–1860." *Quaker History* 59, no. 2 (1970): 106–12.

*Defense of Eld. James White and Wife: Vindication of Their Moral and Christian Character*. Battle Creek, MI: Seventh-day Adventist Publishing Association, 1870.

Dick, Everett M. "The Millerite Movement, 1830–1845." In *Adventism in America: A History,* edited by Gary Land, 1–28. Berrien Springs, MI: Andrews University Press, 1998.

Doherty, Robert W. *The Hicksite Separation: A Sociological Analysis of Religious Schism in Early Nineteenth Century America.* New Brunswick, NJ: Rutgers University Press, 1967.

Dugdale, Richard L. *The Jukes: A Study in Crime, Pauperism, Disease, and Heredity.* New York: G. P. Putnam's Sons, 1877.

Durkin, Joseph T., SJ. *Hope for Our Time: Alexis Carrel on Man and Society.* New York: Harper and Row, 1965.

Durst, Dennis L. "'No Legacy Annuls Heredity from God': Evangelical Social Reformers and the North American Eugenics Movement." PhD diss., Saint Louis University, 2002.

Eastman, Mary F. *The Biography of Dio Lewis, A.M., M.D.* New York: Fowler and Wells, 1891.

Ellis, David M. "The Yankee Invasion of New York, 1783–1850." *New York History* 32, no. 1 (1951): 3–18.

Engs, Ruth C. *Clean Living Movements: American Cycles of Health Reform.* Westport, CT: Praeger, 2000.

———. *The Eugenics Movement: An Encyclopedia.* Westport, CT: Greenwood Press, 2005.

Field, George. *Memoirs, Incidents, and Reminiscences of the Early History of the New Church in Michigan, Indiana, Illinois, and Adjacent States; and Canada.* 1879. Reprint, New York: AMS Press, 1971.

Filler, Louis. "Parker Pillsbury: An Anti-slavery Apostle." *New England Quarterly* 19, no. 3 (1946): 315–37.

Fisher, Irving. *Report on National Vitality: Its Wastes and Conservation.* Washington, DC: Government Printing Office, 1909.

Fisher, Irving Norton. *My Father, Irving Fisher.* New York: Comet Press Books, 1956.

Fletcher, Horace. *The A. B.–Z. of Our Own Nutrition.* New York: Frederick A. Stokes, 1903.

———. *Fletcherism; or, How I Became Young at Sixty.* New York: Frederick A. Stokes, 1913.

———. *Happiness as Found in Forethought Minus Fearthought.* Chicago: Herbert S. Stone, 1897.

———. *Menticulture; or, The A-B-C of True Living.* Chicago: A. C. McClurg, 1895.

———. *The New Glutton or Epicure.* New York: Frederick A. Stokes, 1917.

———. *Optimism: A Real Remedy.* Chicago: A. C. McClurg, 1908.

Flexner, Abraham. *Medical Education in the United States and Canada.* New York: Carnegie Foundation, 1910.

Fowler, Orson S. *Hereditary Descent: Its Laws and Facts Applied to Human Improvement.* New York: Fowlers and Wells, 1847.

Fox, Dixon Ryan. *Yankees and Yorkers.* New York: New York University Press, 1940.

Fuller, Robert C. *Alternative Medicine and American Religious Life.* Oxford: Oxford University Press, 1989.

Gardner, Washington, ed. *History of Calhoun County.* Chicago: Lewis, 1913.

Gaustad, Edwin S. *Historical Atlas of American Religion.* New York: Harper and Row, 1962.

———, ed. *The Rise of Adventism.* New York: Harper and Row, 1974.

Gerstner, Patsy. "The Temple of Health: A Pictorial History of the Battle Creek Sanitarium." *Caduceus* 12, no. 2 (1996).

Gilman, S. C. "Degeneracy and Race in the Nineteenth Century: The Impact of Clinical Medicine." *Journal of Ethnic Studies* 10, no. 4 (1983): 27–50.

Goodwin, Lorine Swainston. *The Pure Food, Drink, and Drug Crusaders, 1879–1914.* Jefferson, NC: McFarland, 1999.

Gosling, F. G. *Before Freud: Neurasthenia and the American Medical Community.* Urbana: University of Illinois Press, 1987.

Gottschalk, Stephen. *The Emergence of Christian Science in American Religious Life.* Berkeley: University of California Press, 1974.

Graham, Sylvester. *Lectures on the Science of Human Life.* London: Horsell, Aldine Chambers, 1849.

———. *The Philosophy of Sacred History Considered in Relation to Human Aliment and the Wines of Scripture.* London: Horsell and Caudwell, 1859.

Grant, H. Roger. *Spirit Fruit: A Gentle Utopia.* DeKalb: Northern Illinois University Press, 1988.

Graybill, Ronald D. *Ellen G. White and Church Race Relations.* Washington, DC: Review and Herald, 1970.

———. "The Power of Prophecy: Ellen G. White and the Women Religious Founders of the Nineteenth Century." PhD diss., John Hopkins University, 1983.

———. "The Whites Come to Battle Creek: A Turning Point in Adventist History." *Adventist Heritage* 15, no. 2 (1992): 25–29.

Greene, John Gardner. "The Emmanuel Movement, 1906–1929." *New England Quarterly* 7, no. 3 (1934): 494–532.

Haeckel, Ernst. *Monism as Connecting Religion and Science: The Confession of Faith of a Man of Science.* Translated by J. Gilchrist. London: Adam and Charles Black, 1895.

———. *The Riddle of the Universe.* Translated by Joseph McCabe. New York: Harper and Brothers, 1900.

Haller, John S., Jr. *American Medicine in Transition, 1840–1910.* Urbana: University of Illinois Press, 1981.

———. *The History of New Thought: From Mind Cure to Positive Thinking and the Prosperity Gospel.* West Chester, PA: Swedenborg Foundation Press, 2012.

———. *Outcasts from Evolution: Scientific Attitudes of Racial Inferiority, 1859–1900.* Urbana: University of Illinois Press, 1971.

———. *Sectarian Reformers in American Medicine, 1800–1910.* New York: AMS Press, 2011.

Haller, Mark H. *Eugenics: Hereditarian Attitudes in the American Thought.* New Brunswick, NJ: Rutgers University Press, 1963.

Hambrick-Stowe, Charles. *Charles G. Finney and the Spirit of American Evangelism.* Grand Rapids, MI: Eerdmans, 1996.

Hamm, Thomas D. *The Transformation of American Quakerism: Orthodox Friends, 1800–1907.* Bloomington: Indiana University Press, 1988.

Hawley, Charles Arthur. "Swedenborgianism and the Frontier." *Church History* 6, no. 3 (1937): 203–22.

Henderson, Mary Foote. *The Aristocracy of Health: A Study of Physical Culture, Our Favorite Poisons, and a National and International League for the Advancement of Physical Culture.* Washington, DC: Colton, 1904.

Herdman, Gerald G. "Glimpses of Early Battle Creek." *Adventist Heritage* 1, no. 1 (1974): 17–22.

Hirshbein, Laura Davidow. "Masculinity, Work, and the Fountain of Youth: Irving Fisher and the Life Extension Institute, 1914–31." *Canadian Bulletin of Medical History* 16, no. 1 (1999): 89–124.

*History of Calhoun County, Michigan.* Philadelphia: L. H. Everts, 1877.

Hitchcock, Edward. *The Religion of Geology and Its Connected Sciences.* Boston: Phillips, Sampson, 1851.

Hodges, Jeffrey Alan. "Dealing with Degeneracy: Michigan Eugenics in Context." PhD diss., Michigan State University, 2001.

———. "Euthenics, Eugenics, and Compulsory Sterilization in Michigan, 1897–1960." Master's thesis, Michigan State University, 1995.

Holt, Niles R. "Ernst Haeckel's Monistic Religion." *Journal of the History of Ideas* 32, no. 2 (1971): 265–80.

Hook, Milton Raymond. *Flames over Battle Creek.* Washington, DC: Review and Herald, 1977.

Hudson, John C. "Yankeeland in the Middle West." *Journal of Geography* 85 (1986): 195–200.

Hutchinson, William R. *The Modernist Impulse in American Protestantism.* Cambridge, MA: Harvard University Press, 1976.

Illingworth, J. R. *Divine Immanence: An Essay on the Spiritual Significance of Matter.* London: Macmillan, 1898.

Imber, Jonathan B. *Trusting Doctors: The Decline of Moral Authority in American Medicine.* Princeton, NJ: Princeton University Press, 2008.

*In Memoriam: Ella Eaton Kellogg.* Battle Creek, MI: n.p., 1921.

Jackson, James Caleb. *How to Treat the Sick without Medicine.* Dansville, NY: Austin, Jackson, 1877.

———. *The Sexual Organism and Its Healthful Management.* Boston: B. Leverett Emerson, 1869.

———. *The Training of Children.* Dansville, NY: Austin, Jackson, 1872.

Jaher, Frederic Cople. *Doubters and Dissenters: Cataclysmic Thought in America, 1885–1918.* New York: Glencoe, 1964.

James, William. *The Varieties of Religious Experience.* 1902. Reprint, New York: Modern Library, 1929.

Kellogg, John Harvey. "The American Medical Missionary College." *Christian Educator,* September–October 1897, 14.

———. *The Battle Creek Sanitarium System: History, Organization, Methods.* Battle Creek, MI: n.p., 1908.

———. *Harmony of Science and the Bible on the Nature of the Soul and the Doctrine of the Resurrection.* Battle Creek, MI: Review and Herald, 1879.

———. *How to Have Good Health through Biologic Living.* Battle Creek, MI: Modern Medicine, 1932.

———. *Ideas.* Battle Creek, MI: Good Health, 1916.

———. *Ladies Guide in Health and Disease.* Battle Creek, MI: Modern Medicine, 1902.

———. *Life, Its Mysteries and Miracles: A Manual of Health Principles.* Battle Creek, MI: Modern Medicine, 1910.

———. *Light Therapeutics.* Battle Creek, MI: Good Health, 1910.

———. *The Living Temple.* Battle Creek, MI: Good Health, 1903.

———. *The Miracle of Life.* Battle Creek, MI: Good Health, 1904.

———. *The Natural Diet of Man.* Battle Creek, MI: Modern Medicine, 1923.

———. *Neurasthenia or Nervous Exhaustion.* Battle Creek, MI: Good Health, 1916.

———. *Plain Facts.* Battle Creek, MI: Good Health, 1917.

———. *Plain Facts for Old and Young.* Burlington, IA: Segner and Condit, 1881.

———. *Plain Facts for Old and Young.* Burlington, IA: Segner, 1888.

———. *Shall We Slay to Eat?* Battle Creek, MI: Good Health, 1899.

———. *Social Purity.* Battle Creek, MI: Good Health, 1887.

———. *Tendencies toward Race Degeneracy.* Senate Doc. 648. Washington, DC: Government Printing Office, 1912.

Kevles, Daniel J. *In the Name of Eugenics: Genetics and the Uses of Human Heredity*. New York: Alfred A. Knopf, 1985.

Knight, George R. "Adventist Faith Healing in the 1890s." *Adventist Heritage* 13, no. 2 (1990): 3–14.

———. *A Search for Identity: The Development of Seventh-day Adventist Beliefs*. Hagerstown, MD: Review and Herald, 2000.

Kuklick, Bruce. *Churchmen and Philosophers: From Jonathan Edwards to John Dewey*. New Haven, CT: Yale University Press, 1985.

Land, Gary, ed. *Adventism in America: A History*. Berrien Springs, MI: Andrews University Press, 1998.

———. "Shaping the Modern Church." In *Adventism in America: A History*, edited by Gary Land, 113–37. Berrien Springs, MI: Andrews University Press, 1998.

Lane, Kit. *Lucius Lyon: An Eminently Useful Citizen*. Douglas, MI: Pavilion Press, 1991.

Le Vay, David. *Alexis Carrel: The Perfectability of Man*. Rockville, MD: Kabel, 1996.

Lewis, E. H., ed. *Allen of Alfred: Some of His Words to His Students*. Waukesha, WI: Davis Greene, 1932.

Loughborough, J. N. *The Great Second Advent Movement: Its Rise and Progress*. Washington, DC: Review and Herald, 1909.

Lowe, Berenice B. *Tales of Battle Creek*. Battle Creek, MI: Miller Foundation, 1976.

Lyon, Rev. George G. "New Theology." *Popular Science Monthly*, July 1884, 320–31.

Mabee, Carleton. *Sojourner Truth: Slave, Prophet, Legend*. New York: New York University Press, 1993.

MacArthur, Kenneth C. "Eugenics and the Church: Answering Some Critics." *Eugenics: A Journal of Race Betterment* 3, no. 12 (1930): 469.

———. "Eugenics and the Church: Eugenics and Unity." *Eugenics: A Journal of Race Betterment* 3, no. 11 (1930): 439.

MacDowell, E. Carlton. "Charles Benedict Davenport, 1866–1944: A Study in Conflicting Influences." *Bios* 17, no. 1 (1946): 2–50.

Macfadden, Bernarr. *Science of Divine Healing with a Key to Health and Happiness: The Cosmotarian Gospel*. New York: Cosmotarian Library Service, 1945.

Major, Nettie Leitch. *C. W. Post: The Hour and the Man*. Washington, DC: Judd and Detweiler, 1963.

Mathews, Shailer, ed. *Contributions of Science to Religion*. New York: D. Appleton, 1924.

Maxwell, Mervyn. "Sanctuary and Atonement in SDA Theology: An Historical Survey." In *The Sanctuary and the Atonement: Biblical, Historical, and Theological Studies*, edited by A. V. Wallenkampf and W. R. Lesher, 516–44. Washington, DC: Review and Herald, 1981.

McGiffert, Arthur Cushman. *The Rise of Modern Religious Ideas*. New York: Macmillan, 1922.

Melody, M. E., and Linda M. Peterson. *Teaching America about Sex: Marriage Guides and Sex Manuals from the Late Victorians to Dr. Ruth*. New York: New York University Press, 1999.

Meyers, D. H. "American Intellectuals and the Victorian Crisis of Faith." *American Quarterly* 27 (December 1975): 585–603.

Meyers, Jay Arthur. *Fighters of Fate: A Story of Men Who Have Achieved Greatly Despite the Handicaps of the Great White Plague*. 1927. Reprint, Freeport, NY: Books for Libraries Press, 1969.

Miller, Russell E. *The Larger Hope: The First Century of the Universalist Church in America, 1770–1870*. Boston: Unitarian Universalist Association, 1979.

Moore, James R. *The Post-Darwinian Controversies: A Study of the Protestant Struggle to Come to Terms with Darwin in Great Britain and America, 1870–1900.* London: Cambridge University Press, 1981.

Murphy, James L. *Reluctant Radicals: Jacob L. Beilhart and the Spirit Fruit Society.* Lanham, MD: University Press of America, 1989.

Muser, Necia Ann. "Home Missionaries on the Michigan Frontier: A Calendar of the Michigan Letters of the American Home Missionary Society, 1825–1846." PhD diss., University of Michigan, 1967.

Numbers, Ronald L. *The Creationists: From Scientific Creationism to Intelligent Design.* Cambridge, MA: Harvard University Press, 2006.

———. *Prophetess of Health: Ellen G. White and the Origins of Seventh-day Adventist Health Reform.* Grand Rapids, MI: Wm. B. Eerdmans, 2008.

———. "Sex, Science, and Salvation: The Sexual Advice of Ellen G. White and John Harvey Kellogg." In *Right Living: An Anglo-American Tradition of Self-Help Medicine and Hygiene,* edited by Charles E. Rosenberg, 206–26. Baltimore: Johns Hopkins University Press, 2003.

*Official Proceedings of the Second National Conference on Race Betterment, August 4, 5, 6, 7, and 8, 1915, Held in San Francisco, California, in Connection with the Panama-Pacific International Exposition.* Battle Creek, MI: Race Betterment Foundation, 1915.

O'Shea, M. V., and John Harvey Kellogg. *Making the Most of Life.* New York: Macmillan, 1921.

Paley, William. *Natural Theology; or, Evidences of the Existence and Attributes of the Deity.* London: J. Faulder, 1809.

Paxson, Peyton. "Charles William Post: The Mass Marketing of Health and Welfare." PhD diss., Boston University, 1993.

Pease, Norval F. "'The Truth as It Is in Jesus': The 1888 General Conference Session, Minneapolis, Minnesota." *Adventist Heritage* 10, no. 1 (1985): 3–10.

Peebles, James M. *Outlines of Dr. J. M. Peebles' Medical Standing and Medical Practice.* San Diego: Peebles, 1896.

Pernick, Martin S. *The Black Stork: Eugenics and the Death of "Defective" Babies in American Medicine and Motion Pictures since 1915.* New York: Oxford University Press, 1996.

Persons, Stow. *Free Religion: An American Faith.* Boston: Beacon Press, 1947.

Pickens, Donald K. *Eugenics and the Progressives.* Nashville, TN: Vanderbilt University Press, 1968.

Pilcher, E. H. *Protestantism in Michigan.* Detroit: R. D. S. Tyler, 1878.

Pivar, David J. *Purity Crusade: Sexual Morality and Social Control, 1868–1900.* Westport, CT: Greenwood Press, 1973.

Pomerantz-Zhang, Linda. *Wu Tingfang (1842–1922): Reform and Modernization in Modern Chinese History.* Hong Kong: Hong Kong University Press, 1992.

*Portrait Biographical Album of Calhoun County, Michigan.* Chicago: Chapman Brothers, 1891.

Post, C. W. *I Am Well! The Modern Practice of Natural Suggestion as Distinct from Hypnotic or Unnatural Influence.* Boston: Lee and Shepard, 1895.

———. *The Modern Practice: Natural Suggestion; or, Scientia Vitae.* Battle Creek, MI: La Vita Inn, 1894.

Potash, P. Jeffrey. *Vermont's Burned-Over District: Patterns of Community Development and Religious Activity, 1761–1850.* Brooklyn, NY: Carlson, 1991.

Powell, Aaron M., ed. *The National Purity Congress.* New York: American Purity Alliance, 1896.

Powell, Horace B. *The Original Has This Signature—W. K. Kellogg.* Englewood Cliffs, NJ: Prentice Hall, 1956.

*Principles of the Battle Creek Sanitarium.* Battle Creek, MI: n.p., n.d.

Pritchard, Linda K. "Religious Change in a Developing Region: The Social Contexts of Evangelicalism in Western New York and the Upper Ohio Valley during the Mid-Nineteenth Century." PhD diss., University of Pittsburgh, 1980.

*Proceedings of the First National Conference on Race Betterment, January 8, 9, 10, 11, 12, 1914.* Battle Creek, MI: Race Betterment Foundation, 1914.

*Proceedings of the Free Convention Held at Rutland, Vt., July 25th, 26th, and 27th, 1858.* Boston: J. B. Yerrington and Son, 1858.

*Proceedings of the Pennsylvania Meeting of Progressive Friends, 1853.* New York: John Trow, Printer, 1853.

*Proceedings of the Pennsylvania Meeting of Progressive Friends, 1857.* New York: John Trow, Printer, 1857.

*Proceedings of the Pennsylvania Meeting of Progressive Friends, 1858.* New York: John Trow, Printer, 1858.

*Proceedings of the Pennsylvania Meeting of Progressive Friends, 1859.* New York: John Trow, Printer, 1859.

*Proceedings of the Third Race Betterment Conference.* Battle Creek, MI: Race Betterment Foundation, 1928.

Reggiani, Andrés Horacio. *God Eugenicist: Alexis Carrel and the Sociobiology of Decline.* New York: Berghahn Books, 2007.

Roberts, Jon H. *Darwinism and the Divine in America: Protestant Intellectuals and Organic Evolution, 1859–1900.* Madison: University of Wisconsin Press, 1988.

Robinson, D. E. *The Story of Our Health Message.* 3rd ed. Nashville, TN: Southern, 1965.

Rosen, Christine. *Preaching Eugenics: Religious Leaders and the American Eugenics Movement.* New York: Oxford University Press, 2004.

Rosen, George E. "The Committee of One Hundred on National Health and the Campaign for a National Health Department, 1906–1912." *American Journal of Public Health* 62 (1972): 261–63.

Rosenberg, Charles E. *No Other Gods: On Science and American Social Thought.* Baltimore; Johns Hopkins University Press, 1976.

Rowe, David L. *God's Strange Work: William Miller and the End of the World.* Grand Rapids, MI: Eerdmans, 2008.

Russell, Charlotte M. "'Most Accursed of Our National Sins: Battle Creek's Churches Confront Slavery." *Heritage Battle Creek* 9 (Winter 1999): 60–68.

Rust, E. G., ed. *Calhoun County Business Directory.* Battle Creek, MI: E. G. Rust, 1869.

Rydell, Robert W. *World of Fairs: The Century-of-Progress Expositions.* Chicago: University of Chicago Press, 1993.

Sabin, Brainard S. "The Progress of Our Faith: An Outline of the Theological History of the First Congregational Church of Battle Creek." In *Our Todays and Yesterdays: A Volume Marking the Centennial of the First Congregational Church of Battle Creek, Michigan.* Battle Creek, MI: n.p., 1936.

Sanford, Dan A. *A Choosing People: The History of Seventh-Day Baptists.* Nashville, TN: Broadman Press, 1992.

Schieffelin, William Jay. "Work of the Committee of One Hundred on National Health." *Annals of the American Academy of Political and Social Science* (March 1911): 321–30.

Schneider, William H. *Quality and Quantity: The Quest for Biological Regeneration in Twentieth-Century France.* Cambridge: Cambridge University Press, 1990.

Schoepflin, Rennie B. *Christian Science on Trial: Religious Healing in America*. Baltimore: Johns Hopkins University Press, 2003.

Schwarz, Richard W. "Dr. John Harvey Kellogg as a Social Gospel Practitioner." *Journal of the Illinois State Historical Society* 57, no. 1 (1964): 5–22.

———. "John Harvey Kellogg: American Health Reformer." PhD diss., University of Michigan, 1964.

———. *John Harvey Kellogg, MD*. Nashville, TN: Southern, 1970.

———. "The Kellogg Schism: The Hidden Issues." *Spectrum* 4 (Autumn 1972): 23–39.

———. "The Perils of Growth, 1886–1905." In *Adventism in America: A History*, edited by Gary Land, 77–111. Berrien Springs, MI: Andrews University Press, 1998.

———. "Reorganization and Reform: The 1901 General Conference Session, Battle Creek, Michigan." *Adventist Heritage* 10, no. 1 (1985): 11–18.

*Seventh-day Adventist Encyclopedia*. 2nd ed. Hagerstown, MD: Review and Herald, 1996.

*Seventh-day Adventists Believe . . . A Biblical Exposition of 27 Fundamental Doctrines*. Hagerstown, MD: Review and Herald, 1989.

Sherbon, Florence Brown. "The Preacher's Part." *Eugenics: A Journal of Race Betterment* 1, no. 3 (1928): 1–5.

Shyrock, Richard H. "Sylvester Graham and the Popular Health Movement, 1830–1870." *Mississippi Valley Historical Review* 18, no. 2 (1931): 172–83.

Sinclair, Upton. *The Profits of Religion*. Pasadena, CA: published by the author, 1918.

Sinclair, Upton, and Michael Williams. *Good Health and How We Won It*. New York: Frederick A. Stokes, 1909.

Smith, Uriah. *The State of the Dead and the Resurrection of the Wicked*. Battle Creek, MI: Seventh-day Adventist Publishing Association, 1873.

Spencer, Herbert. *First Principles*. New York: D. Appleton, 1864.

———. *The Study of Sociology*. London: Henry S. King, 1873.

Spiro, Jonathan Peter. *Defending the Master Race: Conservation, Eugenics, and the Legacy of Madison Grant*. Burlington: University of Vermont Press, 2009.

Stoltz, Garth "Duff." "101 Cereal Manufacturing Companies in Battle Creek, Michigan." *Adventist Heritage* 15, no. 2 (1992): 10–13.

———. "A Taste of Cereal." *Adventist Heritage* 15, no. 2 (1992): 4–9.

Stump, Alan. *The Foundation of Our Faith: 160 Years of Christology in Adventism*. 6th ed. Welsh, WV: Smyrna Gospel Ministries, 1997.

Thomas, Allen C. "Congregational or Progressive Friends." *Bulletin of Friends' Historical Society of Philadelphia* 10, no. 1 (1920): 21–32.

Thornton, Frances. "Harmonia: Memories of the Lost Village." *Heritage Battle Creek* 4 (Spring 1993): 16–23.

Trall, Russell Thacher. *Digestion and Dyspepsia*. New York: S. R. Wells, 1873.

———. *The Hydropathic Encyclopedia*. Vol. 2. New York: Fowlers and Wells, 1854.

———. "July Matters." *Water-Cure Journal* 1, no. 10 (1850): 16.

———. *Sexual Physiology*. New York: Wood & Holbrook, Hygienic Institute, 1866.

Trine, Ralph Waldo. *In Tune with the Infinite; or, Fullness of Peace, Power, and Plenty*. New York: Thomas Y. Crowell, 1897.

*The Universalist Register*. Boston: Universalist, 1890.

Van Buren, A. D. P. "The City of Battle Creek: Its Early History, Growth, and Present Condition." *Michigan Pioneer and Historical Collections* 3 (1881): 347–67.

―――. "Pioneer Annals: Containing the History of the Early Settlement of Battle Creek and Township." *Michigan Pioneer and Historical Collections* 5 (1884): 237–93.

―――. "William H. Coleman." *Report of the Pioneer Society of the State of Michigan* 5 (1884): 228–29.

Vandevere, Emmett K. "Years of Expansion, 1865–1885." In *Adventism in America: A History,* edited by Gary Land, 53–75. Berrien Springs, MI: Andrews University Press, 1998.

"W. W. Prescott, Part 2, 1901–1944." *Lest We Forget: Adventist Pioneer Library* 10, no. 2 (2000): 3–4.

Waggoner, E. J. *Gospel in Creation.* Battle Creek, MI: Review and Herald, 1894.

Wahl, Albert J. "The Pennsylvania Yearly Meeting of Progressive Friends." *Pennsylvania History* 25, no. 2 (1958): 122–36.

Walker, William B. "The Health Reform Movement in the United States, 1830–1870." PhD diss., Johns Hopkins University, 1955.

Ware, John. *Hints to Young Men on the True Relation of the Sexes.* Boston: Cupples, Upham, 1884.

Warren, Wilson J. *Tied to the Great Packing Machine: The Midwest and Meatpacking.* Iowa City: University of Iowa Press, 2007.

Warthin, Aldred Scott. *The Creed of a Biologist: A Biologic Philosophy of Life.* New York: Paul B. Hoeber, 1930.

Washington, Margaret. *Sojourner Truth's America.* Urbana: University of Illinois Press, 2009.

Watkins, Marilyn P. "Civilizers of the West: Clergy and Laity in Michigan Frontier Churches, 1820–1840." In *Michigan: Explorations in Its Social History,* edited by Francis X. Blouin Jr. and Maris A. Vinovskis, 162–90. Ann Arbor: Historical Society of Michigan, 1987.

Watts, Kit. "Seventh-day Adventist Headquarters: From Battle Creek to Takoma Park." *Adventist Heritage* 3, no. 2 (1976): 42–50.

Weeks, Lewis E., ed. "August F. Bloese: Former Secretary to Dr. John Harvey Kellogg, an Oral History." Lewis E. Weeks Series, Hospital Administration Oral History Collection, American Hospital Association and Hospital Research and Educational Trust, Chicago, 1985.

Wellcome, Isaac C. *The History of the Second Advent Message and Mission, Doctrine and People.* Yarmouth, ME: I. C. Wellcome, 1874.

Whipple, Edward. *Biography of James M. Peebles.* Battle Creek, MI: published by the author, 1901.

White, Ellen G. *Child Guidance.* Hagerstown, MD: Review and Herald, 1954.

―――. *Education.* Mountain View, CA: Pacific Press, 1903.

―――. *The Great Controversy between Christ and His Angels and Satan and His Angels.* Battle Creek, MI: James White, 1858.

―――. *The Health Reform and the Health Institute.* Battle Creek, MI: Seventh-day Adventist Publishing Association, 1872.

―――. *Mind, Character, and Personality.* Vol. 2. Hagerstown, MD: Review and Herald, 1977.

―――. *The Ministry of Healing.* Mountain View, CA: Pacific Press, 1909.

―――. *Prophets and Kings.* Mountain View, CA: Pacific Press, 1917.

White, James, and Ellen G. White, eds. *Health: or, How to Live.* Battle Creek, MI: Seventh-day Adventist Publishing Association, 1865.

Whorton, James C. "'Christian Physiology': William Alcott's Prescription for the Millennium." *Bulletin for the History of Medicine* 4, no. 49 (1975): 466–81.

―――. *Crusaders for Fitness: The History of American Health Reformers.* Princeton, NJ: Princeton University Press, 1982.

―――. *Nature Cures: The History of Alternative Medicine in America.* Oxford: Oxford University Press, 2002.

―――. "'Physiologic Optimism': Horace Fletcher and Hygienic Ideology in Progressive America." *Bulletin of the History of Medicine* 55, no. 1 (1981): 59–87.

Wiess, Harry B., and Howard R. Kemble. *The Great American Water-Cure Craze: A History of Hydropathy in the United Sates.* Trenton, NJ: Past Times Press, 1967.

Wiggam, Albert E. "The Most Remarkable Man I Have Ever Known." *American Magazine*, December 1925, 61–105.

―――. *The New Decalogue of Science.* Indianapolis: Bobbs-Merrill, 1922.

Willey, T. Joe. "Kellogg and Pavlov: Portrait of a Friendship." *Spectrum* 14, no. 2 (1983): 16–19.

Wolff, Tamen. *Mendel's Theatre: Heredity, Eugenics, and Early Twentieth-Century American Drama.* New York: Palgrave Macmillan, 2009.

Wu, Tingfang. *America, through the Spectacles of an Oriental Diplomat.* New York: Frederick A. Stokes, 1914.

Young, Norman. "The Alpha Heresy: Kellogg and the Cross." *Adventist Heritage* 12, no. 1 (1972): 33–42.

Zenderland, Leila. "Biblical Biology: American Protestant Social Reformers and the Early Eugenics Movement." *Science in Context* 11, nos. 3–4 (1998): 511–25.

# INDEX

*Italicized page numbers refer to figures.*

BRIAN C. WILSON is professor of American religious history and past chair of the Department of Comparative Religion at Western Michigan University. His publications include *Christianity* (1999), *What Is Religion?* (1999), *Reappraising Durkheim for the Study and Teaching of Religion Today* (2001), and *Yankees in Michigan* (2008).

Milton Keynes UK
Ingram Content Group UK Ltd.
UKHW020845280424
441777UK00006B/124